LEAVING

FOR ME

ALEX NICOLLET
DELON

Disclaimer:
As in any first-person account, the events in this book are from a single perspective, the author's. Though she has wished for psychic abilities umpteen times, she didn't receive them; therefore, the minds and memories of others were not accessible and cannot be fairly represented in this story of her journey. With respect for the privacy of others, she has changed names, a few locations, occupations, and descriptions, but the impact and essence of events is as she remembers them.

FIRST EDITION

Cover and interior design by Gwyn Snider, GKS Creative, Nashville, TN.

Library of Congress Cataloging-in-Publication Data
Registration Number: TXu 2-074-040
Effective Date of Registration: November 06, 2017

ISBN 978-0-9995208-0-2
Ebook ISBN 978-0-9995208-1-9 mobi
Ebook ISBN 978-0-9995208-2-6 ePub

Printed in the United States of America

I dedicate this book to my mother and to the generations of strong women who came before her. Their resilience has given me the courage to write this book and the guts to publish it. Here's to you, ladies.

"You must learn from the mistakes of others. You can't possibly live long enough to make them all yourself."

—GROUCHO MARX

I thought he was just a comedian, not to be taken seriously...

CONTENTS

PROLOGUE

Ever wonder why we do what we do? Particularly, why we stay in an unhappy, unhealthy relationship far longer than we should? We can say we are stubborn; don't like to give up; take commitment seriously. We can even write it off to the fear of change, fear of being alone, lack of self-esteem, the kids, the dog, or stupidity. And any or all of the above may apply. Those are things we think about, wrestle with, reason through. But when is enough too much?

I wish the decision to leave my husband had been like a blow-out in my driver's side tire. Sudden. Air-bag at impact. Instead, the stains and strains accumulated over decades, until the weight of one more lie spun me off balance and over the edge. The straw and the camel became a cliché because that's how it works. There is generally a final thing.

My stumbles, tumbles, and triumphs after leaving an over forty-year marriage haven't all been on the clear road to recovery. I've taken side trips, had flings, dated, danced, laughed, cried and come to realize there is more to love than surviving it.

The chapters that follow are gritty, raw and explicit. Not to shock or titillate you, but if I broke blind dates or first nights or the jolt of venturing out on your own to you gently, it would lack honesty for those of you who will identify with me. And too many of you will.

Along this journey I've come to realize though I was more vulnerable than I believed, I was stronger than I ever imagined.

I've also learned that I'm not alone.

Neither are you.

CHAPTER 1

Over the Edge

I didn't lose my husband of forty-seven years. I know right where I left him, and why. I don't have to remind myself to breathe anymore. Finally. That took a while, as did my new smile. But I like it. It's genuine.

I had a lot to contend with when I left Brad. He was livid. Friends and family were baffled, and I was broken. The last time I'd been single, I was seventeen. Brad was an 18-year-old freshman in college, a track star I fell in love with the summer before my senior year. He was only the second boy I'd ever dated.

I was amazed he asked me out on a second date after he met my dad. When Brad picked me up my father's eyes bored down like the barrels of the shot gun I knew was on the closet shelf. I wanted to wilt into the woodwork.

"Nice to meet you, sir," Brad said respectfully as he reached to shake my dad's hand. I think Brad became my hero that instant when he strangely bonded with my father. I had no idea what a defining moment this was in more ways than one.

There was also no way for me to know that when Brad picked me up that night for our first date, his college girlfriend was on vacation with her family and *I* was the other woman that would one day break her heart. I didn't find out they were still having sex in the back seat of his car six months later *until* six months later. We hadn't said I love you or made a commitment at that point, he pointed out, so it wasn't like he was cheat-

ing. He hadn't lied; he just hadn't told me about her. It was that simple.
Not to me.

I told him I never wanted to see him again. Didn't answer the phone for three days. Didn't intend to. But my father got pissed. He liked Brad by then, a lot. My mom did, too.

"Since you weren't even going steady, how could he be cheating on you?" my dad asked. I wanted to know how my father echoed Brad. When my mother shrugged an assent, I didn't recognize it as the moment she passed on her shit-sweeping broom. The one she used to sweep my dad's shit under the rug and move on. I didn't know there was such a thing. The broom, I mean. Or why she wielded it, or how deft she'd become at handling it.

It's a skill that takes grooming as much as practice. Programming. Idealization. Naiveté. Gullibility. Being in love. Blinded by love and the mother of them all: intermittent reinforcement; one of the most powerful tools of manipulation in existence. The demonstration of this phenomenon that lurks in our back brain, behind reason involves a rat. A real four-legged, hungry one.

There's a ton of clinical evidence of this paradox that offers insight into why victims of physical or emotional abuse not only stay, but crave attention from their abuser. Love, need, even defend them when they've gone too far. It's a club I belonged to because I made a mistake. I didn't recognize emotional manipulation or know that it's emotional abuse. The dynamic applies to work, love, parent and child relationships. Bastards can even use the principle to train their dog. Arf.

After I finally left Brad, I was on a quest. Had to figure out why I'd stayed so long or hoped to hell Betty Ford had a "Believers in Love" wing at one of her addiction clinics. I wasn't going back to him, didn't want to check in with Betty, voluntarily or not, when I stumbled across an article about a lab experiment that took Pavlov's dogs, the bell and classical conditioning to the next level. Casinos pay millions for studies on the psychology of what they refer to as a 'variable reward schedule' that engrains desired behavior, which becomes hard to extinguish.

I hope you're ready for the rat and my revelation.

An understanding of the Skinner box made sense to me. It's a simple apparatus where a rat presses a lever to get a morsel of food. If the rat gets food every time it experiences no insecurity in this base need, it's free to play on the treadmill and interact with others. It is self-assured, emotionally stable.

When the rat presses the lever and only gets a morsel every once in a while, it gradually becomes obsessed with pressing the lever. Eventually, it won't leave it to play or interact with others. It gets depressed. In the most horrid experiments the rat is left to try-try-try until it eventually dies from exhaustion, dehydration, and starvation if too few morsels were dispensed. Gruesome but true. The same principle applies to us and our base needs, whether male or female, to succeed or fail, to be accepted or rejected, to love and be loved.

The attachment isn't to the lever, but to the mind manipulation (I was nice here and didn't say "mind fuck" but that's what it is). And this is exactly what can happen in a relationship between a narcissist or any manipulative person, and an inherently trusting person who can rapidly progress into a codependent and not realize it. This paradox of intermittent reinforcement as it relates to relationships gave insight into how the need for attachment, for being loved, becomes the lever.

The willingness; the need that drives us to sweep the shit under the rug, look the other way, swallow our pride, and choke on broken promises rather than abandon or be abandoned by our relationship isn't where we begin; it's a consequence of adaptation. The rat, the morsel, and the lever isn't logical. It is how we can become conditioned, just like that whiskered creature with its tiny paws becomes obsessed, beyond reason, with the lever.

The one controlling the morsels has a learning curve, too. On a conscious or unconscious level, they're after a desired behavior, reaction or tolerance. They want what they want when they want it. Therefore, they're compelled to discover what makes us laugh or cry, what frightens or makes us happy and, above all, what makes us vulnerable.

As I tried to reconstruct how the dysfunctional-unbalanced relationship I'd fought so hard to keep had evolved, I again became embroiled in my last year of high school in the Sixties. The Genesis of our relationship.

My business teacher had to stop teaching when she was three months along because an obvious pregnancy was a bad influence. No lie. Girls weren't allowed to wear pants or slacks to school, only dresses or skirts, and they had to be knee-length. I went to Coronado, a public high school in Scottsdale, Arizona.

Abortion was illegal, birth control pills needed a parent's consent, therefore a confession. To know for sure if you were pregnant involved the anguish of waiting six weeks after your missed period and the death of a rabbit. Literally. Besides all that, my sister had gotten pregnant when she was in high school. Was required to drop out. Graduated via a G.E.D. She garnered a 'reputation' and parents of her friends no longer wanted her around. Since she was an incredible mother from day one, it was a travesty, but the reality of the times while I was dating Brad. I chose virginity over the trials my sister endured.

"I don't want her," Brad told me, referring to his back-seat fling. "I want you. Want to marry you. Want you to be the mother of my children. I had a weak moment. It won't happen again."

Coming up next is your first glimpse of metaphorical me. Think of this scenario as the blending of the perfect margarita. The base ingredient is freshly-squeezed lime juice.

Pucker-me-up sour.

The infidelity.

Imagine Brad as he deftly pours this lime juice into a shaker of ice. Refreshing. He told me the truth about why he hadn't shown up or called on the night in question. A healthy pour of Cointreau, the sweet-orange liqueur that comes next, is when he tells me he didn't want her. He wanted me to be his wife, the mother of his children.

The tequila comes next. It's the heady part and he didn't skimp on it. He respected that I wanted to wait for marriage, but I was so stirring, so sexual, it was hard on a man.

Sorry, I couldn't resist the pun.

His muscles flexed as ice chimed in the shaker and he skillfully poured it into a salt-rimmed glass. Did it with style. Charisma. The twist he added?

The old girlfriend he'd been with was his best friend's sister. Both still lived at home. That little tidbit was in my way, so I set it aside. Shouldn't have. I didn't sip, I swallowed my first relationship taste of anything stronger than lemonade. I had a warm buzz as he finally wrapped me in his arms and whispered, "You're what I want. Forever."

It wasn't really tequila. It was mind fuck number one.

We were both becoming naturals; the narcissist and the codependent. We were seventeen and eighteen. Neither of us knew that we were forming relationship dynamics that would carry us through hell and back for two-score and nearly ten years of dysfunction. Family helped us along.

My mother waitressed at the Ember Glow, a local diner, and made more in tips than my dad earned in the shipping department at Motorola. They got up early for work, so my father wouldn't allow Brad to come over after 10:00 p.m. But Brad worked nights and weekends at Frank's Union 76. It was the days of full-service gas stations, where you also got your windshield washed and collected glasses or green stamps. He didn't get off until 10:00. We barely saw each other.

My graduation was on a Wednesday night. Brad got the night off and came to the family party at my house after the ceremony. At 10:30 sharp his father called our house phone. That may have been the first time I saw the flash of fury in Brad's eyes that I would come to know too well. Evidently, he didn't hit back when his father shoved him into their glass-patio door that night. The next morning Brad called to tell me he was moving out.

"Can't afford a place of my own so either we get married or I get a room-mate." I didn't know then about the physical abuse Brad had survived, or the consequences we would pay for how he endured. We were young and invincible, or so I thought.

I was business student of the year and had already landed a secretarial job at Ed Post Realty. With his $1.40 per hour and my $275 a month it would be tight, but we could make it. Three weeks later we had our wedding reception in the same family room in which we'd celebrated my graduation.

My smile was genuine then, too. Huge and happy. I'd married the boy of my dreams who I'd known since junior high. We were ready to tackle the world together. Did we ever.

Per Brad's instructions to 'think boy', I gave birth to our first son when I was twenty, our second when I was twenty-two, our third when I was twenty-three, and went from taking dictation and typing contracts to babysitting four children, as well as our own.

Those years were cloth diapers and clothes lines, a budget so tight that finding a quarter in the laundry felt like winning the lottery. We moved ten times in the first thirteen years, moves that included a rickety house on a dirt lot, ten miles from Mexicali. It made our move to a single-wide trailer that was off the ground, relatively bug-free and air-tight, rate a celebration. We played bridge on Saturday nights with friends we made in the trailer park. Had Sunday pot-lucks and picnics. If there was a time I believe we had it all, I think this would be it.

What happened? How do I account for all the years I brandished the ass end of an ostrich? I call them my dumbass years now. In retrospect, hiding from and covering up the lies made me an accomplice and a coward. Even now as I move forward, create a new life, some days regret sticks to me like flypaper, when I think of all the years that I betrayed myself.

I'm not sure when we became ballroom champions of the dance between the narcissist and the codependent. It's a gradual process. I didn't know there was such a dance, but knew the steps, turns, and twirls had begun to make me dizzy and sick to my stomach. On the surface, we looked great. He didn't bully or put me down in public which is good and bad. We looked like a happy couple, but because we did, no one understood when I finally left.

Up until then, now in our sixties, our friends and family thought we had it all: a thriving business, beautiful homes, the means to travel, and lucky that two of our sons worked in the business we'd built. But that was the façade. Underneath was a cauldron of lies and deceit with which we'd lived for decades.

People tell me now how courageous I am; what strength it took to leave Brad after forty-seven years. In truth, it was an act of desperation. My biggest regret is that I waited so long. My greatest hope is that someone out there will benefit from my mistakes and be heartened by the brilliance of life beyond a dysfunctional relationship.

So here you go: a bit more of why I stayed so long and had so far to fall. And a lot about the adventure my life has become since I embarked on my journey to begin again.

CHAPTER 2

Martyr, May I?

As a culture, we re-label behaviors, trend them up. I was born on the brink of the Fifties, when the "boys will be boys" mentality swept lots of shit under rugs that covered lots of areas. My mom lifted the rug and swept the shit under it, chin high. She was Melanie from *Gone with the Wind*—the woman who stood beside her husband, Ashley, and her friend, Scarlett, Ashley's lover emotionally, if not physically. Melanie created her own version of reality, refused to believe either had betrayed her. She protected them from social exile, and then took Ashley to bed even though she knew she couldn't survive childbirth again. She got pregnant and bequeathed her son and husband to Scarlett's care before dying valiantly.

I didn't see her as a martyr. I saw her strength, and that everyone respected her.

I idealize my mother to this day. Her courage, integrity, determination to hold her family together no matter what. It was her job, and in my turn, I picked up the gauntlet. I not only saw myself through my husband's skewed vision, I measured myself by my mom, and I never measured up.

In the Seventies, women looked for answers. Why do these men feel entitled to have fun affairs, then belittle their wife's hurt confusion by snarling, "You need to get a life, buck up, smile, damn it! You're becoming a real drag. I'm home, aren't I?" Self-help books called such men "misogynists." That was better than "cold-hearted bastards." Mine used to add, "Just because you're tied down with kids doesn't mean I have to be." Oh, and this one is priceless: "I never said we were equal. Guys can do things women can't. I didn't make the rules. Society did."

For me, over a decade in a strict New Testament church that clearly defined the man as head of the household and his wife as subservient added sharp lines to the playing field. Brad never went to church with me. I own that one.

I need to add that there were good things about Brad, too. The things our friends and family saw and related us to. Brad was a gentleman. Opened car doors, treated me like a lady. He is brilliant. Fought his way up from the eighteen-year-old boy I married—a boy who made a buck forty an hour—to become educated, accomplished, and financially successful. I credited his success to his extraordinary ability to motivate people. To get them to perform profitably.

But he believes he did it all alone . . . from the early years of beginning a business from scratch, setting up the office, budgeting, to having three sons, ten grandchildren, holidays memorable for homemade meals and gifts, events for friends and family. It all made him look good. Made me look lucky. Everyone respected him. Me, too. He was my hero.

I was truly happy as a wife and mom. Also, frustrated and lonely. But I had an entire bag of tools to explain that stuff away. It was labeled, *If I was better, he'd be nicer. Try. Try. Try*. I could amaze you with my ability to put on my makeup, do my hair, dress, check the mirror . . . and never once look into my own eyes. This is a trick in the codependent's stash.

It's important to reinforce that the bond with the manipulator becomes stronger in response to intermittent reinforcement; crumbs along the *love you, love you not* trail. The desire to please them becomes vital. The fear of losing them relates to survival. It is also what I knew, the world I'd lived in since I turned seventeen. My lifetime ago.

Brad's latest extramarital interest was a sales rep for one of our suppliers. He'd stopped being discrete. He invited her to work-related events at the banks or with other business associates. "I'm helping her out. She's a hard worker, smart. Deserves an opportunity to get ahead. What's your problem?"

He was dating her. He even invited her on a guy's motorcycle trip with four of his friends.

"She's a better rider than most of the guys. Do you think I'd ask her to come if I was having an affair with her? She's just like one of the guys. Smart, has a master's degree, is fun to talk to. You need to go make something of yourself, to back off and get off my back." The way he rattled from one sentence to another without taking a breath spoke volumes.

"If she goes on the trip, I can't do this anymore. I'm done."

He saw the flash of fire in my eyes and knew the next step in our dysfunctional relationship dance. After one nod, it was time for him to sweep me into a waltz, spend a weekend with me at our condo between the Coast Highway and the bluff in Encinitas, California. He knew how much I loved the ocean, watching sunsets slip beneath the edge of the world. I let that sinking sun drag a lot of baggage with it. Out of sight, out of mind. At least that was the objective.

This trip was a far cry from the first time we lived in California, when Goodyear decided to acid test Brad, the rookie. They sent him on his first assignment after college graduation, to El Centro, California. A mere ten miles from Mexicali, forty feet below sea level, it boasts a record temperature of one hundred thirty degrees. We had one car, (and that's a long story), one rather large dog, two sons, and an audio issue with money. We pinched pennies so hard they squealed. Kept me awake many a night, yet I was happy there for nearly two years. Eventually. It took a bit of time and a shift in attitude to get there, but I did.

We'd been married five years by then. I was really good at budgeting, had to be, especially when we wouldn't have the money I made babysitting since we moved.

I'm going to cut myself a break here. I was twenty-two, Brad twenty-three. Our first son, Andrew had just turned two. Ben was six months old and got sick the first week we arrived in El Centro. I don't know if he ate a bug or got a bug from the water. Could have been both.

I'll give the teacher that built the little house Brad had rented points for industry. He built the place himself, on weekends and through a sweltering summer. Maybe he figured with rental income, he could afford to get out of there one day; but during construction he scrimped in wrong places.

The house was on a dirt lot. I'm not exaggerating here. Not a blade of grass beyond us and the irrigation ditch along the road. Dirt in El Centro isn't rich, loamy soil like Minnesota, where I lived until I was nine. If this had once been ocean bottom, and there were grains of sand, I'll bet they screamed out when the heat exploded them into a talc so fine a footstep raised a cloud of dust that Tonto would have been able to track from a mile away. When the wind blew, it seeped under the baseboards and made designs on the asphalt tile.

I still believe the water was the culprit when Ben got so sick that first week. There was a tank for AAA drinking water on the roof, but water for the faucets, bathing, dishes, and cleaning came from the six by six-foot irrigation ditch that ran along the road, siphoned through a three-inch corrugated pipe that ran behind the house. It connected to a tank, maybe five feet high by three feet wide, with a carbon filter. When they dredged the ditch every six weeks or so, bath and wash water from the faucets turned as reddish brown as the Rio Grande after runoff from a storm. It was the early Seventies, clearly before building permits and inspections were required.

The worst hit when Ben couldn't keep anything down. He was too little for that to go on too long. I called our doctor in Phoenix. He said no food at all for twenty-four hours. Ben's stomach had to rest. A spoon full of Coke three times a day to counteract the stomach acid, and see if he'll suck on a popsicle. He had to stay hydrated. After an inch of cherry Popsicle, he threw up pink. I called Brad at work and asked him to bring home a Coke from the vending machine.

Ben had twenty-two hours of stomach rest to go when I made Andrew a bowl of Campbell's vegetable soup for lunch, and I lost it. I was holding Ben. He dove for the saltine crackers I was going to crush in Andrew's soup. He cried. I cried. Andrew cried, and my mother called in the middle of all that. We've all had strange moments like that.

My mom and I took turns and timed our calls. She'd call me one week, I'd call her the next. When I answered the phone that afternoon I cried, "I want to come home."

"You are home, Alexandra. You're with your family, and it's your job to make it a home."

Amazing how a couple of sentences punched me in the gut and straightened me up. *Buck up. Measure up. Get your shit together*, I told myself.

The very nice woman who lived in the farm house about a hundred yards behind us drove us to her doctor's office. After three days, Ben's system finally beat the bug, he recovered, and a little gritty water from the faucets became a trivial thing.

After six months on the dirt lot, we bought a 12 X 60 mobile home with a real air conditioner, hooked up to city water, and celebrated our new home. There was no escaping the damned talc-fine dirt, the heat, or the crickets, but we were off the ground, and the windows didn't weep dirt in a dust storm.

The crickets are a long story for another time, but as a hint: at a given time each year, they descend on the Imperial Valley like a black cloud, render the airport runways too slick to land a plane, and shut down the airport. Huge hordes of them don't chirp; they're like gang-bangers with a boom box and electric guitar screams that sting your ears. Incessant.

In those two years, I learned to appreciate and find contentment in simple things we sometimes take for granted. I'm grateful for that. I learned to make jokes and have some remarkable stories about the adventure of living in an inferno, on a dirt lot, in an old town ten miles from the Mexican border, forty feet below sea level, without even a movie theatre. Funny how not having a theatre stands out, now. But that's enough about the first time we lived in in California. A shiver runs up my spine when I realize that was over forty years ago.

This current relationship resuscitation weekend, we were in our sixties. Brad and I would drive separate cars to our condo in Encinitas. I was going to stay over to attend the La Jolla Writer's Conference. He had to get back to Phoenix for work. I assumed his single nod, before suggesting we go on a weekend getaway together meant he would uninvite his current fling. Tell her she couldn't go on the motorcycle trip and they had to end whatever it was they had going on. In retrospect, I call these "dumb shit moments".

My counselor told me they are programmed responses. Practiced. Programmed insanity.

Thankfully, lying to myself all those years isn't considered a character flaw. It should be.

CHAPTER 3

My Pal the Ostrich

I suppose I always sensed when Brad was having an affair, even though he'd deny it, tell me I was crazy, suspicious, bitter. I got good at explaining things away, looking away so I wouldn't be certain.

I'm letting you in on tricks codependents play to stay in the game, to dance the dance. The Narcissist and Codependent Doo Wop. Problem is, it gnaws on you the way a buzzard chomps on road kill that's dying. Given time, it's hard to tell what the smear on the asphalt once was. Brad had familiar habits when he was grooming or fully involved with another woman. He withdrew from me, avoided eye contact, then became chatty at the wrong times. In recent years, he guarded his phone like it was going to spring legs and sprint away. Though he'd never admit it, if he was talking to one of the boys, he couldn't hand me his phone so I could say hello to them because a text might pop up on the screen from a gal pal. He'd be less interested in sex, more interested in kink. No kissing, just multiple climaxes for me. His was always a sure and vocal occurrence.

My validation.

Sick, but there you have it.

What went through my mind? Was it a marathon and I needed to finish first, or more often? When there're no passionate kisses or being held, great sex can equal validation.

I finally began to whisper, "Don't tell me you love me. Tell me I was good." But never loud enough for him to hear. A salvage maneuver to keep my ego from drowning and my life from falling apart.

Am I wild? Yup. Uninhibited? More so than he is. Confident in my body? Nope, it's the curse of a perfectionist with shitty self-esteem. His current tryst, and at least two other past ones, have been with women who never had a child, let alone three in three years. I'm not fat, but a million sit-ups wouldn't put the snap back in the diaphragm below my belly button, the one that stretches like a rubber band when the baby stretches you out. Generally a size four, never bigger than a six, I look pretty good in clothes, but preferred to make love in the dark. Weeks before we went to Encinitas to resuscitate our relationship, I'd already scheduled a tummy tuck for the fifth of December, five weeks away. Sprucing up to meet the competition.

We had a fun weekend. Sex is our thing. Ever the over-achiever, Brad is good in bed. *We're* good at it. I learned to like rowdy, playful, adventurous encounters, because kissing and passion are not his thing. Never were. Wine. Sex. A walk on the Oceanside Boardwalk. We'd be good as ever. I made a commitment to let go of my suspicions. He vowed to let go of his affair. We were going to start over.

Again. I did this with the same kind of determination I'd use to get back behind the wheel after a bad accident. It's like that.

When our weekend was over, he went back to Phoenix and I stayed in California, writing, printing, organizing myself for the La Jolla Writer's Conference.

The afternoon before the conference began, he called.

"Hi, Hon. I'm heading for the gym. It's been a rough week and I don't want you to worry if I don't call you until later tonight. I might just have a glass of wine. Watch some TV at a sports bar."

The call made no sense; he rarely called early. But I chippered up. "No worries. Sorry you've had a rough week." My end of our bargain was to let go of suspicions and start over.

But when I hadn't heard from him by eight p.m., I caved. I've always had the passwords to his email and credit cards, but I had never invaded his privacy nor, I suppose, wanted to antagonize my peace of mind. His credit card statements go to and are paid through the office so they can charge work related things and build travel points.

I managed to pull my head out of the sand and log onto his Visa account. At fifteen minutes before eight o'clock that evening, a charge of $76.08 had been posted from Cafe Boa, an intimate little Bistro across the street from the Grace Inn in Phoenix. It's only five miles from home. Five hundred feet from the hotel.

At eight-thirty, he called. "Hi Hon. Hope you've had a nice day." He sounded relaxed and cheerful.

"I did. Am packed and ready to go to the conference tomorrow. How was your evening? Did you at least have a good dinner?"

"Quiet, but nice. I went to Keegan's, sat in the bar, had a glass of wine and the cheese plate. Not the best meal, but it tasted really good."

"You might want to call Visa and find out who just used your credit card at Cafe Boa."

"What the fuck! You're checking up on me? You're so goddamned suspicious! I didn't want to tell you I went to Cafe Boa because I figured you'd think I was messing around. I like the place. I was alone. I had a glass of wine, a couple of scotches and an appetizer. I don't even have an appetite these days, with all the stress from work and from you."

All in one diatribe he shoveled aggression, accusation, character assassination, blame shifting, lies and guilt. Told you he was a master.

I could go on, but I'll sum it up instead. The most expensive glass of wine on the Café Boa menu costs twelve dollars. He didn't rack up a bill of nearly eighty-dollars alone, and much later admitted it. I wished I hadn't looked at the visa bill or the menu on the internet. Catching him in a blatant lie shoved me to the very edge of that cliff where I had spent too much of our married life teetering, afraid to fall, afraid to stay put. A stealthy wind approached me from behind.

I knew he'd never leave me and split up stuff. I also believe he believed I'd never leave him. We've gathered lots of stuff since our days in El Centro. But what would happen to me if I stayed? If I just outlived his dick, I'd have lots of stuff, but not even sex to validate me.

I didn't sleep that night, either. I got busy. Focused instead on distractions.

I checked into the La Jolla Hyatt the next morning for the writer's conference. I smiled, pretended to be fine, intense, there to learn. That night, I drank most of a bottle of wine in my room. All by myself. I didn't answer my phone when he called.

Around 3:30 a.m. I sat bolt upright from a fitful sleep. The nearly full moon shone through my window like a beacon. I didn't hear a voice or have a semi-sober out of body experience. But a sentence popped into my head, and I uttered the words out loud "I'm holding myself together with barbed wire."

It was true. Doesn't sound like a revelation, but for me it was a moment of insight. I was stuck, trapped. It hurt to stand still, yet I was terrified to move, venture into the unknown.

The Saturday luncheon was an event with motivating speakers, enviably successful writers who told of their unpublished string of early attempts. The challenges of hitting the NY Time's list. In closing, the moderator took the microphone, explained that we would find a slip of paper and a pencil by our plates. In ten words or less, we were to write the opening line of a new novel. This short sentence was to establish and evoke the emotion of the main character as the novel begins.

Judges would winnow the two hundred submissions down to fifteen that would be read and collectively voted on that night at the banquet. Without hesitation, I mechanically scratched, "I'm holding myself together with barbed wire." It isn't a block buster. I don't even know why or how it won the award. Had my Fairy Godmother intervened? Perhaps ripped the trusty shit-sweeping broom out of my hands and whacked me over the head with it?

No one saw the tears on my cheeks that night as I mustered my best smile and accepted the award. Dinner was outdoors, and it was thankfully lit by Tiki Torches, crystal fireplaces, and dim lights. No one needed to know I had not won. I'd failed. Those words, that award, pushed me off the cliff into the vast unknown.

It's never one thing, but there generally is a *final thing*, the proverbial last straw. What that is, is different for all of us; but when we snap that straw, take that plunge, it is almost never a quick, clean fall. I hit snags and ledges I desperately clung to on the way down.

CHAPTER 4

The Refugee

Who and where was I *before* I became a refugee fleeing my old life? What willed me to become an immigrant, determined to adapt to a new world? Leaving Brad and my home meant more than becoming single in my sixties. If I followed through, I was going to uncouple after nearly half a century, fracture my family, tear myself free from a man I loved. What drove me to where I found myself the night before I left my husband?

It was one week after the writer's conference in La Jolla. Brad had been in Austin on business, so I hadn't seen him since I got home. I'd spent the week flipping through photo albums of when our boys were little. I looked happy. Brad looked proud.

I also went through his emails again.

He had deleted all correspondence with his gal pal from Inbox and Trash. But when I opened his Sent file I found enough threads to shatter what was left of my hero. The exchange server only carried the emails back two years—two years too many. I was glad I read them, yet regretted that they would always lurk in the back of my mind. Stains I could never scrub out.

Brad told his while-at-work-wife she was wonderful, that he didn't know what he'd do without her. She replied, "You're sooooooo amazing. I appreciate you sooooooo much. You're sooooooo wonderful."

The day I had waited and waited to hear how he was doing in the big Member/Member golf tournament, he was emailing her play-by-plays. "I can't wait to get to Phoenix tomorrow and celebrate with you. I know how fun you are after too many margaritas."

I especially enjoyed another email he sent while out of town. He told her not to stay at her office too late, she'd be too tired to pick him up in the morning. Visuals that vilified my hero and made me want to slap the woman who solicited business from us while soliciting my husband. She knew me, knew Brad was married. She came to our company Christmas party and visited with me like I was her best friend. When I think of her I hope Karma is real.

My last night before Brad's return from Austin I was not measuring up to my mother. I wasn't noble. I was curled up in a fetal position in a back bedroom. Holding myself together with barbed wire.

I needed tools. Where in the hell was I going to find a sturdy set of metaphorical wire cutters? My jaws ached from clenching my teeth. I wondered if soldiers in battle go through similar rituals, invoke the same sense, before they shoulder their weapons and prepare to lose their lives.

I would like to say that the next night, when Brad pulled down our long-winding driveway, I was strangely calm. But I think I'd numbed out.

Our home in Phoenix is chiseled into the foothills of Camelback Mountain. The night view never ceased to take my breath away. From Four Peaks across the East Valley, beyond the Superstitions, lights sparkle, shift, move, and dance in the dark. Mesmerizing.

"Let's have a glass of wine on the patio," I suggested. I had already opened a bottle of his Santa Margarita Pinot Grigio and a soft Chianti for myself.

"Great." He was bubbly, smiling, cheerful Brad. His version of flowers and an apology.

"Let me put my suitcase down and use the bathroom. I'll be right there."

We hadn't seen each other since he left Encinitas or spoken since our phone call riddled with his lies and my Visa invasion. As I waited for him on the patio, I slid and fiddled with the linked Tiffany gold and platinum bracelet on my right wrist. I had put it on as I packed my things that afternoon. It reminded me of barbed wire.

On his way out, Brad ruffled Houston, our bullmastiff's, ears and tossed his rope a couple of times. Then he swiped up his glass of wine, sat in his usual wooden rocker, poolside, crossed one ankle over the opposite knee, and announced he was glad to be home.

That was our M.O. We didn't hash shit out; I swept it under the rug and moved on, as if nothing had happened.

I'd lit the fire pit. Ambiance? Warmth? It just seemed appropriate. Fire and water, side by side. The color wheel over the pool light bled the water red to yellow to blue. There was a faint scent of chlorine. I didn't look at Brad, but beyond the negative edge of the pool, out into the desert and the dancing lights beyond.

There was no catch in my voice. No fury. No tears.

"I've made a decision. I'm leaving you."

I wish I could say Brad's explosion took me off guard, but it didn't even startle me. I was used to his temper tantrums. I wasn't afraid of him. He had never hit me. But the hatred in his eyes, his pursed lips, jabbing index finger, and snarl weren't self-esteem builders. I was as used to being bullied as one can get.

"What the fuck! Fuck me! I work my ass off! Get home to this shit! I'm still the one that makes all the money! Don't piss me off!"

I don't remember the rest of what he shouted because he vaulted out of his chair, kicked it halfway across the patio. I do recall watching his phone splash into the pool, gulp and flash once before turning black and disappearing into the depths.

About then I became aware Brad was still yelling. He launched his wine glass beyond the negative edge, into the desert preserve.

I'd told no one of my plan to leave Brad. I didn't want the condemnation or commentary. It was my decision and my step to take alone. I left Brad on the patio that night, without another word. There was nothing left to say.

As I write this I stop typing and fiddle with the Tiffany bracelet. I center the clasp on the inside of my wrist. I haven't taken the bracelet off since that day.

It reminds me that I didn't fall apart.

CHAPTER 5

Family, Friends, and Forgeries

The forgery of my life with Brad was fairly predictable. We pretended to be happy, okay, and forever. It's odd how we can all be convincing performers to conceal our real life from friends, family and work associates.

Our separation should have been about Brad and me, but we turned out to be only the eye of a tornado. The damage was widespread and unpredictable, ripping the façade off nearly everything that surrounded us: our family, our business, and our circle of friends.

Actual tornadoes gain furious momentum, rage so fast and forcefully the body may not have time to adjust to the pressure change. Within a tornado's vortex, a vacuum occurs. Negative pressure and upward winds can literally suck the air right out of person's lungs. Did mine, a time or two. Or three.

The declaration to divorce wasn't announced, or even whispered, but it carried across the winds of change like the bleat of a trapped animal on a dark night. Our family didn't welcome separation, possibly impending divorce news any more than they'd wave down that tornado to rip through all they hold dear. This coming Christmas, a mere seven weeks away, would be the last holiday Brad and I would share in our home, together with our family.

Business was the beast. Two of our three sons have invested their careers in the family businesses, and suddenly we needed a new structure for handling decisions that would affect all our individual futures. Our tornado didn't cut a straight path, it whipped left and right on impulse and circumstance. I couldn't react to his outbursts without risk of shredding everything we'd built.

Relating to friends after separation reminds me of field stripping an assault rifle. Be cautious, deliberate, and don't fuck up reassembly. Friends who care for both of you want to be supportive, yet don't want to take sides. Neutrality can be deemed consent, by either injured party. Open support can be viewed as opposition. It's a backfire situation for them. I didn't totally realize this at the time, and wish I had.

If you consider walking away, it will help to be aware of the storm's reach, but I encourage you to hunker in and weather it if you can. The winds of change also clear the air.

When I walked away that night, I went to the Grace Inn to spend the night. It seemed appropriate at the time. He was calm and a bit sheepish when I picked Houston up the next morning. We didn't talk.

I don't remember most of the drive up north, only that I waited until I reached our home in Flagstaff to catch my breath, and reach for a tissue. The two-and-a-half-hour drive to Flagstaff, north on Interstate 17, has straight stretches, but it also hugs miles of mountainside as it winds from one thousand to seven thousand feet in elevation. From bristling desert to tall pines flexible enough to sway and bend in high wind. I'd left my life behind me. That called for a big exhale.

I finally called to tell my mom and sister that I'd left Brad and realized how unprepared I was for the barrage of questions, cautions, reprimands, and advice I would get.

My older sister, Brenda, fired away with no breaks for a breath, hers or mine. "When are you going to tell the boys? You won't tell them over the phone. Are you and Brad going to do it together? Have you filed for divorce yet? You'd better protect yourself. Don't be an idiot or it could cost you a ton. Have you thought about this? Do you think you're going to find someone who doesn't fuck around? I have a news flash. They're all alike. You just have to stop taking their shit, do what you want. That's what I did." Finally, she paused and asked, "Are you okay?"

"No, but I will be," I exhaled.

She meant well. I was in a freefall that was beating the shit out of me. A sharp branch knocked the wind out of me when I hung up. In retrospect, probably a panic attack. I'd left my husband and believed that was the hard part. I hadn't realized it was just the beginning of our end.

My face hurt. When the urge to sob threatened, I plastered the back-middle of my tongue against the roof of my mouth, hard. Long. There should be a contest for tongue muscle builders. We tear tamers would win, hands down. I may need new enamel on my molars if I keep this up and do hope that taut jaw muscles become the rage, no matter what age I am.

I was now home. The realization hit that the house in Phoenix, our dream house for which I'd picked out every door, window, appliance, toilet paper holder, flooring, lighting, and beyond, would never be my home again. The ache of letting it go was physical, the thought of going back stifling. So, our summer home in Flagstaff became my home, and it is a beauty.

Despite a couple of attempts by the original owners to add a feminine touch here and there, it is a king-log man cave. Elk-hide cornices downstairs sound awful. They looked as bad to me at first glance, but after a while, they fit. You'll have to trust me. I wouldn't have believed it either. Imagine Daniel Boone's joint: sanded, varnished, and bulked up on steroids.

Brass lamps with buckskin leather lampshades, buffed to a glow, sit on rustic end tables beside the living room couch. I threw an old comforter and pillow on the floor in front of the gas fireplace, so I could wrap myself around Houston and burrow my face in his neck in case I cried. Just in case, right? Then I tried to sit on the couch and cover my eyes, but he climbed up, and burrowed his wet nose and soggy jowls between my hands. Good thing we're both washable.

Houston thinks he's a lap dog, but he's over a hundred and forty pounds of muscle and heart. He outweighs me by over twenty pounds and is my self-appointed guardian. Bullmastiffs are a blended breed: sixty percent English Mastiff and forty percent English Bulldog.

This gentle giant's coat is the original brindle color, a golden tan with irregular black stripes, and it was no accident. Bullmastiffs were bred to guard English estates from game poachers. He's invisible after dusk for a reason.

Instinct is strong in him. He looks and sounds intimidating as hell when predators, such as javelina, coyotes, or raccoons approach the yard. But when deer hop the fence in my middle son Ben's yard, lured by moist grass, Houston stands on the deck so still it's hard to tell he's breathing. A straight-backed, majestic statue, he watches over these gentle creatures. They perk and look at him, but soon relax and graze. If I walk outside, they bolt, but not in the presence of their guardian. How they know mystifies me.

Children? The tinier the better. My teenage grandsons toss balls, take him on hikes, and feed him cookies behind my back. My granddaughters crawl on him, peek inside his ears, pillow their heads against him and watch cartoons. Their parents are well advised not to make the little gremlins cry in Houston's presence. He barks once, pushes in between them and the child, and looks up with a 'you don't get to do that' shrivel between his eyes.

Can you tell I'm stalling? The next few hours after I reached Flagstaff were not pretty. I was a muddled mess of grief, relief, fury, and fear. Fear, hell. I was terrified. I'd just turned my entire life upside down and watched it fall out of reach.

Whoever called it 'a good cry' must not have been as exhausted as I felt when I finally lay quiet, watched the flames, pretended the tiny embers warmed my wounds, and that the big flames licking around the fattest logs in the back rendered retribution. Nice if it were that easy, but it isn't.

Houston, who hung in there for the whole, pitiful scene, lay on his side with his back curled against me from my knees to chin. I spooned against the only breathing soul nearby. He was snoring like a freight train. I'd evidently exhausted him, too.

By the time Brad called that night, I was cried out and calm. Numb again? Probably. First, he announced that he wanted couples counseling. Garnering reinforcements to talk some sense into me? Then he launched his offensive.

I'd blown his relationship with his work wife all out of proportion.

They were close friends. He could talk to her about anything. She was smart. Had her masters. Understood business.

"Did you tell her she couldn't go on the motorcycle trip the night you had dinner with her at Café Boa?" I asked.

"You need to do something with your life, so you don't expect me to make you happy. You don't understand our friendship because you don't have any friends." A true professional, he dodges the subject then relies on repetition to reinforce his point, and doesn't slow to allow interruption, as he continues.

"If there's one thing I know for sure, it's that you need professional counseling to figure out why you don't have any friends." His offensive that night was to cast his infidelity to shadowed corners. This was a familiar pattern whenever Brad was pissed at me. The best defense is a good offense run simultaneously.

I didn't have friends? Lights began to pop on and illuminate neglected corners of my life. Brad had never liked my friends, said he had nothing in common with their husbands, threw a few impressive temper tantrums (that included airborne tools) over drop-in company that was not allowed, ever again. I adapted. Most of my girlfriends became wives of his friends, women married to similar men. They validated each other.

I have a hunch that a few of the second wives with pre-nups envy my exodus, but suddenly there was so much I couldn't talk about with them. Cindy's eyes stared off into the distance when she confessed that her husband had had an internet affair just six months earlier. "I'm glad you at least tried to forgive Brad and start over again. I'm going to stick it out, work to save my marriage." She didn't audibly add, "...and you bailed out," but I heard her loud and clear.

I wished her luck. We've stayed in touch in a superficial way.

Two others in the golf group broke my heart. Judy was the first. She called me in tears. "I can't believe you're breaking up. You're the only reason I went to Flagstaff. I don't know what I'll do without you."

I consoled her, told her I wasn't gone, just in a different place, and we could get together anytime. That was the last time I heard from her. I was completely confused when she wouldn't return my phone calls. Now, after a year, I get that she never will. And I wouldn't answer if she did. Recently she wanted to "friend" me on my new Facebook account.

No.

The worst was Sandy. Well, almost. I called to tell her Brad and I were separated, and confided that he'd had another affair. She snapped back, as though rehearsed, "Well, he's always treated *me* with respect. It takes two, you know."

I wanted to point out that it *does* take two for an affair to tear a marriage apart, but the injured spouse was an unwelcome third party. While Brad and his gal pal were in the throes of their emotional affair, or when the headboard was banging off the wall, did Sandy think I was driving him away, or cheering them on?

Why didn't I tell her that? The place where my confidence should reside was hollow.

The worst was a conversation with my dearest friend, Bonnie. She is my rock. An independent, strong-willed, career woman I've looked up to for decades. After I told her I'd left Brad, she sighed and said, "It's too bad neither of you is willing to fight for your marriage."

I quaked, cracked and caved in.

I had been determined not to tell tawdry tales, verbalize emails between him and his at work wife just to denigrate him to our friends, but I lost it. The twig broke. The proverbial shoe dropped. I puked painful details to Bonnie.

"I'm so sorry, Alex. I doubt anyone knows what's been going on, and for years. It's just…"

I felt better, but battered, and guilty. Getting through this with as few regrets as possible was going to be a bitch.

Brad soon adopted tactics that eased any guilt I carried.

My mom felt duty-bound to call him, but when she did, he lit into her about me. In a tone harsh with contempt, he gave her the friendless, dysfunctional profile of her daughter, right out of the gate.

"She does have friends, Brad. Sandy and Bonnie, Cindy, and the group of six or seven women in Canada that she met at that conference. She goes to see them every year."

"All those Canadian women are gay," he flung back.

He snarled. At my mother.

She didn't call and tell me about her conversation with Brad, I heard it through my sister, who was pissed as hell.

"They aren't gay, are they?"

"A friend is a friend. It wouldn't matter to me if they were, but one is divorced, the other five are widows, all mothers and grandmothers. By the way, I talked to Haley last night. They're flying out of Canada in February for Bucerias, Mexico, and have room in their condo for me. I booked my flight an hour ago." I had plans to be on the beach with friends and Coronas, and it felt good. Better than good. An escape.

Funny, but when those dark corners of my life popped with light, the misprints and forgeries glared neon red. True friends stayed, and I am better for the loss of ones that only functioned when I was coupled with Brad. When I asked my mom about her conversation with Brad she stared at her lap, twiddled her thumbs and with gritted teeth said, "I didn't know. I'm glad you left him."

After my first departure, the end of October, I'd agreed to couples counseling, but stayed in Flagstaff for three weeks, before time for our first scheduled session. I then stayed at our house in Phoenix for the December 5th surgery I'd scheduled well over a month before I considered leaving Brad, when I felt compelled to spruce up to meet the competition. Now? I wanted to look good.

Okay. I will own up to wanting, needing to bolster my own self-image. I was going to be single again, but hopefully not celibate. How in the hell was I going to be naked in front of a new man? I didn't strip in front of Brenda, for crying out loud.

Brad wanted life as we knew it back again. He...we pretended it was a possibility. He drove me to the Surgi-Center three weeks before Christmas to perk the girls up and tuck my tummy. I'd slept on the couch, or in the back bedroom when in Phoenix, but I think he still wanted the counseling to help us resolve our issues. Remember, we'd been doing the 'sweep the shit under the rug' routine for over forty-seven years. No wonder that he thought I'd get spruced up, come to my senses, and behave.

Insurance covered my breast surgery, so to tag the tummy tuck on was less than half what it would have cost on its own. That considered, some crazy person fueled by fear and vanity said, "Yeah! While we're going under the knife, let's cut your chest and stomach muscles at the same time." That idiot should have tried rolling on and off the couch and using the toilet before she jumped on that one.

It's a grueling surgery, endured without makeup, with a gremlin that snarled my hair and left bloody drain tubes dripping from my sides. I was actually schooled in how to clean, clear and reposition them for the next ten days. At least the gremlin provided some pretty good drugs. I slept more than I had in a year.

Eight weeks is a long recovery time without engaging those knitted stomach muscles, but mandatory. Between naps, I put earbuds in, Googled "Letting Go" meditations and visualizations. I draped tissues over my ears because tears trickled in and tickled. Drugs also dissolved the walls that guarded my heart and left me ruthlessly vulnerable. To Brad, I was a yo-yo, pushed and pulled, walked, swung, and stuffed back into his pocket for later. I fit neatly into his life. A great accessory. He dusted me off for events, or when he had no other plans.

I couldn't recover in Flagstaff alone, especially since stairs were off limits for those first eight weeks, so I slept in the back bedroom of our Phoenix home. Brad and I ate dinner together, watched TV in the evenings. How could it feel even remotely normal? Why would it not, after damned near half a century? It worked because I was there to fill my slot in his life; dinner, TV after he was done doing everything else he wanted to do. Everyone else.

Sorry. That was mean.

When he brought his gym bag home, I commented on the neatly folded, clean clothes it contained.

"I took it easy on the clothes. Don't want to make more laundry for you."

I didn't laugh in his face, but hid my, "Yeah, right," smirk as I rounded the corner. The smell of bullshit stung my eyes. His workouts evidently didn't require clothes.

I'd like to voice to the spouse who is fucking around that treating someone who loves you badly because you feel bad about what you're doing is a cop-out. Buck up, take responsibility for yourself, your actions, and your feelings. Hang up your cheating shoes, or hit the road; hurt your significant other with the truth. Get it over with. You two can decide to work on your relationship or split up. Just stop the lies and betrayals that tear them to shreds.

It must be hell being unhappy with your partner or spouse, but not willing to let them go until you know you've got a place to go, another person to fill the gap, or to wait until you are willing to split up your stuff. Building the second relationship takes time. Are you compelled to move from one extra-marital affair to another until you lock into the next someone? If you treat your spouse badly enough, will you incite them to leave you, as I finally left Brad? Do you want them to let you off the hook so you're not the one that walked away?

One defining characteristic of narcissism is the absence of empathy. They can't make the connection between how what they're doing makes you feel, and consequently they don't care. And the most important thing to accept is that they don't change, because they never come to realize it isn't you. If they have a flash of insight, it dissipates into the air like smoke from a cigar, leaving residual toxins and a stale odor in their wake as you leave or are left behind.

At first it didn't seem possible. He was so charismatic around friends, family, anyone who admired and didn't challenge him. I had to accept this vital factoid found in just about all literature regarding this character disorder, because it feels like hatred; yet they're masters of hiding it behind a mask, projecting it onto you, their perception of you, and of dropping enough morsels to compel you to work the hell out of that lever.

I gave the lever a break when for me, recovery from surgery turned out to be a two-month reprieve with perks. I smiled when I finally looked at my naked self in the mirror. Who knew you could buy six-pack abs, a renewed waistline, level the ladies and sport a two-piece just from an eight-week event? I'd lost weight down to a size two to four, depending upon the label.

Counseling did not go well. From what I've read, counseling often becomes the stage of vindication for the narcissist/manipulator. Act One of "Sling Mud to Cover Guilt." I gestured for Brad to talk first, air his grievances. I was there because I wanted to demonstrate that I'd done everything I could, more to myself than him, but didn't hold any hope we'd resolve our issues. Not this time. Lame, but I need to own up to my truth, too.

This wasn't our first rodeo. I'd walked out of the only counseling session he'd shown up for when we'd separated twenty-eight years before. His attack was brutal. If I called to see when he'd be home for dinner, I was suspicious, jealous, controlling. A bitch. Everything I did was to hurt, vilify, and be mean to him. The other women were a survival tool, how he coped. I'd stopped calling him, so I'd detached, become distant. Cold. He had me coming and going, and now, here I was again. This time I was braced. I listened while he told Betsy, our counselor, that his head hurt when I tried to talk to him. That I expected him to make me happy. That I didn't understand the depths of his friendship with his while-at-work wife because I didn't have any friends. His eyes narrowed, fingers jabbed a couple of times. In a two-hour session, his mask dropped to reveal a gnarled snarl of contempt for me that he had worked damned hard to hide.

I gained reinforcement, not that our marriage was worth saving, but that I should have left a long time ago. I didn't need him to 'make me happy'. I needed the bastard to stop making me miserable.

He refused to tell his while-at-work wife that it was inappropriate for her to go on the guy's motorcycle trip.

"I won't tell her she can't go. I can't disappoint her like that. She's excited about the trip."

He then looked at and addressed Becky. "This is what she does. Grabs onto something and chews it to death." Then he swung on me. "Why can't you let it go and go on? What's wrong with you?"

Instead of telling his gal pal if she went on the ride, I would leave him, he lied. Told her and his friends he had to go to Vegas on business, and canceled out of the ride. The entire trip fell apart. Our counseling sessions became batter-up sessions, only this time, I wasn't alone. Betsy was there.

On other rare occasions, when too caught to claim innocence, I doubt Brad realized he used the same lines to discount me and exonerate himself.

"I don't know why in the hell you can't let this go," he'd repeat. "It's no big deal. It didn't mean anything. I had fun with it. That's all." It was the same damned lines after every affair. The "it" he referred to was always another woman. And then after lines like those, it would come. Finally. The morsel.

"You know I love you."

That was where I'd snatch up my trusty shit-sweeping broom and go to work. I got so damned good I could do it without abandoning the lever.

But this time was different. I'd read a line that resonated. "When the pain of where you are becomes worse than your fear of change...." The ending was left up to me. I had agreed to couples counseling. I went, paid attention, and nearly everything he said resonated. Not a single thing he said drew me back. Instead, he boasted how accomplished his while-at-work-wife was, to the point that Betsy, the counselor, slapped the table, drilled him down with her eyes and said, "No! Why do you do that to Alexandra? It's rubbing salt in a raw wound."

"How will she know what she needs to fix, if I don't tell her?"

Teeth grind, jaws clamp as I armor up and begin to detach. I intended to fix myself, all right. To do that, I intended to be single in my sixties. Gulp. Before I left that second time, there was something I needed to do.

It was good, and bad. So was I.

Brad really wanted to see the finished product. Me naked. We'd had sex together since I was seventeen and he eighteen, right? I didn't want the first time after my surgery to be my first time with another man. I let Brad test out my new design. He liked it, and I assure you, he enjoyed himself, so I have no guilt. Humph. Amazing how that works. I may be getting the hang of it.

I didn't have sex again for nearly nine months, and that sexual encounter was so bad it set me on course to write this book. Deserved that one, didn't I? Actually no, I didn't deserve that bad encounter, but my mistakes began to illuminate dead ends. Bad decisions made for the wrong reasons turned me around, and shifted the direction I had to take to get out of the maze. I spent a lot of time backtracking in the beginning.

My love for Brad, once my hero, was dying a violent death.

CHAPTER 6

Put Myself Out There? Where?

W hen I stepped off that cliff, mine was not a clean fall. I grasped at branches and rocks, endured scraped knees, wounded pride, and got dust, sand, and grit in my eyes on the way down. I'd stuttered. Gone back to Phoenix for eight weeks to have my scheduled surgery, then left a second and final time the first week in February.

For the next two months, he called every night. I got emails, telling me I was a wonderful person, if I'd take time to pull myself together and be sensible. And by the way, "How much do you weigh now? I just wanted to know so if you were ever disappointed in how you looked I could remind you how good you look at the weight you are now."

His breaking point was Mother's Day in May. He sent flowers, and a card, "I love and miss you." I texted him a thank you, and added, "I wish things had turned out differently."

"You're a hard woman," was his immediate response. I heard his last straw break all the way from Flagstaff that morning. Smelled the dust in the air. Felt the ground quake.

I had often wondered how the work wife coped when he went home to me or we went on trips, while she slinked in the shadows of his life. In the emails between them that I'd found, he'd sent her pictures and videos of everywhere we went on our trip to New Zealand the spring before I left him. The woods where they filmed *The Hobbit*, a winery where we toasted to our wonderful trip.

When I'd handed him those emails he'd sent her, he said, "Well, she's never been anywhere!"

If I'd known about her while we were on the trip, I would have let her take my place. But she already had, right? Or had she? As soon as I left him, and he was available, Brad didn't pull her out of the shadows to stand beside him. He was on the hunt again. Yet, from everything I can piece together now, he didn't cut her loose, either. Not for nearly a year.

His hunt began in earnest after my Mother's Day rejection. Or he had a head start I didn't know about. Either way, within four months he began introducing a new woman in his life to our children and grandchildren. Was she really that new to him, or did she suddenly come out of a dusty closet she'd been in during our marriage? Could he seriously have been seeing two other women at once?

Why I care confuses me when I don't care about him anymore. I get that Brad prying her into my slot in our family after only a few months makes me want to wish pimples and plagues on both of them. I don't want him back. Don't want him to touch me ever again. So, what is it? Do I want him to suffer longer? To go to bed lonely and not have a big pair of breasts (which she has) there to burrow his miserable face in?

Yup. I want to pummel him, not picture him pumping his brains out with someone new.

Come on. This woman is in *my* house. On *my* side of *my* bed. In *my* bathtub, closet, and kitchen. It's an invasion of *my* home, property, and family.

I didn't know about the lever back then; the mind fuck, the back brain that worked behind my back.

My spirits matched the winter landscape in Flagstaff. If it wasn't a prickly pine tree, it was brown, rustled in the wind, or shivered. The snow was old, dirty, and barely sparkled in the sunlight.

If and when you leave your partner, lover, or spouse, you'll need at least one good friend you can vent to who isn't afraid to say, "that dirty bastard or bitch." You also need some single friends. You're now uncoupled. If you don't have either, get a good counselor you can pay to listen and lend support, get in a chat room, carry your phone or an iPad to fiddle with when eating out alone, and a good stereo system to fill empty air space at home.

The internet provides a wealth of information. I had a lot of work to do on me for sure, and the support that comes from realizing you're not alone being alone and lonely, is critical to dispelling isolation. The similarities and patterns of personality disorders in dysfunctional relationships shocked the hell out of me. The wealth of articles about the dance between the narcissist and the codependent resonated. Support is essential, so is laughter - and the laughter will catch you off guard in a good way.

One day I'd like to meet Chely Wright and Rachel Platten. Tell them that listening to their music helped lead me out of the maze. I played *Shut Up and Drive* and *Fight Song* over and over. Sang my lungs out...sometimes when I'd wake in the middle of the night. You can't use logic or even a sledge hammer to bust the lever. It takes determination to disengage and reprogram. Fuck the lever. Get your own morsel. Doesn't mean you'll get back to sleep.

Initially, the codependent's instinct will be to find someone else to fix, help, or take care of, or worry about. You've gotten through this far with distractions. Dulling. Numbing out. Resist the urge. Feel the gap. Fill the silence. Take care of yourself. You're broken.

I also need to clarify something that's bugging me. If thus far I've made men the bad guys I so don't want that to prevail. I love and am proud of my sons and grandsons; I admire men who've changed history, fought for principles, have written books that became lifelines, that walk their dogs, hold their child's hand. I long to be loved by a man capable of loving me back.

Being hurt or betraying another is not gender specific; it is universal to both men and women. When a pair becomes tangled in a triangle of deceit, three is a fucking crowd. And the dysfunction of bullying and devaluing is exactly that. Dysfunction. And because it requires adaptive behaviors, it's contagious.

I need to back up a few months to tell you how I met Jo. The end of the first week in February, after my surgery, I was back in Flagstaff. It was roughly three months after Brad's phone did a pool plunge. I decided I wasn't going to sit home alone and mope.

Healing begins with a decision, then a commitment to action. Debride your wounds, bandage up, and get the hell out of the house. I Googled "Events in Flagstaff," found the First Friday Art Walk, a downtown event where merchants open their doors, serve hot cider or tea, even cookies. How cool is that? There was a comedy show playing at the old 1890's Orpheum Theatre, too. I bought my seven-dollar ticket online. I was now committed.

I'd attended a rally the prior summer for Patty Blair, a candidate for an office on the Forest Hillside's Board of Directors. She's the only person I knew in our community that was single. I looked her up in the roster, called and gave her my "left my husband of forty-seven plus years, want to go out, and wondered if you're in Flagstaff" pitch. Maybe I should have embellished. I left my home, my family and the life I knew behind. *And* him. It was too much information at the time.

"Good for you. No, I'm down in the valley, but call Jo Harris, she lives in Flagstaff year-round."

"I'm not going to cold-call some woman and ask her to go out with me. I'll get a reputation for chasing women instead of leaving men."

"Call her. She's down to earth, was raised on a huge cattle ranch somewhere in the Dakotas. Go ahead, give her a call."

Okay, at this point I'm so lost, I look Jo up in the roster, make my pitch and wince at the dead silence that follows. Empty seconds take on epic proportions before she answers. Three? Five seconds maybe?

"Ah, what the hell. I'll pick you up at five-thirty."

Great. I'm going out on the town, just me and a stranger, but it is a move forward, a step out of the shadow of Brad's and my relationship into a world of my own. A new place, and I'm excited to go.

That's key, too. The knot is still clenched between your breasts at this point, but when you can be excited about something new and different, it works like a chisel.

When I got into Jo's Jeep Cherokee, I did a double take. In the photo she'd posted in the Forest Hillside Roster, light-brown hair curved around her face and draped stylishly to her shoulders. It was straight, with brushed bangs. The rowdy curls that framed her face tonight were clearly the real Jo, not blown out and coiffed for a photo shoot. I liked this version better.

Her high cheek bones, even without much of a smile as she greeted me, made me wonder if South Dakota native blood traced through her veins, but that would have been in direct opposition to her wide-grey-blue eyes. The trace of eye-liner, pale-blue shadow and mascara transformed the home-town wholesome image she tried to pull off, to stunning.

"Are you Russian, Scandinavian or Irish perhaps?" I asked, as she drove skillfully through the winding road towards the main highway.

"My mother is Irish," she answered crisply, as though I'd invaded her privacy.

"Your eyes. Grey, barely blue, are distinctive to Baltic regions; Russia, Finland."

"So, you're a walking encyclopedia?" I know a skeptical sneer when I see one.

"I did research for characters in a book I'd worked on." I can deliver crisp replies, too.

"I don't have a lot of friends. I'm different."

"Evidently I don't have a lot of friends either." My pitched brow, side glance met hers, but neither lingered.

"If this were the 1800's, I'd be Annie Oakley." She gripped the steering wheel with both hands and stared straight ahead. Braced.

"I'd be Calamity Jane," I smiled and shrugged. "She had a great voice and a hot guy."

Finally, Jo smiled. I even heard a soft chuckle as her hands dropped to the inside edge of the steering wheel.

We'd plopped down a cornerstone to our relationship before we turned onto 89A towards town. It was etched with lines that said, "not easily intimidated, respectful, straightforward, and no cliques, bullies, or bullshit allowed." A sturdy cornerstone.

I left Brad's wimpy wife, my alter-ego behind, when I left with Jo. For the most part. She still surfaced once in a while. Good, bad or indifferent, I was myself that night. No bullshit.

Jo was in jeans, a maroon turtleneck and a form-fitting down jacket I'd trade her for. I was in skinny jeans, knee-high boots with buckles, and a bulky-knit sweater. We were dressed for comfort in a cowboy town, not the flash and dazzle of dressed-to-kill.

Jo and I ordered wine and split nachos at the old Weatherford Hotel. Our corner table on the second floor overlooked the balcony and the bustling street below. The front page of the menu touted the town's heated history. Originally and subsequently, the city buildings were constructed of local wood. Handy. Organic. Flammable. After it burned to the ground one too many times, the city fathers invoked a mandate. As of the late 1800's, Flagstaff was resurrected in red brick and mortar, stone, and steel. Traces of cobbled streets still peek from beneath winter-worn asphalt.

Jo, married thirty-four years to a man two decades her senior, has been widowed for three dateless years. Almost dateless. Wyatt deserves more than a mention, but that's Jo's story, not mine to tell. I didn't know anything about him at the time I met her, either, but now I know that though her husband may have been the love of her life, Wyatt was the lust. Jo had no kids of her own, in the past five years had taken care of her invalid husband, then her father, and now her mother, who lived with her. She needed out of the house as desperately as I did. Maybe more.

"My morning exercise is bagging soppy Depends. I'll have to burn the house to get the smell out. By afternoon, I drag packages my mother orders from QVC through the front door. I threaten to take my credit card away from her, but it doesn't even slow her down."

"Cut the television cable, put her on DVD's?" I smile as I tease a possible solution to her mother's shopping addiction.

"She'd report me to my brothers, then call the County Sheriff."

"I'd bail you out."

"Easier to just shoot me now. One more trip through Walmart with her, and I'll pull the trigger myself."

This is where Jo and I began our routine of twisting worries with wit, and making jokes out of shit.

Jo and I stroll through the artistic shops and then head to the Orpheum Theatre for the comedy show. It starts slow as fumbling local talent, mostly college kids, try their hand at stand up. Jo and I laugh as we rewrite a few glaringly pathetic punch lines. We both have a sharp wit and no mercy.

The last two acts make it all worthwhile. The club owner, who's obviously done this before, is funny as hell. Self-deprecating, bold. A little edgy. The last man to stand up had been a Vegas lounge act in his life before Flagstaff. We laugh till our sides ache, and it is the first time I hear Jo's war whoop. She sounds like an ancient Native American rallying the tribe for bloody battle. Not a face in the crowd at the Orpheum that night that doesn't know we're there.

It's these little glimpses of distraction that begin to part the clouds, let the sunshine warm my face once again. A few wildflowers may have sprouted at my feet that night.

The next time Jo and I go out is for dinner at Criollo, a Latin restaurant on San Francisco Street. It is much like the rest of the shops, bars, and restaurants in Flagstaff. Imagine the long, narrow buildings in the old westerns. High ceilings are wood or lined in tin panels. Electric, phone lines and plumbing now thread through galvanized pipe bracketed to the raw, red-brick walls.

When Flagstaff was a summer home, I fit in with the weekend-tourist population. I was in vacation mode and rarely left Forest Hillside. As a permanent resident, I'm still getting used to one-way streets, parallel parking, puddles of pedestrians that move like mercury bubbles, and life in a small town. Once Jo and I order a glass of the same pinot noir, I pour out essential details about Brad and his current fling, his while-at-work wife. I confess that most of my friends and family want me to reconsider. "Go home, get counseling, turn my back while he zips his dick in his pants one more time."

"Your mother didn't utter that last line."

"Nope. That's my line and I'm sticking to it."

"He'll just do it to you again in two years. Or less." Jo doesn't mince words.

"He will, won't he." It isn't a question, but a painful admission. This was mine and Brad's roller coaster pattern, about every two years or so. Jo's reality check chisels another chunk out of the knot in my chest. I don't wrestle with indecision when I slip into bed that night. I've left home twice. Stepped off the cliff, but still clung to a sturdy branch or two, close enough to the ledge that I could crawl back if I decided. Tonight, I let go and fell out of reach.

CHAPTER 7

Boundaries Without Barriers

Setting boundaries is essential.
    Restate and restake them if they are battered.
    Be careful they don't become walls of the cage that boxed you in.
You're out. Lock the fucking cage door behind you.
Never construct boundaries out of barbed wire.

If you leave, you'll be on the run for a while. It's part of the process. You'll slip and skin your knees. Keep a box of bandages and a tube of Neosporin handy. If you ever fall so hard you need stitches, get help. That isn't part of the process.

Jo's crack that Brad would do it to me again in two years screamed a truth, damn it. I was looking for an escape even more now than when I first made my plans to go to Mexico. Ten glorious days in Bucerias with my Canadian girlfriends wove steel into my spine.

I had met these six ladies two years before at a pop-culture Buddhist conference in Richmond, across the bay from San Francisco. Actually, we met in the hotel elevator. I was alone. They never are, even when apart. These are educated, kind, emotionally sturdy women. Five of them weathered the deaths of their spouses, one divorced; all experienced the crisis and chaos that children and family can be, yet are lighthearted and bubbly.

They'd formed a support/meditation group. It worked wonders.

As they picked up the pieces of their lives, they pieced together a meditation-slash-potluck group that came to understand that the past is unchangeable, the future uncertain, and the moment? Well, it's a time to laugh, have lively discussions, read, relax, roam through the streets of the little Mexican town and absorb the culture, colors, music, and fresh sea food. Just when you think they aren't paying attention, they snap a look and call it like they see it.

"If you answer that nasty email you just got or consider sleeping with Brad again, that's completely codependent behavior." Haley didn't mince words, and I listened to her wisdom born of experience.

A few more wildflowers sprouted on that trip, despite me. I did try to drown them in wine one night, announced I wasn't wearing any panties, and got smacked on top of my head by my endearing Buddhist friend from Canada. She's still talking to me and that speaks volumes about true friends. Amazing how these principled, genuine, completely kind women have gumption and grit. Boundaries, without barriers that box them in.

After I returned from Mexico the February after I first left Brad, I spent the rest of the winter in Flagstaff cooking, playing with my sons and grandchildren, working out, and keeping up with Jo. When spring came, I told her that whatever was going on, sign me up.

How in the hell was I supposed to know she was an institution in Forest Hillside, had lived there for twenty plus years, was a record-setting golfer, and a closet party girl so ready to get out that she clearly needed a Mexican bit and a tie down? I saddled up, bought a day planner so I didn't screw up, stocked my liquor cabinet, and became part of a group of five women that planned three theme parties for the ladies group between June and September.

I chose July, Fifties Night, bought boxes of White Castle burgers, made onion dip for chips, ordered Tootsie Rolls, Juicy Fruit gum, and decorations from Amazon, before calling my oldest son for his party punch recipe.

"You used to make Jungle Juice for college parties, and I need punch with a punch."

"That's old stuff, mom. Now there's Drunk and Go Naked."

"Not an appealing thought since it's a girl's only party, but I'm up for rowdy."

A quart of dry lemonade, eighteen beers and a large bottle of vodka makes a brew that goes down like an effervescent lemonade, but packs a wallop. Between the punch and karaoke machine the party took on a life of its own, and I became a more familiar face to the core of golf ladies in our Forest Hillside community.

That summer Jo and I shunned online date sites. No one fixed us up with a friend or relative, and we heard rumors floating around that she and I had a thing going.

"If we find out who started that rumor, I think we should fuck their husband," I boldly announced to her one tequila evening.

"Good idea," was no more out of her mouth when her entire face shriveled. "Eww. What if it's Mazie Collins? Her husband is disgustingly gross."

"Okay, so we'll hire it done."

"You know where to hire a hooker?"

"I know who would." No way was I backing down or copping to incompetence. We didn't hire any hookers, wouldn't, but the banter was fun. I do know who would know, but won't share that, even with Jo.

Friday nights Jo and I team up to play in an event called the Skins game. Fifteen two-person teams turn regulation golf into a free-for-all. One member of each team tees off, the other hits the second shot, and we alternate shots and even putts through the seven-hole game. The craziness comes in because all fifteen teams move down the same fairway at the same time. One team has a karaoke machine, microphone, and speaker tied to the top of their cart. A liquor cart brings up the rear, as we all move down the fairway like a herd of singing, hollering degenerates. Take a practice swing and a shrill horn pierces the air to a chorus of reprimands.

Jo has been on the semi-injured list since mid-July, and it is now mid-September. She has a big swing, hits the ball a mile, but her bicep tendon retaliates. She had repair surgery done twenty years ago and she has been determined to push past the pain this time, rather than admit she needs to go under the knife again. Between massage, physical therapy and wide strips of tape between her shoulder blades, she's gutting it out; but I imagine the surgeon is shaking his head and sharpening his scalpel.

There's a big cocktail party at the clubhouse after the Skins Game. I've looked around the crowd and decided it's nuts to date a member of Forest Hillside, someone I'm sure to see on regular basis after a relationship gone bad. But one Friday night towards the end of September one of the single men asked if he could buy me a drink. I've heard stories about him that plop him in the 'player' category. He's known for dating two or three women at a time, which is not so tough when he has homes in Phoenix as well as Flagstaff, but what the hell, it's a drink at a crowded bar. Conversation went well.

When he pulled out his phone to show me pictures of his daughters, my eyes swung from the screen to his eyes, with a smirk. He'd hit the "photos" button and the first one to fill the screen was a porn shot. A pair of torpedo tits, some woman's mouth, and yup, one more orifice stared back that took the photo from a Playboy pic to Hustler.

He didn't miss a beat, but began flipping through photos till he got to his offspring. I wondered if it was a form of foreplay. Perhaps a test to see if a sex shot shocked me. I resisted the urge to tell him he should Google instructions to organize his photos into albums. What if his grandchildren got a glimpse of Orifice Annie? But it's not my job to reform his errant behavior. Bit by bit I'm learning not to be a fixer. Big progress for me.

Then he came out with a familiar question.

"How long have you been divorced?"

"I'm officially separated, but it's going well." I need a new line, because he mumbled something about having been there, excused himself and disappeared.

What I need isn't a new line, it's an official, law abiding, binding document that states what I already know. I am no longer Brad's wife.

Another tip: no matter how "nice" you try to be, your life may be inside out, with ragged seams showing for a long while after you first decide to leave your partner. For me, rejection, humiliation, and being devalued not only hurt, it festered, then scabbed, only to flare up again. It was time to move forward.

Dating is a dilemma, and I have enough of those still smoldering: like how are the boys and grandkids taking it; that Brad was a bastard in our last mediation; and there is the empty stillness of long nights and days without another human being to talk to. My ego is not strong enough to face the risks and rejection of getting out there yet. So, what the hell am I doing? About to do, if I start dating?

When fall leaves and chill breezes mark a year from my first goodbye, biology blossoms and trumps prudence. I need to be touched, held, and made love to. Am I compelled, like a salmon that fights currents and swims upstream to spawn? Deep down are we all just creatures of inherited memory and instinct? Can we defy natural order to mate, to love and be loved with cunning? Make intelligent choices, like the third ram? He's figured out how to mount and mate without all the drama. I watched a nature video of his performance, but here's a recap of my current hero.

While two male rams tangle horns and tear each other apart to win the lady with heated hind quarters, the third ram mounts her, plants his seed and scuffs away, satisfied yet unscathed. If nature is going to drive me out there, I want sex without challenge or conflict; to be held, kissed well, then to wander back into my habitat for a cool drink, with a satiated smile. No scars, tethers or backward glances.

"Use it or lose it" terrorizes my dreams. What if I go so long without sex that I dry up or can't enjoy an orgasm? I'd be bad in bed and no way does that equal validation. Biology and technology are about to lock horns. The internet rules. Date sites lure me in.

Motivation comes cloaked in the robes of fury sometimes. Like now. I'm pissed that I'm single in my mid-sixties. Shit! Here I go!

I didn't know the abyss went yet deeper. That there was a swamp beneath that lever. The memory still haunts me.

CHAPTER 8

B. J. and His Pal Dick

Married my entire adult life, instead of entertaining temptation, I learned to dodge hits. Avoid eye contact. No lingering touches or personal conversations with other men. Ignore the post in the chiropractor's pants when he makes an adjustment. Also, ignore outright passes from the husbands of friends and the odd relative. Not all men are gentlemen. At one party, a man in our group looked me right in the eye and announced, "I'd like to have an affair with you." One evening, another asked if I fantasized about having sex with him. The answer to that was a blood curdling "Not one fucking time!" that I swallowed, and instead whispered, "No," turned my back and walked away. I didn't cause scenes. I brushed away a hand on my ass here and there and got good at deflecting.

Now I have to unlearn all that and reprogram myself to attract a date again? I'm pissed as hell. Keep the ball bats out of my hands or my soon-to-be-ex's kneecaps better be headed the other direction, and at a dead run. I hate that I'm knee deep in the shitty, over-sixty dating pool.

The last time I was single the only thing that narrowed the dating pool was the fear of handcuffs, a cellmate named Bubba, and my dad. I was seventeen, madly in love with Brad, completely inexperienced and ready for adventure. Now, at sixty-five? The dating pool is only knee deep, murky with married guys, ex-husbands, damaged hearts, the needy, some need to be needed, and unidentified debris largely comprised of egos. They must cover the surface and elbow the nice guys into the reeds. At least this time I have lots of playful sexual experience. Lots.

Jo's been having a clandestine affair with Gerry, the head pro of a nearby golf club, for the past three months. She's been alone longer than I have, widowed, not divorced or on the road to divorce as I am.

"Does it feel okay being with a new man? I asked.

"I kept my eyes closed at first, when we had sex. It was okay, but not awesome. It's getting better all the time," she added, with a devilish wink.

"At least one of us is having sex."

The seam on my skinny jeans reminds me, in the damnedest places, that I miss the weight of a man on top of me, his musky-male scent, the delicious sensation as coarse hair on his body grazes inside my thighs, against my stomach and breasts. I don't need to have my heart tangled up in him to be stirred and satiated. Who knew? I'd have bet money I couldn't pull that off. Toys and tools are for the practice field. Let the games begin!

What delusional thought made me believe that lots of experience with sex would help me find a date or figure out how to date? The Internet date sites rule, but without a rule book. Media used to be a movie, now it's the means of communication from emails to texting to sexting to dick pics, boob and crotch shots. Oh dear. Dorothy isn't in Kansas any longer.

To hell with Dorothy. Right out of the gate, my first time in the new pond, I discovered this current crop of single men have interesting appetites that have nothing to do with culinary cuisine. And I didn't meet this one on any internet site. He came with a pedigree. All of this is leading to my first sexual encounter since I left my husband.

Since Flagstaff is in the woods beneath the Snow Bowl ski run, it isn't strange that this particular man lived in a sprawling home in the pines, not mapped on any GPS. Or that he was way ahead of me in adapting to this new environment, by acquiring products I didn't know existed.

No. I am not referring to Viagra.

He was not an online-date site date, but conventionally sourced. My first date since I was seventeen. It wasn't the first time we'd met. Friends said, "James is such a nice guy." James, not Jim, is a retired neurologist that raised two daughters on his own.

He invited me home the night we met, said, "Don't worry, we'll just sit on the couch by the fireplace and cuddle. No worries." Jo must have overheard him, because the next thing I know she grabs my purse with the same hand she grabs my elbow.

"We're going home now. Tell the nice man goodbye."

But the nice man called me the next day, and the day after that. We met for lunch a few times, and then one night over the phone, he invited me to his home once again. I wonder if he could see my smile, or hear my heartbeat thump in my ears, as I anticipated the next afternoon with him.

"I'd like that."

Before a crackling fire, wood smoke mingling with musk, I stood on the brink of a precipice, determined to take my maiden plunge. Even my grown sons had told me I needed to get out there. "Just dive in, Mom." I had to do it sometime, right?

Grey hair feathered his temples. Distinguished, educated, accomplished, and interested. If that wasn't enough to intrigue me, he was, surely still is, in good shape.

Framed photos of his children and their once tiny handprints in tempera-paint stand on a buffet opposite the wall of windows exposing wooded acres that stretch to the horizon. A bonus of living on the edge of National Forest, I assume. While we talk I only sip the soft red wine. Slightly dry. Nice. I nibble on the sharp cheese and salty crackers he served on the coffee table. Food keeps even half a glass of wine from going to my head. I also need a distraction.

I wait for a cue line. How does this work? Will he ask if he can show me the bedroom? Join me on the couch, slip his arm around me, put the other hand on my thigh, lean over and kiss me? Wait. That's a teenage boy's move at a movie.

I didn't realize how dearly I was about to regard those teen years.

Stretched out in his chair, long legs lazily propped on a roan-leather ottoman, he sets his glass of wine on the table beside him, smiles at me, excuses himself with a wink and a promise to be right back. I hear the bathroom door shut.

Alone, a warm calm envelops me. I stroll around the room, run my fingertips along the rugged-stone mantel. Nothing crackles or smells quite like wood burning in a fireplace. Our dance has begun. It's a dance I know with my eyes shut or open and long to feel my way through. I should let him lead at first. Learn a few new steps, perhaps add a few of my own.

I don't turn around when he comes back into the room. He lifts my hair, softly blows a warm breath, nibbles, and teasingly kisses my neck. I shiver deliciously. He turns me slowly around. A waltz for our first dance. Perfect. The thought that teenage boys should learn the waltz before their first-time pops unbidden to mind. I promised myself I wouldn't compare this man to my past. So, I turn and place my hands against his chest, warm, solid, mind numbing.

I'm not wild about his moustache, but when he wraps his arms around me, leans down and kisses me, his mouth is warm and tastes moist yet earthy, like the dry Cote de Rhone. I slide my hands around his neck, pull him closer, kiss him back. On tip toe, I trace the soft swell just inside his lips with the tip of my tongue. I respond to the different textures of his mouth with mine. Does this never-ever land daze of mine last two seconds or even three?

Whoa! I tripped a trigger. Axed the rope on a catapult. He vaults into action. No blind grope. This guy operates with orthoscopic precision and speed. Our lip lock breaks when I wince.

"Ouch" is involuntary. I get that our waltz is over but don't know we aren't just leaving the dance floor. When he plants his hands on my shoulders, steers me around, pushes me a few steps back and presses me down onto that rustic ottoman, I know we're headed for the parking lot. I relate the parking lot to trashy, backseat, bang-her-brains-out, then dump her sex. This suddenly turned a way worse direction.

His hands clamp my shoulders with a vise grip, and he has vice on his mind.

"The way you kiss I know you like this. That you're good at it."

This is not a Kodak moment, but I now wish I had a snapshot of the look on my face.

Both of his hands move with choreographed precision. One unbuttoned his shirt, the other his pants. A Singer performing a zig-zag stitch. Good grief. Good thing the zipper didn't catch on that! I want to smack myself, because my first thought is, "Nice equipment."

Within seconds, my perch on the brink becomes a free fall. This could have been a pleasant part of our dance. It's where I like to take the lead. But his fast shuffle isn't a lead in.

"Is that all there is, my friend? Yup!" ricochets inside my head like a shotgun blast in a blind slot canyon. He is intent on a one act show. I'm getting nothing out of this but a sore throat and half a glass of wine?

What if I seethe, "No," or better yet, "Hell no!" Am I willing to find out, or have I been stupid enough already? I know from experience that when a car spins out of control on icy asphalt you turn into the spin, not against it, or there's no telling where you'll end up, or in what condition. The instant he tangles his fingers in the back of my hair, the real possibility of being forced, of gagging and aspirating, takes on I-Max proportions.

"What about me screams 'hooker?'" I wanted to shout. If I was a hooker, I'd upcharge for having my tonsils assaulted. Determined that that will not happen if I can help it, I brace with resolve, make an executive decision, palm his pair in my left hand, then curl my fist just enough to take the lead. The bastard tightens his grip on my hair, tenses and squeaks out, "Yes. Pain. I like pain."

Fuck.

How did I get myself in this position? I didn't ask enough questions, though asking "What do you like?" the way Julia Roberts did in *Pretty Woman* would have plopped me in Hookersville. All righty then, I need to pay attention, get this gig the hell out of the trashy sex parking lot, and off the damned ottoman.

"Let's take this to the bedroom." I tried to sound sultry, certainly not as combative as I felt while thinking prone, missionary position and on a mission to get the hell out of there. My tonsils pulsed with gratitude when he reluctantly released his grip on my hair, took my hand and led me upstairs, grumbling, "I don't do oral. Tried it once. Didn't like it." Wow! I was with a completely selfish, sleazebag hypocrite! My skin didn't shiver, it crawled, like I was in a scorpion pit hoping not to get stung at least more than once. And where. I wanted to direct where and where not, to be stung. I wanted the hell out of there as fast as possible.

The crescendo, singular, his, comes upstairs. At least we were back on the dance floor instead of in the back seat in a trashy-sex parking lot; my uterus, not my tonsils center stage. Disappointed the hell out of B. J., who'd asked, "Can't I at least cum all over your face?" No judgement here, folks. It might be your thing. Trouble is, it is not my thing. It is absolutely not a first sexual encounter suggestion, unless you've reached smut-level-seven during fore-play or are on the pay as you play field.

I still can't believe what came out of my mouth a nanosecond after his last grunt. I looked at him with shriveled brows. "Did your ex-wife like sex with you?"

I need to develop filters.

He shrugged. Didn't know? Didn't care? Both, I imagine.

I have practiced moves too, and am headed out the door in under a minute and a half. I wrap my scarf around my neck, take a last glance at the shotgun and shells carelessly left on a shelf in the entry and don't bother to close the door behind me. A flurry of questions that rival a blizzard raging across the South Dakota Breaks raced through my mind, as I stormed to my car.

The dating pool had stagnated into a cesspool when I wasn't looking.

I don't bother with the garage when I get home. I leave my car in the drive-way and charge into the house on a mission. When I finish with my tooth-brush, I trash it, then gargle a pint of peroxide. What in the hell is on the roof of my mouth? Oily, there to stay, and it's numb? When he set down his wine glass, said he'd be right back, and went into the bathroom, the bastard must have put some sort of lotion on his penis to prep my tonsils and diminish a gag reflex? What a guy. Damn him.

I'm still stepping out of my panties when the shower of scalding water stings my skin. I clutch myself with both arms and remind myself to breathe.

Damn it.

I'm a big girl. I'm not traumatized. I'm disgusted and pissed. With him for sure. With myself for being careless and naïve.

Stupid. I have no right to whitewash stupidity with soft adjectives. Sure, I'm disappointed. I wanted to be held, to revel in the feel, the weight of a man, the scent, taste and touch and rush of at least one mind-blowing crescendo of my own. I didn't expect magic the first time, but he didn't enjoy me. He used me.

How am I going to begin again, when now I don't even trust myself?

And then it hits with the force of an avalanche, a blow to the soft spot just below my breasts. That weight and knot is physical, the one that really does make it hard to breathe.

He didn't want me.

He didn't want *me*.

He didn't.

Suddenly "he" wasn't the man I had just left. "He" was the man I'd left behind.

I wiped salty tears from my cheeks with the backs of my hands and stepped directly under the shower. When hot rushing water floods my hair and face, I can't feel tears anymore. I know how to do this, too, how to fade out, let the shower sting my face numb.

No need to feel my way. I just wanted this feeling to go away.

Robin Hood's Sherwood Forest horn trumpets from my phone. The sound signals a text message from Jo, I imagine. A *wake the hell up, shake it off* distraction. I towel off, finger-comb my hair, and for the second time that day, wish I had a Kodak on a selfie stick to capture the stricken look on my face.

The text is not from Jo. It's from someone whom I will forever refer to as B. J., and his pal, Dick. "Great blowjob! Call me when you want me again!"

I want to poke the eyes of each and every one of the ten-happy face emojis strung across my screen.

"Shock does clear the mind," I blurt, the instant Jo answers her phone.

"So, was it shockingly awesome or shocked the shit out of you?"

I give her a graphic rundown, complete with gag and puke sound effects, then read her the text just announced by Sherwood Forest's merry trumpet.

"It got me out of the shower. I thought it was you."

"Do you think he's trainable?" Jo asks, with the best intentions.

"Seriously? I'd need a whip and a box of kinky restraints just to stay out of the gutter."

"So, we need to go shopping?" Jo has a way of ending a question like that with a laugh-inducing lilt. Genuine laughter-to-tears therapy. Bad-sex-to-side-aching hilarity. Girlfriends are wonderful. This particular one? Priceless.

After that encounter, I know I need an education. Once I dress and pour a glass of Chianti, I look online for information. One link led to dating coaches. Wikipedia's definition? "They train clients to meet and attract romantic partners." That's not pimp preschool? The more articles I read, links I follow, the deeper I get into some foul territory.

Seduction was for hookers or true gamers out to hook a man. It sounded a lot like trolling for marlin, knowing when to jerk the line, secure the hook and reel them in. To have a real relationship with a man, the articles read like 'Hoyle's Rules of the Game'. *Learn how to be bait, put him on the hunt, make him chase you, or lose to women who do. Men are hunters*, they chided. They don't want a doe to stand still. Beckon them. They want a challenge, to win a prize the other hunters will envy. No wonder the words 'ego' and 'dick' slur nicely. If you say them really fast a few times, they form the word 'egotist'.

If dating is really just game playing I don't think I want to gamble with my heart and the rest of my life. The muddled puddle of late-date dating became quicksand that threatened a slow descent into oblivion.

I don't want a bunch of rules, or to lock in GPS coordinates and dully follow the most direct path. I want to experience the adventure of being single again, have the courage to stray, explore unmapped nooks and crannies. But I damned well want to avoid horror shows, mind-grazing bullets, and bad landings. At this point I wonder if Webster was on the dating circuit when he defined adventure as an unusual and exciting, typically hazardous experience, and then defined hazardous as dangerous. It's a wicked loop and the new-age dating world is all that and more.

But there is something else. Something more. I also need to learn how to be safe and warm alone on a quiet evening, brisk morning, or sunny day. There must be workable tricks to that, too, and I am damned well going to figure them out.

CHAPTER 9

Bird of Fight

Perspective has one hell of a backhand. Sure, you can shift attitude and outlook through calm contemplation, but the afternoon Willie, Bonnie's husband called, it raised a welt when it hit me. I was so focused on Brad and B. J. Pissed about the past. Afraid of the future. Determined to forge ahead. I forgot to remember that from the proverbial abyss, I can still imagine my world over the next hill, even it if will be a bitch to climb.

Jo and I had been to dinner at the Mariposa in Sedona. The wind-carved rocks, even redder at sunset, are majestic, grounding. The vistas of Sedona bring problem-shrinking perspective. The twenty-mile drive from home winds through tall pines before it drops to trail alongside Oak Creek Canyon; lined with aspens and oaks. Soothing. Beautiful. I was driving on our way home when Willie called.

"Bonnie had another episode. She's back in the hospital."

"Give me an hour and I'll be on my way." I'd be home by seven, could pack a bag and be at the hospital in the valley before ten.

"No. Stay in Flagstaff. They have a bunch of tests to run. I'll keep you posted."

I wanted to be there, but he insisted over and over that I wait. After a fitful night's sleep, I decided the hell with it, packed a bag and headed to the valley before sunrise to see one of the dearest friends I'll ever have. My son Andrew's daughter, Emily, had an 8:00 a.m. soccer game and I intended to use that as my excuse for defying Willie's demand that I wait at home.

This past year had reinforced the value of true friends. I drove to see Bonnie on the fifth of December, a year to the day since I had returned to Phoenix for my body-spruce-up surgery. Over the past year, Bonnie never gave up on me as I stumbled from anger, to despair, to swearing I was happy and just fine; like a crazed teen on a tear through her closet, until everything she owns is strewn around the room in messy heaps and she's too frustrated and tired to try on another thing.

No way was I staying away now. Sorry Willie.

I went straight from Emily's soccer game and arrived at Chandler Regional Hospital before 10:00 a.m. Saturday morning. The instant I saw Bonnie, I knew why Willie didn't want me there.

I stood beside her hospital bed and wanted to wake her, tell her I was there, but needed to get a grip first. I closed my eyes and took slow deliberate breaths that soon mimicked the beat of the ventilator that forced air into her lungs, receded to release it, and gushed again. Relentless.

She was going to be pissed. Willie wasn't ready to let her go. Again. The last time this happened, less than a year ago, she'd made him swear.

"Never let them shove that plastic tube down my throat ever, do you hear me? Ever again! No, no, no, don't you look away from me." She'd grabbed his chin so hard her fingertips turned white.

"I want to die quietly, not live like a mummy with that beast of a breathing machine droning in my ear. Besides, I gag on that damned thing. Promise me."

Willie closed his eyes tightly, and bobbed his head.

She'd reached out and stroked his hand. "If I stop breathing again, please," she pleaded, in a whisper. "Take my hand. I'll believe you when you tell me you love me. If I can't say the words, know I love you, too. Then let me go." Tears trekked down all our cheeks.

I was there because I'd come home from the hospital with them the last time to help her get settled and stock the refrigerator and cupboards, so he could manage while she recuperated. It bought her eight more months with him, so whether she was pissed or not, I imagine Willie figured it was worth it.

Brad and I had known them for over thirty years. We'd traveled together, celebrated birthdays, taken our first family ski trip with them. Bonnie had a way of blending conviction and kindness in her eyes that brought a half smile as my memories of her drowned out the drone of the breathing machine. She'd been a beautiful woman, with an extraordinary figure. Busty, with narrow hips. She wore her naturally curly-blonde-hair short. It framed the little firecracker like a New Year's sparkler. And she was all that.

Bonnie's only child, Chrissy, was seven years old when Bonnie and Willie married. When not at work they were a threesome. From the backyard pool to the beaches of Hawaii or the ski slopes of Purgatory, Chrissy colored, sketched, read books contentedly, and kept up in their adult world. She and my sons are still close.

Bonnie was a high-level executive in a major insurance company who didn't leave her organization and decisiveness at the office. Unfortunately, she didn't leave her pack of Marlboro Light 100's anywhere, either. She tried to quit from time to time, but after a bout with aggressive breast cancer two years ago, she announced in a fury, "To hell with it. I'm going out with a glass a Chardonnay, a cigarette, and a smile, not curled around the toilet, puking my guts out from another treatment or succumbing to whatever my trashed immune system can't handle."

That was Bonnie. She took charge of things. I once told her I admired her command of life. She knitted her brows, tilted her head and said, "I don't command, I simplify. Two words, kiddo: expectations and boundaries."

"Where was I when they handed those out?"

"They don't hand them out, Alex. You create and defend them yourself."

That was a call to arms if I ever heard one. She once told Brad he was a male chauvinist pig and he laughed. He loved her. I don't know how in the hell she got away with it, but I considered her my champion. Definitely my mentor. I had to stop remembering her devotion to Chrissy, the light in her eyes when Willie took her hand, or I'd break down and have to leave the room before she woke up. I owed her more than that.

I clasped her ever-manicured fingers in my palm, gently closed my hand with enough pressure so she stirred and struggled to open her eyes. As if startled from a nightmare, her hand began to shake and her eyes darted, wild with fear.

The instant she feebly reached toward the tube, made a 'No, no' gesture and jabbed toward Willie with her index finger, I realized it wasn't only fear, it was the fury I'd expected. I was afraid, too. Did this mean she'd live on a ventilator? For how long? Given artificial help so she wouldn't die, only struggle day and night to breathe? It was as though these questions bled through the primal fear in her eyes.

"You want them to take the ventilator out?" I asked, overstepping my bounds to defend my friend.

She nodded so hard it's a wonder she didn't wrench her neck. Willie popped to her side, grabbed her hand, petted it, and said "Sorry. Sorry." Ten times in a row until the word became only a single sound. His eyes met mine, not hers. I lifted my chin, tilted my head and looked back at him, a gesture that was pure Bonnie. His chin dropped to his chest, like a priest mumbling over a rosary. "Sorry. Sorry. Sorry. I couldn't let her go. They thought maybe…"

Crying with a tube down her throat threw Bonnie into wide-eyed gagging, choking that galvanized all into action. I flew out the door for to call for help.

"Take it out. Get the tube out," Willie commanded the instant the nurse rushed into the room. That calmed Bonnie long enough to let the rhythm of the machine resume. She closed her eyes and whimpered with each breath.

Willie and I went into the hallway while the deed was done.

"You've done all you can do, Willie. I wish Brad had loved me one iota as much." I hate that I compare everything to Brad.

Without the tube Bonnie still couldn't talk, but tried to whisper. Mine and Willie's hearing was not acute enough to make much out, but we both knew the magic words. Last night over the phone, I'd suggested it was time to call Chrissy. It's a long flight from Memphis, and he needed her here, as much as Bonnie did.

Willie gripped the bedrails like a lifeline as he leaned to her ear.

"Chrissy will be here tomorrow. Alex is going to pick her up at the airport."

Magic does happen, though sometimes it's only visible when tired eyes open and sparkle just enough to let you know. Perhaps Bonnie made each breath linger. Matter more. The edges of her mouth that curled in a smile said it all.

Bonnie turned her head toward me. I leaned over, smoothed the hair tangled on her forehead from the ventilator strap, and kissed her lightly on the cheek.

"Hey baby girl," I winked and smiled. I had on a white tank top and a blue and white checkered flannel shirt loose over the top that fell over her hand when I leaned in. She gripped my flannel shirt in her fist, her eyes darted to mine, and she whispered each word in a single burst loud enough for me to hear.

"Take care of my girl." Chrissy was Andrew's age, forty-six. If something happened to Willie, too, she'd be alone.

"You know I will." Damn it. I couldn't stop the tears, but I wouldn't allow myself to sniff or wipe them away.

"You know I will," I repeated.

Bonnie's hand dropped and sleep brought comfort and rhythm to each shallow breath. At least I thought she was sleeping.

"Our girl is going to hang in there and wait for her girl to get here," I told Willie. "I'm going get us both a Starbuck's from downstairs."

The aroma of steaming fresh coffee was wonderful. Willie and I stood across the bed from each other.

"Seen any good movies lately?" I asked. When there is nothing you can do, common conversation can help fill the void.

"Nope, mostly football and reruns. She loves to watch the old movies over again. How was Emily's soccer game this morning?"

"She's amazing. So fast. She's the youngest girl on the team, but has those long legs." Andrew had taken after my mother's family. He was six-foot five and owned up to two-twenty. "She made three goals that should have been five. The other two shots hit the goal posts."

"Was Andrew's ex there?" She and Andrew were nearly four years into a bitter divorce.

"Yes, and so was her mother, brother, sister-in-law, and stepfather. A regular gathering of the clan."

"I'll bet that was awkward."

"Not as awkward as it would have been if Brad had the time right. He thought it was a ten o'clock game, instead of eight a.m. and was bringing his new girlfriend along. I'm glad I missed that. Haven't met her yet. I'm in no hurry."

At that instant, we realized Bonnie wasn't asleep at all. Her right hand strained to lift ever so slightly from where it laid across her stomach. Her index and ring finger slowly curled down and yup, that middle finger stood tall, a totem pole of defiance. It was the best bird flip I've ever seen, or ever will.

Willie and I laughed so loud the nurse leaned around the corner to see what was up.

"It's a long story," I said, "But this girl is amazing. Still sparky and sassy as hell."

Bonnie held on through the night. At noon, when I left for the airport to get Chrissy, she looked peaceful, her breathing shallow, but smooth. Their reunion was heartwarming. Not a dry eye in the place. I was so proud of Chrissy. She reassured Willie he'd done the right thing, making them remove the breathing tube. "This is what she'd want, dad."

It was time for the three of them to have these last moments alone. I wiped Chapstick on Bonnie's lips, kissed her forehead, and said my last goodbye.

CHAPTER 10

Training Camp

O nce I was through traffic and across town, I called Jo on my way
back to Flagstaff.

"I want to go out tonight. Maybe Josephine's. We can order a bottle of wine and make a toast to Bonnie." Maybe there was a catch in my voice,
something that gave me away, because Jo didn't press for details. She knew.

"We'll do her proud, Allie. I'll make a res and pick you up at six. Drive
safe. See ya tonight."

Josephine's is on the outskirts of downtown Flagstaff. It's in a once stately
house with a grand porch, rickety stairs to a pitched attic I never fail to bump
my head on, and has excellent food. I was proud of myself for toasting Bonnie with a sincere smile and telling Jo fun stories about her with no tearful
scene the rest of the patrons wouldn't understand. On our way home, Jo
needed to stop by Fry's grocery store to pick up a prescription for her mom.

Four chairs faced the pharmacy counter at Fry's. I sat down to wait while
Jo retrieved the prescription. I leaned forward and squinted to check out
the impressive display of condoms beneath the counter in front of her. The
colorful boxes bragged about reservoir tips, tickle tips, ribs, and came in flavors. Suddenly I couldn't stop laughing long enough to talk. I tried pointing,
but finally had to pick up a purple tickle-tip package and hand it to her.

Her brow lift, head tilt, slow-blink look as she shook her head, told me she
thought I'd lost it. Gone over the edge of insanity.

This wasn't ordinary laughter; it was the idiotic, so hard I could hardly breathe till my eyes teared variety. I don't remember the exact time, but still wonder if that was the moment Bonnie died. It had to have been within minutes. I had bottled it up, held back my heartbreak and tears, so they must have found escape through irrational laughter. How could I have been laughing when she slipped away? How could I not have cried my goodbye?

The holidays chased preparations for Bonnie's Celebration of Life and I raced back and forth between Phoenix and Flagstaff trying to keep up. I was beginning to think I suppressed too damned much; anger, grief, my withering libido. I needed relief and release before I exploded.

Supplementing nature is more daunting than I expected. I soon determine that I don't need a therapist, I need a dating coach and a personal shopper. I not only decide to try reverberating stimulation, I need supplies, just in case an opportunity does arise to have sex. Shouldn't be that tough, should it?

I'm shocked that Walgreen's security doesn't arrest me as I tuck personal lubricant in my cloth Whole Foods bag I'll unpack at checkout. The poor bag is beige and lays limp in the bottom of my cart. With furtive glances down the aisle so I can bolt if anyone starts in my direction, I scrutinize a baffling array of those non-latex catch-all's they call condoms. What in the hell *is* a "tickler?" It looks suspiciously like a hangnail. Wouldn't that hurt? I wonder if my ex has a favorite for his little trysts.

Then a hair-prickling jolt shoots through me. What if Brad didn't glove up, went straight skin, fore and after, into one of his playmates? Eww! I put my mouth on that! What if he'd just been *inside* her? Had I tasted another woman and not known it?

I abandoned my cart and shopping bag at the end of the aisle but didn't bolt out the door. Instead the flats I wore with my skinny jeans clicked with finger snapping rhythm as I walked to my car. Ten minutes is all I need with him. I won't kill him, but he'll have some well-placed lumps, bumps, and scars to remember me by.

This is not a Walgreen's shop. I don't care who sees my car in the Fascinations Adult Store parking lot. I'm mad, on a mission, and need professional help in an environment with like-minded clientele.

Like-minded? Seriously? Once inside the adult toy store, I can't bring myself to make eye contact. It's never a good thing when one bears the look of a deer in the headlights. What in the hell is that? I don't touch it, but skew my neck, bend over, and try to find a definition on the box. It is in Chinese. Where would it go?

And to do...what?

Okay, another "take a breath" reminder moment. Evidently, I'm not past that point. I stop in a corner to compose myself...and there they are. A flavored variety of numbing throat sprays. B. J. was a shopper in this aisle for sure. Damned good thing he didn't try to insert those little black rubber rectangles into my mouth that, according to the illustration, wedge between back molars on both sides, I imagine, to prevent teeth from engaging in oral activity with too much zeal. That entire afternoon with him may have been drastically different. I'd have fought that.

I snap back to those packaged wedges dangling on a hook in front of me. What if he erupts down her throat and she aspirates that shit? Would he throw her in a pool or submerse her in the bath and say she drowned? If she survived, would she gulp down Robitussin DM to help her cough it up? Clear her lungs?

I overhear a slightly overweight, fortyish woman talking to young man in his mid-thirties. He has a black hair, tan skin and a name tag. The store clerk is the first thing I can actually identify. Except for the huge variety of male appendages in silicone. Those I recognize.

"I had recurring yeast infections from a cheap dildo my boyfriend brought home," the fortyish woman began.

I headed for the door at a too-brisk pace. That's it. I can't do this alone. I need at least one friend, tequila, and a ride home. We'll Uber all the way.

This became another defining moment, one in which I decided to look at being single as a vehicle, not a surly circumstance. I've been miserable. Flip from happy, to bawling, to blaming myself for not leaving Brad earlier.

The transition isn't just about dating, it's about adapting and developing. I'm moving forward, no longer spinning my wheels in the muck of regret, loneliness, and a live libido. Okay. Once in a while, but I'm not, couldn't possibly be, the only one floundering out here in this new singles world.

It's wild, but almost all of us are compelled to get our feet wet in the dating pool while hoping we don't drown. Luckily, Jo is capable of turning my tales of woe into uproarious laughter. Most of the time.

She and I have begun to gauge moments and memories not by episodes, but by WTF's per hour. Her Cherokee 4 X 4 bears a bumper sticker with bold letters WTF. Tiny letters beside each initial spell out Welcome to Flagstaff, instead of our mileage-marking What the Fuck. We do flounder, but we're having fun.

This journey is workable. Our lives, losses, loves, and laughter are all part of it.

CHAPTER 11

Herding Cats

A fter B. J., I absolutely need a guide to dating and dancing this new dance, before I get a speeding ticket for WTF's per hour. I decide to begin by ferreting out information about first date etiquette; first sexual encounters; when, where, and hopefully how to avoid WTF finales.

One Saturday night near the end of November, Jo and I were downtown Flagstaff and dateless. I realized I should have worn my snow boots when I splashed from a puddle into slush and then slipped on an icy patch on the sidewalk. Jo grabbed the back of my jacket, but didn't let go when her left foot hit the ice. We landed in a heap in front of the Patagonia clothing store on the corner of Aspen and San Francisco. It was bone-chilling cold, and we were now wet and probably sporting a few bruises as we scrambled to our feet. Why we laugh at stuff like that I don't know. Thankfully it was only a short walk on a clean sidewalk to Criollo, still one of our favorite restaurants. It's small, cozy, age-worn, red-brick walls welcome us.

Our server brought two steaming cups of Mexican-Irish Coffee. A light froth of whipped cream floated bravely on a brew that contained hot-black decaf, Irish whiskey, tequila, and a spoonful of sugar. We clutch our mugs so they warm us both inside and out. What's not to like about a drink that is functional, decadent, and delicious?

"Okay." Jo poked the polished-log tabletop. "If we're going to get out there and start dating, we need rules. Number one, you and I don't have sex with the same man. Ever."

"Agreed. So, we need to catalog our conquests?" My throaty laugh scoffs. "Like there are going to be too many to remember?"

"Maybe."

"Wow. I love your confidence."

"And let's not join the same online date site either," she added.

"Match.com or eHarmony?" I wanted to give her first choice.

"Those are under fifty soup bowls. I'll do SeniorsMeet and you do Our-Time. I did a little research for our fact-finding mission." Jo has a move—a slight right head tilt coupled with a left-leading hand-toss and tiny shrug—that speaks volumes. It was decided.

"I did a little research, too," I told her. "At last count, there are over nine hundred and four online services to service the singles scene. Chew on that for a while." I shriveled my nose when I added, "This is going to totally suck, you know."

If a woman can possess a cocky look, Jo is that gal. She'd been single until she was twenty-six, with no Mexican bit or bridle to slow her down.

"The word 'suck' reminds me of Ollie Karlsson. Won't forget that man." She followed that up with a pronounced lip pop and stretched both arms out and up in a slo-mo triumph pump.

"Oral Ollie?" My repeater-laugh kicked in. A tad higher-pitched, with a full smile.

"I called him Munchy."

That's it. I hurry for the bathroom before I wet my pants and realize our laughter level has turned a few heads.

"Okay, I'm back. So, let the Ollie story begin."

"After high school, I got to live in one of the vacant hired-hand houses on the ranch. Ollie worked on the South Dakota oil rigs. He used to cut his headlights, turn off his engine and coast when he got within a hundred yards of my place. I didn't know my dad knew about him until I flipped on the porch light one night. My dad had screwed a red bulb in it."

"How old were you?"

"Early twenties." She shrugged, then continued without a pause. "Munchy was like none other. He tutored me in how to give it, so I'd get all of that. He was worth every lip smacking move."

"Did your dad ever say or do anything about it? Other than the red light?"

"Oh yeah. He figured if Ollie was going to do his daughter, he could do a few things around the place, too. When he spied Ollie's truck he'd run down hollerin', "Hey, son. Give me a hand with a few things?""

"You're kidding."

"We lived nearly forty miles from Deadwood. My brothers had moved off the ranch by then. If he was stuck with a girl, my dad felt entitled to draft her dates."

"What happened to Ollie?" I asked Jo.

"I dated him for a while until he took me home to meet his folks. At dinner, his mother asked him, "How many children do you hope to have, Ollie, dear?""

He put his big paw around my shoulder, and said, "At least six, Ma."

"I never went out with him again after that. Shit. Scared the bejesus out of me. Six kids? Me? I don't think so."

Until I turned nine, I grew up in *Happy Days,* in a suburb of Minneapolis with a stay-at-home mom, no fences, a park across the street and a father that drove an ice cream delivery truck for Northland. Sometimes it seems as though Jo and I were raised on different planets.

As Jo's story ended, I attempted to revert to the topic at hand, but I tend to sober up and settle down pretty quick when I travel back in time. It's not a bad thing at this point. I'm afraid our server is going to cut us off for being too rowdy, anyway.

"I don't remember how long Brad and I had been married when I first heard about oral sex," I began. "I couldn't believe people actually put their mouths in toilet territory. Either way, I went back to the Joy of Sex pages and boned up on it." My shoulders draw up toward my ears and stay there for a ten count. "Sorry, I couldn't resist the pun."

"I'm sure you'll run into those willing to direct. I mean, B. J. would be happy to give you lessons."

"According to his text, I don't need lessons. He evidently likes it rough and

I bridled myself not to leave imprints on that son-of-a-bitch. 'Yes! Pain,'" I squeaked. "'I like pain.'"

Jo laughed so hard she choked. I stood to smack her back, and mouthed, "We're going," to our rapidly approaching waiter.

As I stepped outside and drew a breath of crisp air, I realized that somehow, I felt empowered by my trip to the proverbial parking lot with B. J. How in the hell does that make any sense? Depravation dementia? A "good girl" pat on the head from a pervert? Maybe that I have a raunchy experience under my belt?

I have work to do. Lots of it. Nice that no eggshells crunch under my feet when I'm home and alone.

By the next morning, Jo was registered on a dating site called Seniors Meet.com. I built my profile on OurTime.com; both are sites for singles over fifty. Woo Hoo!!

There are lots of things to discuss with you about the details, and how not to be derailed out of the gate. How to spot a "hook up only". Useful information if you want more than that, and useful if you decide if a hook up only is your thing, at least for a while.

I don't respond to a 'no photo' profile. Probably married guy.

Some will say 'Serious Relationship Only' is what they're after. I hesitate at this point, unless there's something stellar in their photos or information. There's a slot to click on the types of relationships you're looking for such as: Serious, Casual, Travel Partner, Friendship. You can click them all. Most do.

Keep in mind, a good man may be looking for friendship first, but he rarely wants to stop there. Me either, so it works when listed as part of the group, but 'friendship' as a stand-alone...means it's a hook up only. Could turn out to be a friend-with-benefits or a one-night-stand. I always wonder if these guys are married, or in another type of committed relationship to which they're not committed.

You have to make up a name tag for yourself, as do they. I don't respond to "4doghungfun" or "Handlemehot" sorts. Use your own judgement.

I pass when they don't bother with more than a two-line profile such as, "I'm fun sexy and looking for an in shape adventurous woman." I left out the punctuation, because they generally don't bother with it. There are more of those type of profiles that send you a 'like your photo' hit than you'd imagine. Safety is a real concern here. It's vital to realize you have the right to make your life choices, not just to do what anyone expects of you. Be fair, honest, and have fun. Life changes when you uncouple. Sometimes tough to take, but every once in a while the rush of freedom whistles through the cracks in playful way.

I'd shocked the shit out of everyone when I left Brad. Good for me. They caught up. Real relationships possess depth and meaning. Our relationship was a dry creek bed with flash flood warnings. No longer being part of a have-to-share pair is a new adventure. Adventure is a word aptly defined as "an unusual and exciting, typically hazardous experience or activity." Again, Webster outdid himself on that one.

For me, the adventure took a nasty turn when my now-single self turned to my magnified makeup mirror for a close-up. If I thought it would do a damned bit of good, I'd weld a placard that shouted "Wrinkle for Wrinkle! Aging Equality!" and pump my fist in protest as I marched across the trashy lawns of the testosterone purveyors. But it would be a waste of time. Besides, I don't know where the bastards live. Aging is gender biased. Grey hair and crow's feet can make a man look distinguished. The same lends character to women, but it is rarely considered the same sort of sensual.

Instead, I made an appointment with Dr. Rowley, a magician who promised to transition fat from my hips to hide smile lines and plump my lips.

Let's be clear. There is nothing poetic about the procedure. Adventure? I'll tag this one a harrowing experience.

CHAPTER 12

Fat~~Peel~~Scab ~~Squeal

ecember seems to be my 'spruce up' month with Dr. Rowley. Here I
was, going back, a year later. I drove myself down to the valley the
night before my appointed procedure. After two hours in traffic to
contemplate raping my face a mere two weeks before Christmas, I came to
the conclusion that vanity has morphed into a creature that slithered into the
dark recesses of my brain to blind rational thought.

In my pre-check appointment, I tried valiantly, but could tell by nurse
Rhonda's pursed lips and wrinkled brow that she didn't negotiate.

"We will not let you leave here after the procedure without a driver and
someone capable of taking care of you."

"That has my sister Brenda's name all over it." I concede defeats like this
one with a gush of air that flutters my bangs, then smile and try not to look
like a bitch. I don't explain to Rhonda how excruciating it is for me to face
anyone without makeup on, but vent my fears on my sister that night. Her
spare bedroom is one of my Phoenix landing spots. It's nice.

"I hate to be seen without makeup," I told her. "My eyebrows are a
blanched blonde and don't show up without brow pencil. Even my lashes
have blond roots and look positively naked without mascara."

"You're an idiot."

"Without lipstick, I…"

"I know." Brenda threw her right palm up. "You look like a cadaver. I'll check your pulse every once in a while." She lifts my chin with the crook of her index finger. "What in the hell beat your self-confidence up so bad?"

My bottom lip quivers. I sniff, lift my chin free of support and attempt a smile.

"Brad chased other women because he's an asshole, not because you weren't pretty enough."

I scrub my lips together to keep my damned bottom lip under control, pat her shoulder, and bolt for her spare bedroom—my recovery room after tomorrow's procedure. What in the hell is going on? Has the Ghost of Lost Love Past materialized to haunt me?

That's the thing about big sisters. A closed door means enter at will. She found me flopped face down and diagonal on the bed. Not the first time in our lives, either.

"Roll over. I brought us couple of beers." We prop pillows against the headboard and stretch out our legs. No eye contact is good for my bleary blues.

"So, tell me, Allie. How much more are you going to cut, lift and generally assault yourself?"

"I don't know," I half laugh and cry. "Maybe Rowley will inject some self-confidence tomorrow when he does my face. Damn it. Twenty years ago, I was determined to age gracefully."

"You're fuckin' that up, little sis." She scrubbed the top of my head with her knuckles, settled back and grasped her beer with both hands. "Think you'll ever get back together with Brad?"

"No. If I stay pissed at him for as many years as we were married, I'll be a hundred and thirteen. Serve him right. Besides, I'm way stronger now."

"I can see that."

Damn it, I hate that factitious downturned-mouth, single head-shake, then double-nod move she does.

"I am stronger. I just want to look hot." This time, my smile just happened.

"Okay then, I'm in. Let me see your tummy tuck scars. Have they turned white yet?"

She hands me her beer, thumb-hooks my stretch pants, and leans in for a close-up. Only a sister would or could get away with a move like that.

"Hum."

"What does that mean?" I emphasize 'that'.

"Looks good."

The next morning Brenda insisted she was going to sit in the waiting room and wait it out.

"Brenda, please don't waste your entire morning in the waiting room. Just drop me off. Please." For a little sister to prevail over a well-meaning but bossy big sister is a feat in itself. She finally agreed. The receptionist promised to call her for a pick up when the procedure was finished. I felt like a fifteen-year-old about to get a tattoo. Luckily Kohl's had a blowout sale and Brenda had a twenty-five percent off coupon. Motivation is everything.

Nurse Rhonda watched me down pills that would make this in-office procedure as painless as possible, then led me to a room while the drugs took effect. Nobody believes me when I tell them I'm very sensitive to anesthetics of any kind. My dentist thinks I metabolize them way too fast. It was soon clear I don't respond to these brain-tamer tablets in the usual fashion either. Ten minutes after I downed them, the only thing lower than my spirts were my inhibitions.

"Two Vicodin, a Xanax and I'm weepy," I texted Jo. "Hate that I was never enough. Scared shitless of never being enough. Wow! I thought drugs are supposed to be a fun trip! Who pays big bucks, risks their kidneys and liver to get low instead of high? Still waiting in a little room for the pills to take effect. WTF? Hope we get started soon."

Jo's return text flashed. "Oh dear!!! You are more than enough! Listen! It was not about you....it was never about you! Know that and relax, go with the flow. You are beautiful and will be highlighted now. I reserve the right to call you fat lips till the swelling goes down. No free rides!"

"I can never go back to that doctor's office," is the first sentence I mumble on my way out after the procedure. Brenda is laughing too hard to hear me as she steers me towards her car.

Turns out Xanax and Vicodin wring words out of my mouth the way a potent laxative empties one's bowels. In the operating room, I got a vicious case of diarrhea of the mouth.

This is the doctor and his staff that tucked my tummy and lifted the ladies a year ago. They've seen me naked. Know my shaving habits. Good grief. Now they know how desperately I miss sex, but not my ex or his harem. I told them about B. J. and his pal Dick. My funnied-up version. OMG. They said not to worry, I was entertaining. They did laugh. A lot. And I have no choice but to go back there for my follow-up appointment. It's part of the deal. Oh well. I was under the influence and not responsible, right?

Besides, the doctor shut me up when he brushed this gooey paste in a clown circle around my mouth. He called it a peel, but within a week I figured they should rename it a strip job. I blistered. Soon my mouth and surrounding area resembled the bum end of a baboon. I patted on green concealer to hide the red, resisted the urge to scratch, pick, and peel more layers of skin than any biology book professed I possessed.

Jo laughed herself silly.

CHAPTER 13

Cabo Escape

A short five weeks after my fat-plumping procedure, I leave snowy footprints and wheel tracks behind me as I pull my suitcase up the driveway for an overnight in Phoenix. By late afternoon the next day, Jo and I step off an American Airlines flight into a fantasyland. Flagstaff seems a million miles away.

We landed two weeks at the Playa Grande in Cabo San Lucas, compliments of two couples who decided not to use their timeshares this year. We reimbursed them their annual maintenance fee, equal to a two-queen bedroom at the Holiday Inn in Clovis, New Mexico, for the Penthouse Suite sporting two masters, full kitchen, a forty-foot patio and a gift shop that stocked Don Julio Blanco tequila. The ocean air and delicious dinner of fresh fruits and vegetables on the salad buffet are just what we needed that first night.

The resort is on the Southeast corner of a peninsula wrapped in the arms of the Pacific on one and a half sides, the Sea of Cortez and a marina on the remainder. After dinner I unpack, shower, and slip into a short, satin nighty. I step onto a sliver of railed patio outside the open sliding door in my bedroom. Distant music from the beach wedding we had watched at dinner is carried by the breeze that brushes my skin. Rays of moonlight shimmer across the rippled black ocean. I love the scent of salt-air mingled with sea shells and sand and am incredibly lucky to be here.

I climb into bed, begin reading *The Carrie Diaries* on my iPad, and stupid tears come from nowhere. I'm happy! I have two incredible weeks in this paradise. What in the hell is wrong with me now?

"Same thing," rattled around inside my head like an echo. It started when I thought of going to the pool tomorrow. Would I look good in my swimsuit? Would any of the men find me attractive? I have a mind, gravitate toward intellectual discussions, yet am consumed with how I look, who will look, and what they'll think. It's that stupid lever, and me looking for the validation morsel.

Brad left me for a while, a long time ago. Almost three decades ago, when my boys were still at home, money short. The memory triggers the taste of desperation on the back of my tongue between my molars. Like many of you, the thought of being separated from my sons during Brad's custody time, of finding a place to live that I could afford on my own, juggling work and home, was daunting. I gained confidence over the months of our separation, and went back with him for what I felt were the right reasons at the time. How's deciding I'd have slept with Attila the Hun before I let the boys go during court-authorized visitations? I didn't know about narcissism, manipulation, absence of empathy, or rats, morsels, and levers. And I believed Brad's declaration of love and promises that all would be different, for rational reasons. I held out hope at least.

What I want you to know is that I realize how lucky I am this time. I'm grateful that my children are grown and that I could afford to leave. I expected it would be easier on the emotional front, too, but those things don't fix the ache of loneliness, or fill in the gaps between regrets when I found myself thirty years older, a lot worse for the psychological damage, and alone.

Emotional abuse doesn't have a price tag or dollar limit. It takes a devastating toll, whatever your income bracket. Sometimes we stay in a dysfunctional relationship because we can't afford to leave, other times because we have so much to lose. Financial security created opportunities for me at the same time it demolished excuses, and made it harder for me to believe I was worth salvaging.

I crawled out of my bed in Cabo that first night to see Jo's light on and went to stand in her doorway.

"You look like a phantom from *The Shining,*" She drew her head back.

"I'm sixty-six and alone."

She blinks volumes when she cocks her head like, "Are you nuts?" After all, she's a sixty-four-year-old widow.

"I have to cast myself as bait to find a man I don't want to keep?" I added.

"Catch and release, baby. We both know better than to wanna keep 'em."

"You were with David for over thirty years and he adored you."

"Let's face it, I was twenty-six, nearly half his age when we married. He raised me, spoiled me, molded me into what he wanted. If I find a codger old enough to try that trick again, we'd have seven doddering years before he hit a hundred. You and I are in the real world now, and that dating pool has a rancid stench."

"Decaying bodies of women over sixty?"

"Probably. We need a cocktail."

It took about ninety seconds for us to be on the patio, stretched out on lounge chairs, with a short glass of Don Julio Blanco mixed with Ruby Grapefruit juice.

"I want to invent a sexy, mature man, hot as hell, smoldering eyes, equipment that makes me shudder at the sight," I say, holding my rippled glass up for a toast.

"He and his hunk of a pal live in isolation, waiting for us to snap our fingers." Jo steps into my fantasy.

"They're at our beck and call. We don't share or switch off, by the way," I add.

"Never." she shudders. "We have no guilt for not calling, but when we do, they'll magically appear."

"I want to be wanted. I want to be held, touched, to make love."

"Stop screwing up a really hot fantasy, will you?" Jo snapped back.

"But then I want him to go away. No more broken-heart shit. I want my freedom." A feeble attempt to redeem myself. "Think I'm becoming a guy?"

"I think we should cultivate our fantasy for the entire female population. It would sell like hot cakes."

I dragged our fantasy to bed like a security blanket trailing behind a thumb-sucking toddler. I evidently dropped like the dead onto my pillow, because my next conscious thought was, "Our patio faces East?" I always think of the ocean facing west, but the Pacific wraps around our peninsula and captures both sunrise and sunset. This sunrise looked like a nuclear explosion that touched everything from me to the horizon. I scrubbed my eyes with my knuckles, blinked and looked out my curtains again. *No wonder people once thought the world was flat.*

After coffee, Jo and I packed our beach bags, clapped our flip flops down six flights, exchanged cards for huge towels, procured lounge chairs and umbrellas, and then placed our order with the ever-present waiter.

"Our biggest job today is mustering the guts to pull our cover-ups over our heads," I said.

"Glad that's over with," Jo huffs, smoothing her towel across the lounger.

"I'm not making eye contact with anyone. My ego can't handle it."

"I have an extra ten pounds you could use. Stop bitching. We both look hot."

We turned a couple of heads. Sometimes women want to elbow a man for raking us with their eyes, but today it happened a few times, and it felt awesome.

A string of cascading pools to our backs, ocean spread before us, and by lunchtime, plates of fresh sea bass tacos balance on our laps. We'd have a Corona, but pledged to postpone our Mexican happy hours until after one. I take a bite, then tap the screen on my iPad as I browse the Ourtime.com website, checking in with my roster.

"Okay, my most intriguing offer yet," I announce. "A good-looking man, sixteen years younger. Told him I was heading to Cabo for two weeks. He says, 'Invite me! Want you!' All righty then," I said. "Can't say I am not intrigued."

"Why wouldn't you be?" Jo blurts with a puff of air.

"Because what would I do with him when he sees that twenty-two-year old on the lounger two to your left?"

"Unless she lets him move in, he won't wander far."

"He looks great in the tux, red carpet background."

"Probably profile perjury. Somebody else's picture. Bastard."

"His bio says, "I'm gainfully employed and open to the future." What in the hell does that mean?"

"He wants a sugar tit to nurse, to house, and to feed his sorry, tight ass."

"You have a way with words, Jo."

"I'm just being real here."

"Well shut the fuck up." I lean in a whisper. "I'm entitled to at least a few fantasy moments before you shatter my ego, illusions, and libido."

In the vein of research, I message him that the Cabo trip is booked up, lots of snow bunnies in search of warm waters and weather. I asked him to define "open to the future." Surprised me again, he did.

"It means my job allows me to go wherever I want, whenever, with whomever. I'd love to meet you! Here's my phone number, xxx-xxx-xxxx text me!" Then he did it. Added the deal breaker. "I like older women."

My wounded ego contorted into a slobbering demon bent on devouring me. I grabbed my keyboard as viciously as I'd brandish a wooden cross. Wait a minute. To some guy sixteen years younger, I was an older woman. What in the hell was I so sensitive about?

I show Jo his bio, let her catch up on our correspondence. She looks at me like I have three eyes. "What in the hell are you waiting for?"

"Any idea what my sons would say?" I cocked my head and shiftily narrowed my eyes.

"It's not their life. It's yours. Besides, Andrew's last nightmare was fifteen years younger, and how much younger is Ben's girlfriend? The one with the two-year-old?"

"Twenty years." My sinister thoughts turned to sheepish ones.

"Exactly when do you want to start living on your own terms?"

"Right after I order a couple of Coronas. It's ten past one. He likes older women?" I squeak out. "I'm not just a woman anymore. I'm an older woman. Yuck." My brow furrows in earnest as I turn to Jo.

"Have fairy tales gone the way of pay phones and love letters written in longhand? Did Cinderella catch Prince Charming doing the sixteen-year old milk maid, sue for divorce, and not live happily ever after?" I ask.

"Whoever coined the 'happily ever after' ending didn't know shit. Come on. Let's get wet."

We step into the hot tub for fifteen or so minutes, dry off and are ready for the Coronas plunged into a bucket of ice waiting beside our loungers.

"I know I'm obsessed with sex, but other than being used by that bastard, B.J., it's been a year." I drag the last word through a long bed of hot coals. "A lot of people go through life with intermittent sex. I just wasn't one of them."

"Me either. And don't kid yourself into believing a couple of Coronas will make you stop craving sex. They'll ramp our libidos up till we might wonder if that beefy guy four from the left over there can still get it up."

"Shoot me now." I said.

"I'll cut you off if you start to drift his direction."

"I'll trip you, and hand you another beer. By the way, I signed us up for the Beach Party tomorrow night."

"It's damned time we went to a party. Once we're roasted to medium rare, let's shower and walk into town. Find something "beachy" to wear. And another thing. When a man looks at you, look back, will you?"

"Promise. I'll be on the lookout." I smile like I mean it, but my stomach knots.

More than once we've walked through a bar, restaurant or on the side-walks of downtown Flagstaff and she'd ask, "Did you see the way that guy looked at you?"

My honest response is usually, "What guy?" Nearly half a century of deflection programming. I need to reboot and update my systems. Cabo is a million miles from my old life.

CHAPTER 14

I Finally Looked Back

In town Jo found a fuchsia and black wrap-around skirt, a silky top, and a fuchsia accent scarf. I found a pair of palazzo pants that hugged me in the right places, a strapless royal-blue tank with subtle inch-wide ruffles and a pair of glittery sandals I could manage to walk a few hundred yards in before I'd need to be carried, dragged, or to tiptoe barefoot. Ish. The need for orthotics created a cute shoe challenge, but for one night, I'll gut it out. We went down to the beach party early, hoping to get a table near the bandstand.

Mexicans know how to throw a party; I'll give them that. Two gaily dressed women signed us in, clamped wrist bands (not exclusive to American bars and ball games it seems) on us, led us to a table with rows and rows of Jell-O shots and/or mouthwash-sized paper cups filled with tequila—but not through the roped entry. Evidently 'seeks o'clock' would be the magic hour. Until then we could do shooters, roam the grounds or beach, and wait for the hands of time to do their vertical stretch.

"Why not?" Jo winked as she downed a liquid shot and then popped a Jell-O shot.

"Why the hell not?" I followed suit. "Later, if I've done something you know I'll regret, just give me a few more shots so I won't remember it, and then keep your mouth shut. I won't want to hear about it, either."

"Deal. And ditto. Tequila can be a real a memory scrubber."

"Andrew's last girlfriend said tequila is the only alcohol that's not a depressant. What's to be depressed about when you can't remember shit?"

"Oh darlin'. You've never woken up in a room, wondering where the hell you are, or who the out-cold guy sprawled across your legs is."

"Evidently you have."

"Huh," Jo grunted. "It's amazing I made it past my twenty-first birthday."

We sat on the beach wall, slipped off our shoes and dangled our feet to wait for 'seeks o'clock'. We were both laughing when it happened.

I glanced left, over Jo's shoulder, and my eyes met those of and a nice-looking man in a long-sleeved blue T-shirt tucked into khaki shorts. It felt like two magnets snapped together. Jo's admonition to 'look back' screamed aloud in my head, so I didn't look scared or look away until I gave him a sidelong nod and a smile.

I was on a roll. When the rope dropped, he and a guy friend of his sat down at what I thought was the best table, facing the band. I was already two shots of tequila into this party when he waved us over to sit down. Jo sits on my left. Dan introduces himself and his friend, Dan. I catch my right brow before it pitches cynically, but can't help wondering if they're being cute, or possibly keep an alias simple so they don't screw up after a few drinks. Then I stop myself. Am I looking for a way out before I'm into more than hello? No wedding rings or band lines on tan hands.

Jo settles the name distinction to avoid confusion. Like Queen Elizabeth granting knighthood, she taps her index finger towards the man next to me, calls him Daniel. Another air-tap towards his pal, whom she dubs Dan. Dan instantly offers to get drinks. When he returns with our two Coronas, he sits down on Jo's left with a broad smile. No lack of confidence there. We've coupled up before the band has set up onstage. I have 'first day of school' jitters and swear to myself I'm going to relax, damn it.

I'm dying to talk to Jo, but can't. Turns out Daniel has had a time share at Solmar Resort next door, for ten years. He's been to the weekly beach party a dozen times, but it is new to Dan. Once the band kicks up, talking above coffin-sized speakers no more than ten feet to our left is a test of hearing acuity and voice projection I don't pass.

Good grief, Daniel is on his feet, hand out, and clearly wants me to dance. I slip off my sandals and let him lead. I always laugh when I attempt to dance.

My ex didn't dance, so my only experience was pre-seventeen, kitchen floor bandstand-style moves my older sisters taught me.

Thankfully, dancing these days doesn't require much beyond a sense of the beat and a few repetitive foot moves, so I manage. It feels good to smile. When Daniel takes my hands, and spins me in a turn, I can feel my laughter and feel the sand trashing my forty-dollar pedicure.

Everyone is called to form a line, grip the waist and hips of the person in front of us, and step-kick in a single circle to the beat, much like a cha-cha, in circular motion. Daniel would later tell me he liked clamping his palms on my hips as I moved. His firm grip didn't escape my notice either.

We dance at least half a dozen times. Daniel is a perfect gentleman. His friend, Dan, is all over Jo; arm around her, hand on her knee. Leaning in to talk over the band came with soft-slow kisses on her neck. I'm in awe of the way she laughs and takes it in stride. Responds with her hand on his knee even. She's one hell of a flirt.

Lessons. I'm a rapt student taking lessons.

We all laugh as we watch some 'too big yet brave', and some 'too in the tequila' attempts at the limbo contest. The M.C. is a born comedian. None of us can decide if the drunk Polynesian woman in a slinky dress, hair falling to hips that gyrate kinetically, is a hooker or gold digger, but she's definitely in this for the cash.

"If the mutt-faced old man with horn-rimmed glasses is her sugar daddy, he better have his credit card handy," Daniel hollers above the band, not caring who hears him.

I'm wiping tears of laughter from the corners of my eyes when Jo leaned towards me. "Should we ask them to our place for a drink?"

I mouth, "I don't know," shrug, and shake my head in utter confusion. My guy is a good dancer, nice to talk to, but no sparks fly between us.

Jo grips my knee, leans in and whispers, "Okay, I'll ask my guy; yours will follow. Drinks only. They don't stay. Deal?"

I answer with an open-hands nod. Holy shit! My dad would have shot me!

Daniel and Dan go by their place first and show up with a bottle of Manhattans or Cosmos, something with a red tint that I don't dare try tonight. Jo and I opt for Don Julio with Ruby Red Grapefruit juice. Our new standard. I make mine light, with lots of ice. The four of us take drinks out to our patio. The damned moon, almost full, casts pure white light across the Pacific. It's bright enough that we cast faint shadows on our patio.

Dan has a hand on Jo's back, shoulder, or knee the entire time. Daniel is nice, but doesn't touch me. I figure he's being a pal to his pal, but not interested in me. After a long while, Jo and Dan walk inside our condo. Now I'm scrambling for conversation. I've had a fun night, but my gritty feet yearn for a hot-whirlpool bath.

Jo's dead. I'm going to pummel her for leaving me out here alone with him.

I stand up first, brace myself against the railing, grip it as if it were a lifeline actually, and focus on moonlight strung across the ocean. I hope he's going to follow his pal. Instead, Daniel reaches inside and across me, takes my left wrist, pulls me into him, circles me with his other arm, leans down and kisses me.

Where in the hell did this come from? He doesn't stop. The kiss, a breathbreak, and then he palms my head in his huge hand, tightens his fingers in my hair just enough to tingle. A John Wayne move, and I melt just a little into him, tiptoe and kiss him back. It's a reflex. I react to him, his heat, the pressure of his hands, his mouth, his breath.

Suddenly he ups the ante. His long arms reach around me, lift me into him and the word "kiss" doesn't define the sensation. I am well aware that after just dinner and a few dances this isn't romance, but I've been without a man's hands on me for so long I don't care.

Maybe ten minutes later Jo pokes her head out the sliding door. "Dan went back to their place, and I'm going to bed." She closes the door and drapes so quickly I want to pummel her all over again, but only for about the eighteenth of a second it takes before Daniel takes me in his arms again.

"Can I stay?" His voice is husky with passion. I muster all the common sense I can salvage, shake my head and wonder if I'm out of my mind. I want to pull him into my bedroom and on top of me, not send him packing.

That I want to let a man I've known less than three hours devour me sobers me back to sanity. We stay together on the patio beneath that gorgeous moon till I passed the thirty-year mark for times I've been kissed. Brad rarely kissed me, even during sex. He never kissed me like this. Ever.

Finally, Daniel takes my right hand in his left and presses it palm down against an impressive erection. "See what you do to me." One crisp, impressive statement.

I gulp a breath, look up into his eyes, and fumble my hand back against his rock-hard chest. Everything about his man is solid except his mouth. So soft. Passionate extremes of hard and tender. I've deleted and then clicked this part back in ten times. It is tacky as hell, but I promised to be honest and the truth was, that between his warm mouth, stirring moonlight, tequila and intense arousal involved, I liked the confirmation that we both knew what we wanted.

"Jo and I made a deal."

"If I can't stay, can I call you tomorrow?"

He's too smooth to be anything less than a player, but he's a player who's hot as hell, a sure thing, and I'm in Mexico for a fling. I've only relinquished my first name. As I grip the pen for dear life to keep my hand from shaking, I write my cell number on the back of a grocery receipt.

Daniel simply gives me his card. Over the ripples of a windswept sky is his full name, Daniel R. Macon, Retired 747 Captain, email, cell, and an address in Alaska.

I want to race into Jo's room. Her door is shut, probably more for my benefit than hers, in case I welched and led Daniel into my bedroom. I so want to race in, hop onto the bed like Rizzo, Frenchie, and Sandy in the movie *Grease*, and tell her all about it, but go instead to my room wondering if I'd been smart, or stupid. Since I didn't want to be tied up in a relationship, it was casual sex or no sex.

Jo is a tad sullen the next morning on the patio.

"So, what happened with your guy last night?" I ask. I've been dying to find out.

"He was a candidate for the Astronauts program. Would have been on the Challenger if he'd made it."

Dan had been an Air Force pilot during the Vietnam War. Daniel a fighter pilot and Commander in the Navy who launched off and spot landed on air craft carriers. Both men became commercial pilots after the war and retired from American Airlines.

"Dan idolizes your guy," Jo continues.

"He's not my guy," I quickly correct.

"Whatever. Dan says Daniel's the kind of guy other pilots look up to."

"You two talked, laughed and made out on the patio like a couple of teenagers at a drive-in," I say. "What happened?"

"We went to the kitchen to get another drink and he says, 'Daniel is here through next week, but I fly out at six-thirty tomorrow morning. I want to make love to you now. You're so beautiful...' Blah, blah."

"You could've welched on our deal, you know, unless you're bugged about Gerry."

She and Gerry had been seeing each other on and off for almost a year. He wanted to marry her and move in, she wanted him to call her back when he said he would. Gerry was notorious for plastering her with 'I love you' passion before and during sex, saying he'll call her tomorrow and then evaporating for a week. They had developed a regular routine, and established that telling the truth was an attribute Gerry needed to tune up.

"I don't think so," she sighed. "There was something about things Dan said. And he was over the top. Said he wished he'd met me twenty years ago. His life would be so different." Jo winces and looks over at me. "I'd just met the man. That he wanted a different life was a trigger. I finally asked if he was married."

"Shit."

"Withholding that little tidbit drops Dan in the 'liar, cheater' snake pit. Bastard," Jo stated with a resolute eye lock.

"I should have asked Daniel, too, I guess."

"He's not married. Dan wouldn't fess up to it and then lie about your guy."

"He's not my guy," I insist.

"So, he was a gentleman when you said no?"

"He palmed my hand against a forty-five-degree flagpole I was afraid would escape his waistband, asked again, then asked for my phone number. Whooh!"

"Stop bragging. So, he was ready, took charge, but disciplined enough to take direction?"

"Yup." I rocked and waved both hands beside my face and chanted, "I'm gonna get laid. I'm gonna get laid."

Heaven help me I've made my sons swear they'll never, ever read this book. Just then, my phone rang.

"I'd like to take you to dinner tonight. Do you think that will be a problem for Jo?"

I felt bad about leaving Jo alone and on her own for a fraction of a second before accepting. "How many times have you dumped me for dinner when what's his face, Gerry, drops by for a service call?"

Jo knows it's a rhetorical question, and laughs. "Good grief! I've heard you bitch about no sex for over a year. It'll be a relief to do the laundry tonight. You're finally going to get laid!"

"What should I wear? Classy, but provocative? I brought beach clothes, not first date, out-to-dinner outfits."

"Wear something easy for him to take off you. Not too many buttons or belts. Nothing that leaves imprints on your waist line. Sandals, you don't want your feet to stink from leather loafers or sneakers."

"You're bad."

"No. Experienced." Her throaty laugh is the best.

"I'm actually going out on a date. I'm scared to death. Remember," I scramble, shaking my finger for emphasis. "He only asked me to dinner."

"He wants you for dessert." Jo laughs at my naiveté, so I rally, pitch my right brow, and wink.

"This I know how to do." I don't hide the blush on my cheeks.

At six on the dot, six-foot-two Daniel arrives to pick me up. Halfway on our walk to the restaurant, along a glittering view of the marina on the Sea of Cortez, he takes my hand in his. I squeeze his just enough so that he knows I like this.

He orders a vodka, soda, and lime. His brow furrows when I ask for iced tea. I had drinks the night before, so he knows I'm not a teetotaler. I can't blurt out that I don't want anything to dull my sensitivity to sensations.

What? It could be another year of sexual desolation. If I'm on target, tonight is a night I want to experience completely. Not a single anesthetized nerve.

I don't remember exactly when I notice how at ease I am. Perhaps when I realize he looks at me, not out the window, when we talk. If he asks a question, he waits for my reply. If this is what a player does, all men should get team jerseys and suit up.

I order the mango-drenched sea bass and he orders the same. We learn about each other, share silly moments. Laugh a lot. Sincere or practiced, I enjoy the game. Determined to live in the moment, I don't ask about his ex or relationship status. He's single, is here alone, but that still leaves a lot of relationship turf uncovered. I don't offer any information about my not-soon-enough-to-be-ex, cozied up with his now live-in girlfriend, either. I want to matter, not be defined by my past.

Daniel spends summers in Ketchikan, Alaska. In winter, he lives on a lake near Atlanta, raises horses, and travels. He has a son and daughter, and grins from ear to ear when he talks about his grandsons. "Those two rascals terrorize my daughter," he adds, leaning back as he laughs.

"I have three boys within three years of each other and consider myself a survivor." I don't embellish or share details of how I'd squished poop through a strainer in the bottom of the toilet to find a swallowed nickel. Either I found it, or the doctor would have to. From potty training to marathon ball practices and games, from driving permits to proms, there was rarely a dull moment.

"They looked like little angels when they slept." I manage to keep a straight face as I hug my arms across my chest and rock gently side to side. Daniel tilts his head down and looks suspiciously at me through his brows.

"I loved to watch them sleep, brush their hair back, kiss their little foreheads," I gush even better than Betty Davis faking emotion before I narrow my eyes and get real. "It restored my faith that there was hope for the little heathens. Confirmation that we all lived through another day."

Daniel roars, slaps his hand on the table. "I was almost ready to force a fifth of Scotch down your throat to dilute the bullshit."

"Merciless little creatures, aren't they?" I ask rhetorically. "Don't tell your daughter it doesn't get better when they grow up and go to high school. College even. Then come the speeding tickets, minor in possession of liquor tickets, fender benders, her car on empty when she's late for an appointment.

More than once a grocery or clothing store clerk looked at my check and asked, "Are you Andrew or Ben or Jason's mother?" I flashed Daniel my best full-tooth, hand-toss smile along with my practiced reply of, "Why do you ask?" I'd practiced it a lot. "How was I supposed to know if they had a daughter or a death wish for one of my sons? Did you terrorize your mother, too? Is it a guy thing?"

"Naw. I was an angel."

"While you slept." It was my turn to laugh, signal the waiter and teasingly ask for a fifth of Johnny Walker Black to dilute the bullshit.

I figure Jo just might be clairvoyant, because after the server's expression confirms he thinks we're crazy, he asks us if we want dessert. My eyes meet Daniel's and we both smile.

My cheeks aren't the only parts of me on fire.

CHAPTER 15

My First Fling!

When I planned the trip to Cabo, I paused every once in a while, to fantasize about having a passionate affair. A 'no strings' fling I could sing about in the shower, because I try hard to love my single life. It would be one of my old-woman-in-a-rocker memory-moments. I collect those, gauge experiences and encounters by how I'll reminisce about them when my world has become small and that rocker moves faster than I do.

I'm quiet on the walk back to Daniel's room. How can I talk when my mind is breaking the sound barrier? I glance up at his silhouette in the moonshine and think, he's actually broken the sound barrier in a fighter jet. My chest thumps softly against my arm. No need to check my pulse, only my pulse rate. Am I going to have a heart attack? Is this what they mean by 'breathless'? I'm trying to relax, be casual. It's not working.

With both hands, I clutch the tequila and grapefruit juice Daniel hands me once we're inside his condo. I couldn't turn it down. Last night he'd said he didn't drink Tequila, so he must have gone shopping today. For me. We settle on his patio. How long is he going to drag this out? Make me wonder and wait? What will *his* first move be? When? He's telling me about the marlin his friend Dan caught day before yesterday.

I smile. Nod. I can't concentrate on a fish story. How in the hell is he so relaxed, sipping his vodka soda, talking away? Because he's not new at this.

I'm not new at sex, but I'm new at first time sex with someone I haven't known since I was an adolescent. I'd met Brad in seventh grade, for crying out loud.

When Daniel reaches out, puts his hand on my knee, traces his fingers on my skin, a familiar flush arouses me. This dance I know. At least I think I do.

Wait a minute. I had that thought when B. J. kissed me, too. Thought I knew the steps to his dance, but he was a bad dancer. Okay. He was a selfish prick who taught me a lesson. I determined that I'd find out whether the next man had a waltz, tango, or drop down on the ottoman and open wide performance in mind before I found myself in a compromising position again. Daniel and I are still outside on his patio. There are people in the hot tub. Now is the time to find out.

Palm up, I tuck my fingers beneath his, pull him toward me as I lean in.

"I need to ask you something." I wonder if I sound as unsettled as I am. Either way, I'm determined.

"Since I left my ex, I've had one encounter with a man, and it was bad." I say the word 'bad' like I would describe a bad steak, or bad golf shot: with a wince. I don't want to sound overly dramatic. "I'm a big girl, wasn't traumatized, but regret I didn't ask him what he liked, or wanted before I was in a vulnerable position. So…" I draw out the word, look up at Daniel with 'please understand and be patient with me' eyes. "What do you like and want?"

Webster could put a snapshot of Daniel's expression to this, next to the word 'confusion'.

"I want to make you feel good, to enjoy yourself and to enjoy me."

When I trap my bottom lip between my teeth, smile, and my head cocks playfully, no dictionary is needed to define how I feel. Daniel pulls me to my feet, envelops me in his powerful arms. Magically, my fears melt like candle wax touched by a flame. In a dizzying sensation of warmth, moist breath, soft lips, I don't just drop my guard. I need an exorcist.

Daniel isn't simply sex, he's raw passion, a taste and feel I've never experienced. Not ever! He brushes his lips across mine. I trace my tongue just inside his lips, his breath melts away rational thought. His mouth becomes more insistent; his tongue leads me gently. He draws the air from my lungs.

His mouth devours mine. A goddamned gentleman who lifts me into his arms, tells me I'm beautiful while he grips my arms over my head, controls me. He drives me beyond boundaries, releases passion I didn't know I'd strained to harness.

The man ripped the bridle off, tore the bit out of my mouth and set me free.

When we finally settle side by side, I can see his chest rock, feel his heart pound. I swirl my fingertips through the soft hair on his chest as I nestle against him. His hand slides down my back. He pulls my body against his. As we tell stories about ourselves, I feel him laugh. He grew up just thirty minutes from where I grew up in Minnesota. It went from odd to strange when we discovered that our street numbers were sequential.

"That's strange, 3741 and 3742," I earnestly observe. "Sure you didn't have a detective delve into my sordid past today? Make sure I wasn't a trunk murderer, or commune cult follower? Then make up stuff like that?"

"Not me," Daniel said with conviction. "I've experienced that kind of crazy, and it was bad." He did dramatize the word bad.

"Your ex-wife?"

"Not one of my ex-wives. This one lived with me for a few years, a few years ago. When I broke it off, she cyber-stalked me, trashed my house, and that was the least of it."

"Not *one* of your ex-wives? How many times have you been married?"

"Four."

"And you've also had live-in girlfriends?"

"I'm a hopeless romantic. What can I say? That crazy one was younger."

He left himself wide open here. 'That' crazy one? Ex talk was worse than a wet blanket on a cold night, but I couldn't resist one more question. He left this one hanging out there, low on the vine. Ripe fruit.

"How much younger?"

"Thirty years."

"What a dumb shit." I couldn't help myself. I laughed so hard I had to sit up to keep from choking.

"I know. I know." Daniel rose to his elbows sheepishly.

I put my hands on his wide shoulders, push him back, nestle into the nook, trace my fingertips down his chest, then tickle my palm across the soft brown hair on his tan chest. He's like a Teddy Bear, only better. Nicer, warmer. If I'd been intent on keeping Daniel, looking at a long-term relationship, this new information would be cause for pause. Hell, it would have caused a road block. Set up a detour. Instead, this cinches that he's a fling. Not the real thing. I think I might be learning how play without investing in the team.

Slowly, deliberately, he slides his fingers under my hand, interlocks them with mine, lifts my bent arm over my head as he rolls to hover over me, lowers his mouth to kiss me, and somewhere in the back of my dreamy mind a bell rings, signaling round two.

It's two in the morning when Daniel walks me along the cobbled path, over the short arch-bridge between the sides of the resort, and back to mine and Jo's condo. All the way, I look forward to his goodbye kiss. You'd think I'd had enough kissing, but in fact I sense a lifetime of catch up might never be enough. When we get to the door I turn, in anticipation. I only get a brisk peck on the lips, "I'll call you tomorrow," and off he went back down the cobbled path and over the arched bridge, into oblivion.

Is he angry because I can't go out with him again tomorrow night? It's already Friday. Carol will be arriving at one in the afternoon. She's only staying four nights, but it's a girl's trip. Trust me, Carol will purse her lips and bore a hole in me with her burning blue eyes if I even suggest dumping her and Jo for a date on her first night here. But maybe I could manage?

Saturday, Willie and Bonnie's daughter, Chrissy won't be arriving until ten-thirty at night. Carol can burn and bore, but I made a date with Daniel 'for an early dinner' Saturday. So, what's with the peck and bolt behavior? Did he need to go to the bathroom? He just went. It's four a.m. in Atlanta; surely, he doesn't have a girlfriend to tag up with. Then it dawns me.

Maybe all players have on and off switches, like phonographs or radios.

"So, play me, Daniel," I whisper to the breeze that feathers across my pillow.

CHAPTER 16

A Fling is a Really Good Thing

Questions plague me all the way home from Cabo. I figured, why not have sex the second night after we've met? This was a fling thing. Only this man to wrestle with, not a single 'relationship' rule in play. Then he did it.

"I want to see you again. Can I call you after we get home?" Daniel hadn't rolled completely off me after the second round of our second time together before he dropped that bomb.

I sort of meant it when I answered, "Yes. Sure." A double positive is a sure sign my subconscious had blurted that out, leaving reason in the dust. Damn. Relationship rules pop up like weeds as I mull this affair over during the plane ride home.

I started this relationship with Cabo Daniel back assward but had the time of my life, so no regret there. I didn't ask Daniel if he had a girlfriend at home. Didn't care, and I'm not proud of it, but still. No regrets. I know he's not married. That would have been a deal breaker. But if I ask him his relationship status now, he'd probably think *I* want relationship status, am fishing, reeling, dragging a net to catch him, and I'm not.

So how do Daniel and I test out 'friends with benefits' without any relationship rules? How does one have a physical relationship without trust enough to ask questions, or build trust, without some relationship boundaries?

To hell with it. I'm tired of tie downs, rules and tethers. I'm amazed I can shut my eyes, relive the scent, touch and feel of him without any gnawing worry about if or when he'll call. I do however, send him an email.

"I want to thank you for taking me to dinner and on the beautiful sunset cruise. Being with you was a wonderful surprise. If I never see you again, know I will never forget you."

The day after I get home, Daniel calls, and his voice sounds like sex. I smile involuntarily, especially when he repeats, "I want to see you again."

I invite him to Flagstaff when he returns from his four-week trip in Europe. I've come to realize retired pilots, especially ones with the seniority he has, revolve around the world like gnats around a wad of bubble gum.

If all went well, I'd pick Daniel up at Sky Harbor to spend the last weekend in March with me in Flagstaff. I hope he does come to visit me, but won't sit, wait, and wonder. I've got a date for dinner the day after tomorrow with Prescott Dave, a fellow I've been chatting with on OurTime.com for weeks. He seems like a nice guy, also a retired pilot. Go figure. Besides, I don't know what I'll do with Daniel if he wants more than companionship and sex, but damn it, I want that at least. Again, and again.

I am a circular funnel of confusion. I want sex, and companionship, but not a permanent, full-time man in my life. Then I wonder if I've resorted to lying to myself, to protect my still-healing heart. Being held, kissed, and touched was even better than sex.

Most of the time, I love my freedom, waking at sunrise to turn the stereo on, start my coffee maker. Then Daniel held me, kissed and made passionate love to me, and now I want that in my life, too.

Even over the phone, he radiates passion. I have a sneaking suspicion I've discovered a secret to affairs. Lust can feel like love, but without the hazards of heartbreak. No barbed wire. No guilt for just playing either, because I know he's a player who dates younger, way younger, twenty to thirty years younger. He can. It has its hazards, but also its perks.

I'm a risk. Even though he repeats admiring statements about a lot of things, he can do the math. In ten years, I'll be in my mid-seventies. He'll be damned near eighty, but I doubt that his age crosses his mind as a hindrance.

Ocean blue pills can make things rise like high tide. I wonder if testosterone contains an ego-boosting additive, and estrogen, or the lack of it, is corrosive to self-esteem?

As the sound of his voice over the phone arouses me, I determine to keep that man as temporary in my life, as I am in his. I prop my feet on the ottoman in my living room, and burrow back into the pillows on the love seat with a wicked smile he can't see over the phone line. I intend to enjoy Daniel when he comes to visit. A friend with benefits. No relationship complications.

Can I pull it off?

CHAPTER 17

Have a Good Life

No more had Daniel left on his trip to Europe, when the FedEx driver dropped a package outside my door. Hmmm. I'm an online junkie, ordering everything from my vitamins to clothes to coffee pot descaler. I hate to shop when I can click things to my doorstep. Anyway, I opened the package automatically to find a pair of five-inch Stilettos, black, with rhinestone-studded soles and heels. The packing slip bore Daniel's name and address. So, he was serious about his foot fetish, then.

I put on a pair of fish net thigh highs, slipped into the Stilettos, and snapped a photo of my reflection in the Cheval mirror that stands in the corner of my bedroom. Then, I cropped it down to reveal just above my knees to the floor. A snapshot that didn't reveal my wobble as those damned heels sunk into thick ivory carpeting. Who walks in these things? I can tell you for sure, it wasn't the person who chose the thick carpets or flagstone floors for my house. I could damage myself.

Within seconds of my messaging the picture, he responded with rave reviews. For nearly two weeks I heard from him morning and night. Unfortunately, because of the eight-hour time difference between Flagstaff and Europe, I eventually turned the ringer off on my phone when I went to bed so his messages didn't wake me.

Then suddenly, instead of telling me how much he missed me, thought about me, wanted to see me again, when I woke and looked at his texts I was disheartened to be communicating with a rather boring news broadcaster. I got weather forecasts, photos of scenery as he passed by, and been here, done that documentary texts. I wondered if he met someone and was having a fling. Another fling, right? Or were my insecurities showing?

I didn't tell Jo about the shift in his communications. What if it *was* just my insecurities? I don't want to be broken, so frayed by insecurities I unravel like a cheap knit shawl. I need a reference to measure expectations, from unrealistic to basic things I should expect. I especially don't want to tell anyone he may have moved on without my knowing it. I vowed I wasn't into the man, but by this time I figure I'm better at lying to me than Brad was. Whah! That thought tastes so damned sour in my mouth I have to clear my throat and get a firm grip on a cup of strong coffee.

Daniel is scheduled to come to Flagstaff shortly after his return from Europe. Will he change his plans? Will I want him to stay the hell away? If I ask him what's wrong, am I stepping towards him as he backs away? Is playing dumb better than being stupid? Again?

It is a good thing that I was busy over the next few weeks, that my heart and mind needed to refocus on my mother. She deserved every ounce of my attention, but only managed to edge Daniel out while I was awake. Dreams and morning musings were filled with memories of his touch, the rush he gave me, the hope that just maybe there was a man out there that would and could love me.

So, I'm grateful that for the past few weeks, I'd been back and forth to the valley to take shifts staying with my mom. Thankfully she didn't break anything when she fell those two times. She'd dropped to her knees, ended up on her side. From the back, her hips now bore the tilt of a listing ship, the right side visibly higher. Her ninety-six-year-old bones were too frail to withstand the major adjustment to put her back in alignment. She gutted out the pain without comment, but every once in a while, would audibly catch her breath at the same time her teeth clenched, the creases inside her cheeks deepened, like clay gouged by a blunt blade. Damned tough for her to endure. Not easy to witness in someone I love and want to shelter.

She was too unstable to be left alone, yet pleaded with us to give her time to get her strength back before calling in a caregiver.

"Once I'm on assisted-living, they won't let me go to the dining room without a caregiver. I'll end up in here or in the hallway waiting for one of them to wheel me around. Please, give me some time to get back on my feet."

Brenda and I talked about the uncertainty that mom would ever regain her mobility, but we were determined to help her try. We put a schedule together. Brenda's daughters and granddaughters pitched in and we took turns spending the night. I pulled four weekdays in a row, so I could spend the last weekend of March with Daniel in Flagstaff.

Though his communications were still distant by comparison, he was anxious to come to Flagstaff, and then asked me to go to Cabo with him again only a week later. He had a bonus week on his timeshare that his son was going to use, but he'd cancelled out. So, I was to pick Daniel up this coming Saturday, March 26th, for two nights, then fly to Cabo the following Saturday to spend a week with him.

"Let's see how much trouble we can get into without your girlfriends along," he'd teased. Whatever is going on with him, he seems determined to close the distance between us geographically, at least.

We made these plans before my mom fell into 'wait and see how it goes' status. She told us she thought the physical therapy was helping. Ten repetitions of lifting one foot at a time, a mere foot off the ground, exhausted her.

"Don't live to be this old, Alexandra," she grumbled one night, when she finally gave up trying to get into bed and shuffled towards her self-lifting recliner to spend the night.

It wasn't the first time that watching my mother and the other aged people in her complex stirred my mind and heart to a boiling cauldron of determination to live like I was dying every goddamned second. I'm in the last trimester of my life. Wasting time is no longer an option. It wasn't the final straw in my decision to leave Brad, but it brought enormous weight to bear in breaking that straw. It influences how I will react to Daniel. I determine to savor fulfilling moments, even though I know they are fleeting.

I also decided to start building a self-extinguishing stash of something, hiding it somewhere, and doing the deed of taking myself out before I became too decrepit to execute it. I believe I'd muster the courage to endure the pain, to protect my children or grandchildren, but not to ensure my own limited existence in a nursing home, nursing bedsores, and producing nothing but bags of soggy Depends. Okay, that was insight into my mind, values and capabilities, because I'm not joking, or trying to be funny here. I'm serious as hell.

I never discussed my dead-end plans with my mom. She lost her oldest daughter, my sister Karen, to cancer, nearly ten years ago. Mom made it clear she did not want to outlive Brenda or me. Her directive came with her strict mom look and voice, an edict, not a request. Brenda and I figured we'd better defy death to keep from pissing her off, but really knew we never wanted to see her heart broken like that again. She took Karen's death with squared shoulders, silent tears, and strength she felt she owed all of us, but I feared if I'd put my ear to her chest, I would have heard her heart shatter.

Me and my demented determination to call it when I'm ready, proved I was more like my mother than I realized. While Daniel and I were on the road to Flagstaff, Brenda called.

"We just checked mom into the hospital. She has pneumonia."

"How could it happen that fast? She didn't even have a cold."

"It's evidently viral and landed like a ton of bricks. They put her on oxygen."

"I'll head down. Can be there in about three hours."

"No need to do that," Brenda insisted. "She's stable, on medication that stopped her coughing. Besides you're bringing your guy to the airport day after tomorrow. She'll be fine. See you when you get here, now go have some fun for me, too," she commanded in her big-sister tone.

Daniel and I drove the beautiful winding, twenty-mile road to Sedona the day after he arrived. We walked trails at Bell Rock, toasted margaritas in an open-air bar overlooking the main tourist street. We lathered each other up in the shower, then made passionate love for hours. When he finally settled to slow-sleeping breaths, I regret I didn't buy stock in Viagra.

Monday morning, I dropped Daniel off at Sky Harbor for his return flight to Atlanta. If all was well with my mom, the following Saturday, I was going to meet him in Cabo. A week of sun, sea, and fun. It's amazing how fast life moves whether we want it to or not.

My mom was doing better. They moved her from the hospital to a rehabilitation center. She'd sounded tired but okay when I talked to her on the
phone.

On my way from the airport, I called ahead and talked to my niece, Kelly,
who'd spent the night on the pull-out couch in mom's room. I wondered why
the night shift? Was there something they weren't telling me? But Kelly was
reassuring.

"She's doing better," Kelly said. "Physical therapist gave her a breathing
treatment first thing this morning and the pneumonia seems to be breaking
loose, one disgusting cough at a time. She even fed herself half an omelet."

There was traffic. Always traffic in Phoenix. I stopped for an Americano at
Starbucks. Forty-five minutes after Daniel kissed me goodbye at the airport,
I kissed my mom's cheek, brushed her hair back and woke her to say 'hello'.
She was lying on her right side, facing the window.

"Where is Brenda? I want to talk to both of you." She didn't lift her head,
but tilted it enough to meet my eyes.

"She's on her way. Kelly said your breathing treatment loosened your chest
this morning and you fed yourself breakfast. You're one tough cookie."

Her chest heaved and quivered when she tried to take a deep breath. She
opened her eyes, but stared at the wall across from her bed, not trying to turn
and look up at me this time.

"I'm tired. I don't want to do this anymore." She paused for a few breaths.
"No more therapy. It hurts too much. No more medication either."

Timing is everything, and hers was always impeccable. She no more finished that sentence when the physical therapist walked into the room. The
tall-lanky woman snapped on her first, blue-latex-free glove when I held my
palm up and walked over to her.

"My mother said she doesn't want to do this right now. It hurts too much."

She nodded, and asked, "Should I send in social services?"

I was confused. I'd expected her to tell me all patients in her condition hate
therapy because it hurts, and to tell me she'd be back in a while to try again.
Maybe just 'let her rest, I'll be back'. Were social services going to talk her
into bucking up and enduring another treatment?

"I'm sorry mom." My back molars stung, I bit down on them so hard. I was sorry she fell not once, but twice. Sorry she got pneumonia. Sorry it hurt to breathe. I took a few deep breaths of my own, as I sat back down on the edge of her bed and sandwiched her hand between my palms. I looked over my shoulder, my eyes wide, lips clenched in a tight line, when I heard Brenda and Kelly talking as they walked into the room. I'll never forget the look on their faces as they stopped abruptly and stared back at me.

"Our girl here sent the physical therapist packing," I said, trying for a teasing tone, as I patted mom's hand. Brenda pantomimed that she thought mom had stopped breathing, that I scared the shit out of her. Now that's an act I won't soon forget.

"Are you all here?" my mom asked, waiting for confirmation before bothering to open her eyes. I had no idea she was so weak. How did she get this weak when she fed herself breakfast?

"I'm tired," she stated in a soft, but crisp voice. "I do not want to do anything else to prolong my life. No more medication. No more food, water," she ended that sentence by spitting out the word "therapy," like it burned her tongue.

"But mom," Brenda began, but didn't get far.

"No." I'd never heard my mother yell, or seen her lose her temper. She never needed to, because she had this tone; not loud, but firm and final, we all knew it was just that. She didn't use it often, but I never saw her lose a battle once she did.

As my mom's wishes sunk in, two women walked into the room and introduced themselves. They were from social services, and I was beginning to understand. At ninety-six, and having lived the past four years in an independent/assisted-living home, my mother knew she had choices, and knew exactly what she was facing. She'd witnessed it many times over, the beginning of the end. She'd seen friends go quickly, while others were spirited off to the dreaded nursing home they simply called, "Graythorne." She'd talked about Alice and Hal, just the other night.

About a week ago, while I was with her, she had a long night after a bad day. The shuffle to the bathroom was a chore, intensified by a bladder infection. She was worn out. Her gaze became an unfocused stare.

"Do you remember Alice, the woman across the hall?" Her mouth had barely moved, as though words became work to express unwanted thoughts.

"Wasn't she the southern belle?" I asked. Alice's Alzheimer's was advanced. She rarely left the apartment she shared with her husband, Bob, but the few times I'd seen her, she'd introduced herself like I was a long-lost friend. "Hello darlin'. I'm Alice, from Charleston," she'd repeat each time our eyes met. I replied, "It's nice to meet you, Alice," each time. Alice and I exchanged the same words eight times in fifteen minutes. My mother told uproarious stories of playing bingo or carpet bocce with people whose short-term memory had flown the coop, as she called it. Because my mother had the patience of Job, the troubled gravitated toward her.

"Alice had been such a pretty woman, so prim and proper," mom told me that night. "Last week she ran up and down the hallway butt naked and screaming. They took her to Graythorne." She turned toward me, her brow shriveled, eyes narrowed in anger, not curiosity.

"What happens to people's minds?" she asked.

Few things render me speechless, but there are times like that one.

"She was gone within three days. They're having a service for her this Saturday."

"Do you want me to take you?" I asked.

"No."

I lowered my gaze and peered through raised brows. Mom had long been Florence Nightingale of the complex, comforting the sick or dying, and the ones they left behind. Not this time.

"Then there's Hal," she said, now staring at her lap. "He didn't survive the heart attack, but the paramedics brought him back. He went to Graythorne six months ago." She knew I knew about Hal, so I wondered if she was talking to me, or herself.

"Marie went to see him a few days ago. She said the whole left side of his face droops. He can't feel the drool, or wipe it if he could."

"A stroke?" I asked.

"A sharp mind buried in a corpse."

Hal, a widower with no children, had been a WWII fighter pilot, then an engineer. A tall, lean man who told great stories and had a real, 'seen it all, done more, not afraid of shit' spark about him that charmed everyone. He'd been in mom's complex for over a year before they took him to Graythorne.

"A life well-lived deserves better, Alex." I wanted to turn away as I nodded, but couldn't abandon her eyes.

Her fingers gripped the arm of her chair till the tips turned white.

"He once told me he was afraid to sign DNR authorization or put the orange, 'Do Not Resuscitate' paper by his refrigerator door. We're supposed to do that, you know, but "Who knows, maybe I can cheat death another time or two," he said.

"Maybe it felt like giving up. Hal was a fighter."

"Hal fucked up."

That I'd never heard my mother use the 'f' word, ever, added impact. I knew then exactly what she meant.

Now, as she lay on her side in this bed at the rehabilitation center, I had trouble focusing on the two women from social services that had come to talk to us. The young African American woman, mid-forties I'd guess, asked Brenda, Kelly, and me to take a seat on the nearby sofa. She pulled up a small chair beside the bed and began to ask my mother a series of deliberate questions; her name, date of birth, things to verify she was cognizant, aware and responsive. Then it began.

"I understand you want to stop all efforts to prolong your life. Is that correct, Mrs. Mills?"

"Yes." My mother answered with crisp clarity. The questions continued, along with statements that stripped our hearts raw.

"You understand that without food, water, and your medications, that you will die."

"Yes." By now, mom was getting impatient and short. Brenda tried to intervene a couple of times.

"Mom, do you know what you're doing? Shouldn't we talk about this? Talk to the doctor?"

"No."

Then my mother turned her head, eyes searching, until she saw me.

"Hal fucked up."

"Yes," was all I could manage to reply. If I had any doubt about her intentions, those three words dispelled them. She still had control, and she was determined to exercise it. The gravity of this particular choice was final.

"What?" Brenda blurted.

"I'll explain later," I told her, as I leaned down and took my mother's face in my hands. I winked and smiled. She gave me a downturned smile back.

At this point the question lady intervened. "Your mother is awake, fully aware, and of sound mind. I hope you will support her wishes, because once she's declared and confirmed them, as she has, it's now my job to advocate for her, the patient."

It was clear mom was on a determined path when she slowly reached across to tap her left shoulder. The square shape of her pacemaker was visible beneath her fragile skin.

"Turn this thing off."

As soon as the social worker nodded her assent, I asked her to step outside with me.

"My mother is pacemaker dependent. Completely dependent."

"But her chart says..."

"I don't care what it says. I was there when they did the ablations. First, she had Bradycardia, where her heart would pause over eight seconds, then the A-fib kicked in. They couldn't medicate to slow the A-fib and risk her heart stopping from the Bradycardia, so they ablated all the nerves and made her pacemaker dependent."

I was amazed at the ability of social services to implement my mother's declaration. Hospice was involved within the hour. The pacemaker representative, a somber and reluctant young man, confirmed my assessment, then turned her heartbeat down to thirty-five per minute. The family had begun to gather in mom's room. Willie, Bonnie's husband was there, too. He was family to all of us. I'd called Andrew, Ben, and Josh, and then texted Brad. We were all there, except Ben. He lived in Prescott and was in bed with the fever, ache all over, nasty respiratory flu that had tackled my mother. He wanted to drive down despite it, but would have exposed all of us and possibly others in the facility. I could tell he was crying. I put the phone to mom's ear, so he could say goodbye.

"Don't give up, Grandma! Fight! You're not ready to die! Fight!" He was desperate, sobbing. Tears trickled into the well beside her nose. I pulled the phone away, rushed into the hallway.

"Stop it! There is nothing any of us can do now. She made her decision and needs our support. She damned well deserves our support. I'm sorry. I know you love her. We all do. I'm so sorry you can't be here."

One by one all twenty of us put a hand on her shoulder, hugged and held her, told her we loved her, and put our ears close to hear her whispers. It's an amazing thing, such wrenching heartbreak mingled with strength and support from her, for her, and for one another.

The best was when it was Willie's turn. He kissed her cheek, and in his ever-familiar style said, "Hello my dear. it's Willie."

"I'm going to see Bonnie," she said, with the lilt of a small child excited to be on her way to her grandmother's house.

"Tell her hello for me." Willie somehow managed to make it into the hallway before he broke down.

Then mom lifted her head, looked up at me and asked, "How long is this going to take?"

I think I mumbled something like, "I don't know," but honestly, I can't remember. There are moments that take our breath away and moments like that one, so consuming we react by instinct, but they leave a blank spot in memory when they pass.

Mom finally fell into a restful sleep. The woman from hospice told us it sometimes takes weeks.

Weeks? There isn't enough wine in the world to help me watch her anguish away, one breath, one managed-down heartbeat at a time, for weeks.

Everyone except Brenda, Kelly, and I filtered out to go home for the night. Andrew made a grocery run and brought back salt and vinegar potato chips, and a bottle of wine for Brenda, Kelly, and me. We would stand vigil.

I fear dying alone. Brenda feared mom would die in a dirty gown, so she insisted on giving her a bath that made our mother anguish and plead, "Please. No," as they rolled and shifted her to accomplish the task.

I found the woman in charge of her hospice care and pleaded with her to make it stop. She dispatched more medication more often. One bottle of wine was too much, a case was not going to be enough for the three of us tonight.

Brenda and Kelly went to the cafeteria to get a sandwich and bring one back for me. Mom and I were alone. I held her hand, kissed her cheek and said, "I've always loved you," and I had. I thought she was asleep or wouldn't have put my cheek against hers. Let her feel my tears.

"Have a good life," she whispered. Not asleep, just too tired of final good-byes.

"I will, mom." At first, I wished she had told me she loved me again, but I knew she did. Had never doubted it. She knew Brad had broken my heart. He broke her heart, too, but hard as I tried to be upbeat and just fine, I didn't fool her. I was better, but it would take a while before the scabs healed.

"I will have a good life, mom. I promise." Grit and determination burrow in at the damnedest times in life.

"I'm going to be better than okay," I added.

"Have a good life," were the last four words she would ever say to me, or anyone. She fell into a medicated sleep, too far away for pain to reach her.

At four o'clock the next afternoon, twenty-seven hours after she made her first announcement, sleep gently whisked her through the door to eternity, breathlessly.

Death isn't tangible, yet the pain and passion of it swirled around me like smoke that burned my eyes. I could hear each shallow breath enter and escape through my nostrils. A reminder that life goes on? I stood beside my mother's bed holding her hand, and tried to grasp that I could see her, touch her, but she was no longer there.

Breathless. Lifeless.

Perhaps the business of life pulls us away, keeps us from being consumed by the passion death ignites on purpose. Instead of discharge papers to sign from the rehab center, I watched Brenda sign release papers for our mother's body.

The next morning Brenda missed the turn into the funeral home and made an impressive "U" turn to get us into the parking lot. Our appointment was a blur of package choices, discussing how many death certificates we'd need, and trying to focus on instructions how to post an obituary for the newspaper, online. Writing it was another task.

As I handed over my credit card, I wondered where my mother's remains were, but didn't really want to know. She was now in the hands of people who would never see the warmth of her smile, the resolve and love in her blue eyes, hear the sound of her voice, or inhale the faint scent of Este Lauder's Youth Dew perfume she loved. They were only in possession of the residue life leaves behind.

I returned to Flagstaff the next afternoon. I've had to barricade emotions too many times on that damned drive, northbound on I-17. I called Jo, and she talked to me most of the way. She has enough hilarious stories about her cat, Happy, to fill a cross country trip. I wasn't that far from Flagstaff when she said, "Wait a minute. Hold on, I'll call you back if I lose you."

"I don't want presents," she insisted, clearly talking to Happy, the male cat that captured her heart, house, bed, and about anything else he wanted.

"I don't like lizards, especially after you've chewed their tails off. Get outside while I catch him. Shoo." Her voice is audible, but distant. I hear the cat door snap closed and imagine her swirling to find the four-legged gift Happy had proudly carried through it only moments before.

"Gotcha," she chirped. Great, now she's talking to lizards.

"You must be falling out of favor with that feline," I tease, once she returns to the phone. "His gifts are getting smaller."

"Bastard. He's like a bad boyfriend that hauls in take-out, when you had a nice restaurant in mind."

"Speaking of bad boyfriends, when was the last time Gerry brought you a present or picked up a check?"

"That wasn't nice."

"I get dispensation, I've had a steeped-in-reality, rough week. I'd rather piss you off than see him hurt you again. Besides, I need a distraction and Gerry's an easy target."

"He wants to get married."

"He's wanted to move in and get married from the beginning. Now that your mother's in a retirement home in Arkansas, he dreams about parking his truck in your garage."

"Where are you?" Jo asked.

"Coming up on Munds Park, so twenty minutes out."

"I'll pick you up at six. I want to toast your mother. Didn't know her well, but she was one hell of a woman. I want to acknowledge that with her daughter, a woman of substance she was proud of."

"Stop already, I'm driving," I sniff. "I'll be ready at six." It doesn't escape me that she shifted the topic so fast I have whiplash, but that's Jo. It was four-thirty, and I needed a long, hot bath and fresh makeup. I had not planned overnights in the valley when I dropped Daniel at the airport. I'd garnered a toothbrush from one of the nurses, but had no makeup. Without it, my face is the bland of a true blonde; the roots of my lashes are blonde, my eyebrows too. Blush, mascara, and eyeliner are tools of transformation. I'd brushed my teeth but not washed my face as I avoided the mirror for the past two days.

Spruced up, I still felt like someone had beaten me with a broom when Jo picked me up. I struggled through dinner at Josephine's. Excellent food, a delicious bottle of pinot noir, but we talked about my mother; the creases of her smile, the strength she possessed when my father and sister died. So many memories. I want to remember, don't want to forget a thing, but not all at once.

"I've been immersed in the memories these past few days. I need air."

"Sorry. I bet you do. Are you still meeting Daniel in Cabo Saturday?" she speed-shifted topics like a race car driver making a hairpin turn.

"Yes. Crazy as it sounds, I'm going. I can't do anything else for my mom, except keep my promise to have a good life. Besides, I want to run away for a while."

"Was there anyone to hold or hug you yesterday. After she died, I mean?"

My lips drew a strong line as tears dripped over my lower lids like a damn whose spill gates were clogged, so it overflowed. I shrugged. Brenda and Kelly's husbands were there. Odd the times being single feels like you're on another planet. Alone.

"Jason met me in the parking lot of the rehab center as I was leaving. He came through downtown traffic as soon as I called him. I bawled on my youngest son's shoulder like I was his child. He patted my back and just stood there with me until I gathered myself."

"Jason's a good man, Allie. You did good." Times like these I know Jo regrets she didn't have any children. I wondered who held her when David died. Or her dad shortly after.

"Here's to your boys." Jo held out a half-full glass of wine for another toast.

"Thank you." I toasted and took a sip. "What happened to my topic change? I'm on emotional overload here in a public place. Let's talk about Gerry so I rush to your defense. Channel the high tide of emotions before they smother me."

"Defend me against Gerry?"

"Damned straight."

"Is he that bad?"

"Tell me something good and admirable about him."

"He has a big dick and a hard body."

"Besides the big dick, Jo. Character attributes, kindness, respect for you, for himself. You buy the groceries, tequila and beer..."

"He cooks dinner," Jo jumps to Gerry's defense. No big surprise.

"And you clean it up. Have great sex, then he tells you he loves you, that he'll call you tomorrow."

"But he doesn't call. I wish he wouldn't tell me he'll call." She thrusts her fist in the air. I want to put a club in it. "Just wave goodbye when he leaves, but he always says he'll call and then I don't hear from him for three days. Sometimes a week. Why does he do that?"

"Keeps him in control, you in a one-down position. You're not behaving, Jo. He wants to get married and move in."

She rolled the stem of her wine glass between her open palms like she was working a piece of silly putty into a rope. David, her husband, had adored her. She was his trophy wife, twenty-four years younger, an athlete that became an advanced scuba diver, a championship golfer that made him look good, and he looked on her with pride and admiration. She was naïve to a user like Gerry. I knew I was cynical, yet also fiercely protective of my best friend. I also wasn't wrong about Gerry.

They'd been dating since a year ago last August. The first thing he wanted to do was open a joint checking account so they could both make deposits, and write a single check for expenses. Only he kept forgetting to make deposits.

He drank beer and tequila at her house, but never brought any with him. When they went out to dinner he never picked up a check.

I keyed into comments he made, like, "Yeah, I'll be a working stiff all my life, but you retired when you got married, didn't you Sunshine." It wasn't a question, it was a dig. Covert. Worse than out in the open and head on. Jo wondered if she should feel sorry for him, or guilty because David left her financially secure.

I identified too well with Jo's initial reaction. Taking put downs personally is programming. Dangerously dysfunctional programming. When I asked her what was good about Gerry, she immediately said the sex. In a crude way, Jo's way, but it was about the sex.

Why do we trick ourselves into believing if the sex is good, they love us, and the relationship is solid? Is good sex a mind fuck? Or is it validation? Do we decide if they enjoy sex with us, we're good and the relationship is therefore solid? That would certainly invalidate guys getting off on porn and hookers. No love lost there, right?

Can we simply trick ourselves into believing the intimacy of sex is enough?

The next afternoon Jo and I stopped by The Toasted Owl for dinner on our way home from a grooming run. I'm getting ready for Cabo, and she never turns down a foot rub. Our nails look good as we hang our purses over the chair backs near a window.

The pink and purple cushions don't go with the vintage green Formica and chrome table. To call the decor Shabby Chic would be kind. "Comfortable" is accurate. No table and chair set is the same in this old-white-wooden house with blue asphalt shingles. Some chairs have padded seats, others are wood. A couple of lawn chairs in the corner? Garage sale stuff, but it works. We like the home cooking, real veggies, and locally brewed beer from The Mother Road, the brewery across the street that doesn't serve food.

"What?" I shrug as I sit down and scoot in. "You think I need to call Daniel and tell him about the men I chat with on Ourtime.com?"

"You know that's not what I mean. I just wondered if you'd told him."

I shift my open palms in front of me, as though balancing an off-balance ball. "No way do I need to tell him about Prescott Dave and Cave Creek Ken." I try to keep Jo up to date on my active date-site guys, both research and what just might be the real thing someday, but I am not compelled to share with the men I'm dating, or the ones I'm communicating with on date sites.

"Fuck no. It's not the Sixties anymore and you're in your sixties. You aren't sleeping with them, are you?"

A little side note here. Jo and I have a lot of pent up aggressions, suppressed heartache, and loss that needs to gurgle to the surface and wash out to sea. Her "energy therapist" said so. With each other we talk shit, raunch up any and everything. It's a pressure-relief valve we push, pop, and vent through. Otherwise, most of the time we conduct ourselves like ladies. Except sometimes with Ted. He's one of us, deserves an introduction and a chapter of his own. I'll introduce you to him soon.

For now, Jo is raking me over the coals before we order a beer.

"No. I'm not sleeping with either of them. I've gone to dinner with Prescott Dave, poor guy. Made him so nervous his hands trembled. Shook the head right off his beer."

"I'll wager that's not the head he wanted to shake for you."

"That was gross. I barely know the man, and," I sigh big here, "he's not my guy."

"What about Cave Creek? And by the way, when are you going to stop referring to these guys by where they're from instead of by name?"

"Identifying them by where they come from keeps me grounded and them at a distance. I'll name them when I'm ready for something more personal. Anyways, Cave Creek slid into exclusively research territory last night."

Jo tucks her chin and lifts her brows into her ever-curly bangs and shrivels her lips in a way she should stop doing before the wrinkles stick.

"Last night he tells me wants to drive up from the valley and take me to dinner. He made a reservation at the Drury Suites for the Friday after I get back from Cabo."

"That Friday night is the first Skins Game."

"I know," I say as I cross my hands in a 'time out' gesture. "It gets better.

He tells me he likes to snuggle, requested a king-sized bed and...you're gonna love this. He sleeps naked."

"Ish," Jo chirps. "Way too much information, some of it pure bullshit, from a guy you've never seen."

"Yup. He seems like a nice guy, and we've been communicating for a few months, but only on the OurTime site. I've never heard his voice or seen him, but he's ready for a naked night and sunrise?"

"Well, even with the price of a hotel room, you'd be cheaper than an overnight hooker."

"Exactly. If I was for sale."

"Or desperate."

"I'm neither. Well..." I draw out. "I'll always wonder who was more anxious to get into bed our first trip to Cabo, Daniel or me."

"Are you going to screw Cave Creek? On the hotel, I mean? If you string him along till that Friday, he can't cancel and get his money back."

"I've thought about it."

"Well, don't. You'll feel like dirt and I'll have to listen to you try to redeem yourself. He's probably just some horny old guy that wants to get laid. Figures you won't turn him down if he drives all the way up from the valley and pops for dinner and a room."

"Or he might be a pervert. Can't discount that possibility after my encounter with B. J. Once that bedroom or hotel room door closes, we're vulnerable." I drip a downturned smile and shrug. Innocence is a tough gesture to manage without a smirk.

"There's that," Jo said, swaggering her shoulders. "Being single makes me damned glad I married an older man, and spent my hot bod years on beaches and golf courses as generally the youngest woman in the group."

"I know dating sounds adventurous, but sometimes it feels like a job. Daniel was easy. Met at a party, had a few drinks, danced, enjoyed the entertainment, and then he did this John Wayne scoop me into his arms and kiss me till I needed to come up for air move. Oh my gosh."

"Swell." Jo raises her brows and tosses her head like a bobble head doll. "I had his buddy trying to jockey me into the bedroom before his six-a.m. flight back to his wife."

"You did get the raw end of the deal that night. But you swept the poor fella off his feet."

"Right." Jo dragged out the word and nodded as though confirming a great discovery. "He wondered how different his life would have been if he'd met me twenty years ago. Wanted to write me, tag up again once we got back to the states. That was all before he fessed up to being married and on his way out at dawn."

"Weren't you tempted to give him a tumble, before you found out he was married, I mean?"

"He was tall and scrawny. Not my type. I like 'em beefy."

"And well hung. I know." I hold my hands up in a 'stop, this is too much' gesture, then couldn't suppress a little chuckle before I looked down my nose and locked eyes with her.

"Were you being true to Gerry? Just possibly?"

Jo shrugged. "I don't think so. I dodge that talk. I don't want to have that talk, but maybe," she shrugged. "I'm not interested in messing around with anyone else."

"An undeclared exclusive then? Makes sense, because you have to entertain the idea of being a one guy gal before you want to discuss it, right?"

"Right."

"But you had the date with Dane, the great dancer you tagged up with on OurTime, before we left Flagstaff."

"That might have been what made me decide."

"Decide what, Jo? That you don't want to date? That you only want to date Gerry? You two are on and off more than my six-burner stovetop when I cook for a crowd."

"You went to dinner with Prescott Dave three days before Cabo Dan came to visit. You have a date with a naked man in a king-sized bed in less than two weeks, and day after tomorrow you're on your way to Cabo for a fuck fest, and you're ragging on my on-and-off relationship with Gerry?"

"You're an easy target."

"So are you, Goldie Locks." Our laughter caused half the restaurant to look our way.

Jo and I managed to get back to ourselves for a while. We both decided that dating is a bitch.

"Reading online profiles reminds me of reviewing resumes to fill a key position. The first time you meet, you're both interviewing, evaluating, while trying to be your upbeat self." I do this palms-lightly-upward gesture, and flash a cartoon smile, trying to make lite of the reality.

"We need to leave our baggage at the door, yet everything about who we are, the road we've traveled is in those bags. And that's a good date, because you are both interested in the other. How we ended up single always comes up, but I hate when they start out with breakup stories, or call their ex a crazy person, or worse. And then if nothing clicks, you have to struggle through an entire meal, maybe dessert. Then there's the question of who pays the bill. What to do when they take your hand, ask to see you again. Walk you to your car or kiss you goodbye."

"And what to do if you liked them, and they don't like you."

"There's that," I confirm.

"I knew if I lived to be David's age, I'd be alone for a long time."

"I'm sorry, Jo. I know you miss him."

"So, I had a man who adored me. We both knew I'd be alone one day. You have three sons that love you. You're not alone, girlfriend."

I nod and drop my chin. I lost that one, because I wouldn't trade my boys, for any relationship. She has regrets too. They all fall into the pit of the past.

Jo sticks up for me. I don't know how I'd have gotten this far without her. She senses my edge and resurfaces the subject from past to present.

"You're gonna get laid again, girl. And soon, unless you fuck it up with 'Brad' thoughts."

Brad? I wasn't thinking about Brad. I still haven't told Jo about the sudden change in Daniel's texts and calls so she's fishing. I plop my right elbow on the table, set my chin on the heel of my hand, fist to my cheek as I look into Jo's eyes intently.

"Are there enough of them in the dating pool? Secure guys, in our age specific pool?" My hopes aren't hanging on Daniel. He's still in the fun-fling ring that circles the drain of my dating pool, and I intend to keep him there, even in Cabo.

"Nope. I think the good ones are either married or date younger, Allie. Because they can."

"That's not an encouraging thought."

Jo scrunched her face and shrugged.

"We're on our second beer," I gush. "And I just ordered a kale salad to keep flab off my thighs and ass. You make me wish I'd ordered a greasy Reuben with fries, because in all likelihood I'm wasting my time wading around in this slimy dating pond."

"Your ass could use a Reuben. I'm busting out of my size sixes, so no bitching allowed." She waves to the waiter, with both arms overhead. "Cancel the kale and get this girl a Reuben and fries."

"I'm on it," the young man gleefully announces. Eager beaver NAU students make great servers. They deliver drafts with an "I wish I could join you" grin, and they hustle.

My mouth started watering before the plate hit my placemat.

Jo simply shakes her head. "So, what did Daniel think about your house? It's not an ordinary place, Allie. Did you freak him out when he walked through the door with his overnight bag?"

"The house was Brad's obsession," I say, "not mine. Besides, you could look at it as a reclamation project." I grin, wrinkle my nose, and hope nothing is stuck between my teeth. "They harvested trees from that huge Yellowstone fire, ones cut in the fire break, others too damaged to survive. The house is a tribute."

Every log is exactly eleven and three-quarter inches in diameter. Why not twelve? I haven't a clue. The tongue and groove ceilings are light oak; the log walls a rich redwood. Flagstone floors dominate. The house is elemental—wood, stone, glass and mortar. I don't know when it happened, but I fell in love with it.

Once alive, the walls echo a will to survive, to still matter. I want to be strong like that. Polished with new purpose.

CHAPTER 18

A Rush, a Flush, and a Flipping Crush?

Four days after my mom died, I boarded an American Airlines flight to Cabo to meet Daniel. There was nothing I could do for her now, except keep my promise.

I found it. Him. The perfect relationship. Daniel is exactly what I wanted. Everything I asked for. He's the mantra I chanted over and over to myself. I wanted great sex with a nice man.

A man I enjoy talking to, traveling with. We like the same movies, and food and wow. I have a hot friend with benefits that travels, raises horses, has a boat on the lake outside his front door. He has a wave runner that spews a rooster tail, also a summer place in Ketchikan, Alaska, and flies the world free on his 747 Captain's retirement program. I forgot the Harley. Of course, he rides a Harley. He's been around more than the block. He's left footprints around the world, and knows how to do casual sex with a great smile, I might add.

That's me with my 'paint everything rosy' wand in my hand. I honed that down to an art in my last four decades with Brad. But guess what? As much as I want to learn it, love it, I'm gonna flunk out of flings and freelance fucking. The old adage, "Be careful what you wish for, because you just might get it," hit me. Splat. My entire plan did a face plant. I want a man that wants more than sex, or I'll embrace and enjoy being single, damn it.

Reality is, on mine and Daniel's first fling in Cabo, the sex was amazing. The way he held me before, during, and after. Told me that the chemistry we had was so rare. This time, he met me in the lobby of the hotel when I arrived but didn't hold my hand as we walked to his condo. He pulled my suitcase between us.

Perhaps if his texts and tone of voice hadn't gone flat, I'd have let myself, my heart open enough to let him wheedle his way in. But…they did go flat. I armored up. Took a step back. Then twelve. It worked. I don't do the dreamy, what-if scenarios when we lie in bed. I keep him outside on the porch, in partial shade. If I wish for anything in those quiet moments, it's that some-day someone will love me, truly love me, and I'll be open enough by then to love them back.

I'm screwed up. Fucked. If I play the odds I will never find the love of my life, in love with me. We singles have to catch each other between marriages and relationships. If I trip over the man of my dreams, will I mow him down and keep running?

There is one absolute. The Principle of Least Interest absolutely applies at this point. The person *least* interested in the relationship controls it. This is where the tug of war comes in.

It's called dating, and so far, there seems to be nothing natural about it. It's a game with many rules; let him lead, women shouldn't initiate a date or buy him a gift. There are rules about how to dress, when to put out or give up, and how long to stay or clear out afterward. Dating is daring, but shouldn't it just be fun?

If I say, "that was fun" or "sounds fun," one more time, I will puke all over both of us.

Great. Just great. I popped out of working on this manuscript to check my email and JerryGeeWhiz sent me a message on the dating website, OurTime. com. He's reaching out. I tapped on his photos and there it was, the bloody corpse of an elk, mangled legs, neck, and antlers strapped to the back of his ATV. He's mounted behind the handle bars, peering through his brows with eyes I don't want to see focused on me.

The next photo in his cache was a bore-down glare into the camera, not a smile, a Jeffery Dahmer "I love hunting, killing, and carrying home carcasses." Holy shit. Sorry to be so crass, but no other word is adequate.

I broke the date with Cave Creek in time for him to cancel his reservations at the Drury Suites and not incur charges. He can sleep naked in a king-sized bed somewhere else. Besides, I rarely do sunrises. I'm a night owl, not an early bird. I'd had lots of long, fairly deep communications with this man I never met. Never would meet. We both needed the company at the time, just not someone I want to be up close and personal with...naked.

Prescott Dave sent me texts the entire time I was in Cabo with Daniel. Now I'm the one guarding my phone so Snoopy hugging a heart doesn't pop up on screen for Daniel to see, but I'm not cheating. I'm dating. Unless you've had the 'let's be exclusive' talk, you owe them respect and courtesy, but not fidelity. This is what all the articles preach, and the counselor confirms. It doesn't feel right, but who am I to question the process?

I ask Daniel if everything is okay? I just lost my mom, and I'm more upbeat that he is. I'm determined to be upbeat for now, but still.

"Yeah sure, everything's great. Are you having a good time, Sweetie?"

"I am," I reassure him, and decide I'm going to enjoy the rest of the week with a nice man, in a beautiful place and stay in the moment. I need to know that if he left me here and flew home today, I'd have the good sense to enjoy this on my own. It's the only way I'm able to be okay. I'm determined to make warm, happy memories, not whittle away moments that will surround me with shavings of regret.

Our last day in Cabo felt like we were strangers. Bad sex in the morning, and at the airport he apologized for being in a bad mood, dropped me at my gate, and went to sit at his. Over and done, just remember the fun? If I know anything for sure, it's that it's a waste of time trying to puzzle him out.

At times like this, dating sucks. It reminds me of trying on clothes, but nothing fits or feels comfortable. It is however, better than being with my ex while he's sharing sexts, sex, and expensive Scotch with yet another of his work wives and then telling me I'm crazy, suspicious, insecure, and fucked up. His affairs were like a hop on and off merry go round. I became dizzy and dysfunctional as hell. That's how it works, I think. To cope with a dysfunctional relationship, you have to adjust rational behavior to irrational. Dysfunction perpetuates dysfunction to function...now there's a conundrum for you.

I avoid making eye contact with the woman beside me as I settle in my window seat on the flight from Cabo to Phoenix. I open the Kindle app on my iPad and try to read, but my mind is like a constipated bowel, unwilling to let shit go. I'm still furious that I'm out here single at sixty-six, but I intend to learn the art of being damned good without a man. Happy, calm, productive, creative, fabulous. A mission.

I can do this.

I'm absolutely terrified that I can do this.

CHAPTER 19

Leave Them Before You Love Them?

The day after I got home from Cabo, Daniel called.

"Great trip Sweetie. When can I see you again?"

This was a WTF moment I gauged going at criminal speed. What was going on? On auto-pilot, I dove for my shit sweeping broom. Don't forget the sneaky back-brain, the rat and the lever. If that isn't enough.

Something must have been troubling him when we were in Cabo, I reasoned. Something he didn't want to share. Maybe whatever it was is resolved, and we can have a good time together again. Was my faulty programming, to sweep shit under a rug, still functioning at full speed?

Don't answer that. I know for certain that healing, rebuilding a new life is not a snap. It is a process. But if I intend to date without drama or expectations, enjoy the moment, then why not see Daniel again? Maybe this time I'll make it about me, and my new life. Whatever my motivation, less than two weeks later, I boarded American Airlines Flight 610, Phoenix to Atlanta, to spend three days with Daniel. Jo and I crafted a "Goin' South" trip to follow it up.

Once in flight I focus, intent on throwing all inhibitions and fears out the window into the fluffy clouds beneath me. I like him, but am not in love with him, so have nothing to lose. What I have is three days to make memories able to stir me, even in my rocker on the very small porch, where I imagine I'll live once my age and activity cinch my world to a tiny, barely manageable space.

I don't want the complications of a relationship. At the moment, I like my single life. I need to convince myself of this, for sure. Perhaps a perk is that companionship and sex are within reach, yet don't tether me. I would miss the excitement of our here and there affairs.

I imagine the taste of Daniel's mouth, the heat his hands and body radiate. I don't want him to be gentle, worry about pushing me too far, too fast. I want to stir his wild side, see what he's capable of once set free to follow his desires and instincts. Hell, I want that for myself. At least I thought I did.

As my flight neared Atlanta, I made my way down the narrow aisle toward the back of the aircraft. I soon wonder if the bathroom mirrors on an airplane are meant to instill humility, or if I really have that many wrinkles under my eyes when I smile?

I need to let go of my bad self-image, fears, and inhibitions. I wonder if 'confident me' ever existed. Is this the ultimate treasure hunt? The search for something I buried beneath shovels of doubt and fear? The reflection of resentment in Brad's eyes, then his longing for other women? My oldest sister's determination to label me worthless, to shove her hand in my chest, slam the door in my face, and tell me no one wanted me around? I know now this is sibling stuff, especially when she was six years older. I'm sure I was a pain in the ass to a sixteen-year-old girl, when I was a ten-year-old tag-along. It still hurt.

I wonder that I'm rebelling, running wild, because I never did? Or because I can. Because I want to know what it feels like, free to be and on my way to have an affair with a man that lives in Atlanta. I want to experience what it feels like to be with a sexual, passionate, powerful man. Whew, I need to slow down and settle down, let him lead, and tighten the reins on my libido.

As I made my way toward Baggage Claim in the Atlanta Airport, Daniel met me at the escalators with open arms and a huge smile. It felt good to brush my cheek against his chest, even for a moment. We had three days together. I intended to enjoy the city, the scenery and the man I was with.

His house on the lake was beautiful, so distinctively him. Art and décor from his travels. It seemed everything had a story, and Daniel is a born storyteller. He's also an extraordinary chef. The flaming Halibut that scorched the stainless stove hood melted in my mouth, and I'm not a real fish person.

"Navy-blue-satin sheets?" I teased, the first night we snuggled in. I'll always remember his throaty chuckle and that cushiony nook as I melted against him. I wondered if these moments happen to couples who've been together for a long time. After the new had worn off.

Brad held me like this in the very beginning. He even told me a scary bear story one night. I laughed and felt loved. I don't want to remember those times, especially here, in another man's arms. I've learned to think of the lies Brad told me, the faces of other women. A volleyball game when he benched me, and played the girl he was playing around with. But I don't want to think of Brad at all, tonight, in Daniel's arms. Talk about spoil the moment. There is so much not to remember.

The next afternoon we took Daniel's boat past inviting coves, and he gave me a history of the lake he'd lived on for over thirty years. We listened to a great band at the marina while we had dinner. Under the stars as we made our way back across the lake that night, I realized that I needed to be cautious. Everything about being with him felt good, but I knew better. I didn't build a wall between us, but settled for a moat with a sturdy bridge I could cross at will.

It was too chilly to linger in the moonlight once we got back, so he turned on the stereo, made us each a tequila with grapefruit, and asked if I played pool.

"Yes, but not very well." These are five words I rather regret, in retrospect. I'm not very good, but good enough to win two out of three. I scratched on the eight ball or would have skunked him. It was funny at the time. I think.

We woke to a fine drizzle that still misted as we went to the stables to saddle up his horses. By the time we saddled up, we rode in the rain, on slick Georgia clay roads. We ate burgers and fries at Five Guys, then had dinner with his friends at a cozy restaurant near the lake. Daniel was entertaining me. I knew I was a guest, but was good with that.

Dating, I reminded myself umpteen times.

We hold hands, kiss, tangle ourselves in those satin sheets, yet we're not intimate. Dating has too much dimension for definition.

My last day, I didn't need to be at the airport to intercept Jo until 5:00 p.m., so we had time for one last adventure. I never liked motorcycles, but straddling the seat behind him felt safe, and he's one hell of a windbreak. He skillfully wound country roads past century-old barns, houses with porches with rocking chairs, bicycles, and smoke curling from chimneys. In the little Bavarian town of Helen, we had pretzels with beer cheese dip, and some German beer I don't remember, beside a rushing creek, under sprawling shade trees. It would have been a great day if he hadn't stared off into the distance quite so often, or hadn't avoided my eyes.

How could I have such a wonderful day, yet be grateful it was time to go? Jo and I had a ten-day road trip planned, that we called "Goin' South". We'd make a loop from Atlanta to Memphis, to see Chrissy, then on to Nashville, and Chattanooga, and back to Atlanta airport for our return to Phoenix.

It's a little sad that my last memories of Daniel will be of him barking at heavy traffic, grumpy again. He drove me to the airport during rush hour. I'm proud, because I felt that I was gaining ground. My shit sweeping broom was secured in a corner, and I'd detached the tether that flung it into my hands so readily. I'd enjoyed the activities of the past three days, glad I'd come to see Daniel, but as glad to leave him behind. He would be a warm memory.

If curiosity weren't such a bitch, I'd have left it at that.

CHAPTER 20

Goin' South

Jo and I met at the car rental counter at the Atlanta airport, both ready to head 'em up and move 'em out. She'd spent the past ten days in Fayetteville, Arkansas with her family.

"I have shingles," she announced, as we hoisted our suitcases into the trunk of the Nissan that would be our ride on the trail through Georgia and Tennessee.

"You always get them when you visit your mother. How many trips to Walmart this time?" Shopping is better than comfort food or alcohol to her mother. Jo's visits provide opportunity, transportation, and a trusty credit card.

"If I hadn't abandoned her and if I came to see her more often, she wouldn't have as much shopping to do."

"Guilt trip is free of charge, I assume."

"Not free. These goddamned shingles are the price I pay. Shoot me now."

"Hell no. I'll drive. You navigate. Get your ass in the passenger seat. Three deep breaths and let's hit the road, girl."

So that you don't think I have no compassion for Jo's mom, I'm compelled to explain. Jo's mother had a stroke thirteen years ago, and Jo's taken care of her physically and financially, ever since. Jo also props her up emotionally by supporting her mom's online shopping addiction, hands-on treks to craft stores, and the ever venturesome aisles of Walmart. Jo could market the series of pep talks she delivers to her mom with a lilt, but a nasty rash of shingles are the going price Jo pays for her appearances.

Jo was raised on a six-thousand-acre cattle ranch, with two brothers and the ranch hand's two sons. She could drive a combine, shoot, rope, ride, and wrangle cattle as well as any girl in the state, but couldn't bake a pan of biscuits without burning their bottoms or blistering her fingers. I doubt her mother has forgiven her. I wonder that Jo's mother wasn't a little jealous of the respect Jo earned from the men in the family.

At twenty-six, Jo married a bigger than life corporate executive. A man a year older than her mother. Jo and David traveled the world, hosted lavish parties, played golf together, scuba dived in exotic places. From the look in her eyes in a few photos I'd seen, I have a sneaking suspicion that Jo's mother had a crush on Jo's husband that nearly squeezed the life out of her.

"Shake it off, Jo," I said, once we'd cleared the Atlanta airport maze. "First stop is the grocery store for a Styrofoam ice chest and supplies."

Turns out the south is still segregated, at least its beverages are. You can't buy liquor in a grocery store and can't buy chips and salsa in a liquor store. Interesting arrangement.

"Gotta love the south," I told Jo. "We can buy enough liquor to drink ourselves into oblivion, but not in the same place we buy mixers, fruit and food to buffer it from running rampant through an empty stomach."

After two 'U' turns, we finally found a rather seedy looking liquor store. I parked next to a Toyota pickup.

"Come check this out," Jo said, her bottom lip protruded, as her brows raised.

Instead of replacing broken side mirrors, two pieces of plywood just their size, had been painted silver and screwed to the mirror brackets.

"Original equipment?" I teased.

"God, I hope not."

Duct tape attempted to seal sheets of plastic wrap where the back window once was.

"How do you lose a back window and both side mirrors without trashing the truck?" I asked.

"In three shots would be my guess."

"And he's buying whiskey." I didn't make eye contact with the scrawny man carrying a liter of Jack like a football as he passed us.

The drive out of Atlanta was a freeway free-for-all. All signs of southern chivalry evaporated once rubber hit asphalt. It felt like southern California freeways, peak season, on steroids. No sweat. I'm a veteran, but I was afraid I'd have to peel Jo off her seat back pretty soon. She grew paler by the minute.

"You can drive a bull dozer, deliver a calf caesarean and stitch up the cow, but a little traffic and you're on the verge of an anxiety attack?" I laughed, but she was dead serious.

"Get us out of here, and I'll buy dinner."

"Well hold it together, Sunshine. You're navigating, and if we miss an exit, we could be caught in this maze for days." I didn't make any sound, but my nose crinkled and my shoulders shook as I laughed on our way out of the brutal Atlanta traffic.

Two and half hours later, we approached the shadows of Birmingham, Alabama's skyscrapers. Slivers of the setting sun darted between the tall buildings like shiny swords. We had a room reserved at the downtown Marriott, and would head to Memphis to see Chrissy in the morning. We arrived before noon and went directly to meet Chrissy for lunch. She gave us a quick tour of Memphis high points.

It was good to see Bonnie's only daughter for a couple of days, enjoy BBQ with her and her boyfriend, and meet some of her friends. Our last day in Memphis was Sunday, May 8th.

Chrissy and I spent the first Mother's Day of our lives without our mothers, together. She knew and loved my mother, as I did hers. We probably had one too many mimosas at brunch but didn't care. We were glad to be together, especially that day. It was that night, when things got lively. Maybe weird would be a better word.

Jo and I went back to the Marriott for a few hours before we were to meet for drinks at an East Memphis patio bar. Chrissy called with a request, while Jo and I were in the hotel hot tub.

"Tom and I wondered." She paused and drew a breath. "We don't want to invite our friend, Jimmy tonight without checking with you and Jo," she said. I wondered why in the world she'd need to check with us, before inviting a friend along.

"Well," she drew out. "Jimmy can be inappropriate. What the hell, he can be crass and just plain offensive sometimes, but we love him."

"I can't wait to meet him," I answered with a laugh.

"Are you sure?" Chrissy asked. "He might walk up to Jo and say something like, "nice rack" and I don't want her mad at me."

"Jo can handle herself and it sounds like it might be entertaining."

Boy, did I underestimate the man Jo later dubbed as 'Backdoor Jimmy'. Like an unruly child, he could use a stern hand and Jo was just the one to give it to him.

Chrissy picked us up at our hotel and we met Tom and Jimmy at an East Memphis restaurant with patio seating, fire pits, and conversation cozies to enjoy drinks before dinner. The weather was perfect, as long as I kept my sweater on. At first glance Jimmy looked pretty benign; late forties, clean cut, average height, not trim, but wore a tucked in shirt well. On the ride over Chrissy told us he was recently divorced and had two kids in grade school. As it turned out, she could have shared a bit more information, but that might have taken the fun out of getting to know Jimmy.

He didn't garner my attention initially. Chrissy and her boyfriend, Tom did. Her fingers curled over the edge of her arm chair and her chin lifted ever so slightly, a gesture that reminded me of her mother, Bonnie. Something was up. I soon learned that her boyfriend's ex-wife and her mother had just walked past our group, and sat down at a table for two, barely earshot away. Both Chrissy and Tom shifted from relaxed to casual alert. Jimmy broke the tension as deftly as a bush guide swings a machete.

I'd barely taken two sips of my cranberry juice when Jimmy looked Jo up and down, then focused on me. Now he had my attention.

"You're telling me you won't lick that?" Jimmy locks eyes with me and juts his chin at Jo.

Jo and I looked at each other and then shook our heads like bobble head dolls. I winced. I couldn't see Jo, but she probably shriveled her face, too. Well, that certainly broke the ice, it even thawed Tom and Chrissy out. Chrissy shrugged, tossed her hands in an, 'I warned you' gesture. And so, it began; my opportunity to interview a single, middle-age man from Memphis.

"How long have you been single, Jimmy?" I asked.

"About a year." Even better. He was recently divorced. Probably still raw, which I hoped meant that he'd be less complacent about living life alone. I took a long drink from my cranberry juice and dove right in.

"Have you dated much since you've been on your own?" I try to get his eyes off Jo's more than ample breasts and get him into the conversation.

"Naw," he slurs, southern style. "Don't need to. Besides, dating is expensive." Jimmy reached for his beer as he continued.

"Drinks, dinner, a show or a movie, a guy can easily pop a hundred bucks. Maybe two if she orders an expensive wine. Then if she thinks you're relationship material, she won't put out until after three or four dates. I can find a top-notch hooker for less than that. Besides, I got hooked up."

"With a hooker?" Jo blurted.

"Even better." I worry the corners of Jimmy's mouth will latch onto his ears his grin is so wide.

"Swingers love singles. You two ought to try it."

"You were invited to join a swingers group?" I asked with trepidation.

Jimmy nodded. I glanced a Chrissy, who dropped her chin and peered at me through her brows. I know. She warned me, right. But this is a side of being single I'd never heard about, not from a real person.

"Were you invited by a woman or a man?" I pried along the edge.

"A husband. Men in this group are into cockholding." Jimmy's grin had transformed into a smirk. He enjoyed shocking the shit out of us, but I was fascinated. If cockholding was anything like hand holding, I got the general idea. I couldn't have been more right and wrong at the same time.

Evidently the men into this, husbands in Jimmy's circle of swingers, want a man like Jimmy to pump and grind their wife's front and back doors, while they stroke themselves and watch. When Jimmy finishes, the husband mounts his wife and rides her like a gold belt-buckle bull rider, intent on showing her he's not only the last, but the best she'll have.

"Voyeurism with a full contact finally," Jo said. I wondered what the wives thought about this. Used? A happy two-for-one night? Saddle up cowgirl. I'll take a bye on this scene.

When Chrissy got up to go to the ladies' room, I kept an eye on Tom's wife. If she'd followed Chrissy, so would I, but there was no such drama. I almost matched Jimmy's brashness with my own. I had questions about Viagra and condoms, men's expectations, turn-ons, turn-offs, a ton of things I had no man I could ask…until now. Please bear with me. There was no topic off bounds for Jimmy, so I decided to research away.

Jimmy was passionate about sex, the physical sensations and release he got out of it. Nothing more. Reminded me of a man so addicted to beer he didn't care what brand it was or what receptacle it came in.

He stripped Jo raw with his eyes. Made crude gestures with his tongue until she did a hand wave pass from breast to thigh and said, "Don't even think about it." As she pulled a elbow back, leaned back and put her left foot on the fireplace. What a brat.

"Are you into kissing during sex?" I wanted to redirect him and wanted him to answer 'no', so Daniel would be real, even if just for those moments. The sensation of passionate kissing was new for me. Overwhelming. Erotic. Wonderful. I wanted Jimmy to tell me the truth, but at the same time wanted to plead with him to lie, if he was going to shatter my illusion.

"I like a woman's tongue on my dick, not down my throat. That's one of the perks of swinger sex, I don't have to pretend to be hot for the broad. They just want me to fuck her hard, inside and upside down."

"Nice." Jo made that sound dirtier than anything Jimmy said.

"You've evidently tried Viagra, so I have questions. Does it ensure your performance every time? Even if you don't find the woman attractive?"

Chrissy's brows shot up, when her boyfriend, Tom, answered.

"You have to be attracted to the woman or somehow turned on, then it brings back teen years." By Tom's throaty chuckle and one cornered smile, his memory of teen performance was good. Chrissy made a three-point overhead glance then shook her head. Her way of exiting the conversation without leaving the fire pit. I was sure Daniel had taken it. He was seventy, not seventeen. But even he seemed surprised when he was ready for round three our first time together. I didn't want it to be because of a blue pill. I wanted to be what aroused him, so I welcomed Tom's informative contribution.

"Is it the same for you, Jimmy? What if you show up at one of those swingers get-togethers and aren't attracted to the woman you're hooked up with?"

"I'm more situational than Tom here," Jimmy laughed. "Fucking another man's wife is a turn on, especially when he watches me do it."

"So, romance and passion aren't motivations for you," I half laughed.

"Not since I walked in my bedroom and caught the best friend fucking my wife."

CHAPTER 21

Text-Sext Disasters

Ｔhe last night of our trip Jo and I went to a great seafood restaurant in Atlanta. I can't remember the name to save myself, but it was a famous, 'have to go to' place. That's why we shouldn't have been surprised by a now familiar list of menu choices.

"Everything is buttered, battered and fried, or just plain fried. Again," Jo gushed the last word, as she peeked over the edge of her menu. "They fry tomatoes, okra, green beans, pickles, bread, fish, shrimp. I don't even want to ask what else they fry. I've had enough."

"We knew this. We've known this for nearly two weeks. Lick it and stick it on our ass food, but it tastes great," I teased. "It's time to go home."

"Yes. Before we have to go shopping because we can't button our jeans." Sometimes she sounded like a beleaguered child. This was one of those times.

We had a great waitress. Silvy was all smiles and sass. We visited with a couple from Minnesota that sat in a booth across the aisle. They were on a second honeymoon after fifty years of marriage. It was nice way to spend the last night of our trip.

We returned the rental car at the airport, and took the hotel shuttle back to our room around 5:30. We'd take it to the airport in the morning, had it all mapped out. It should have been a tidy evening; watch a little TV, and it started out that way. But, there was nothing but news or commercials on the few channels offered. So, I plugged in my iPad, logged onto Wi-Fi, logged into Amazon Video, for Season One, Episode One, of *Outlander.*

"This series has it all, sex, violence, passion and intrigue. We can stream one uninterrupted episode after another," I announced. By 8:00, we were on number three.

"I can't believe they show this stuff on television," Jo gasped, clapping her hand over her mouth during an explicit sex scene.

"They're in a Medieval Scottish castle. It's cold and damp. They want sizzling hot." I laugh. "The beauty of pay for view channels," I added. "You know, for someone so savvy and sexually uninhibited, you can be completely naïve. The ranch-raised girl who believed in Santa until she was fourteen is showing."

"But not on television, something kids can watch in their homes for crying out loud. Put it on pause, will you?"

I shivered at the scrub of tightly sealed Styrofoam as she pulled the lid off the $2.50 cooler we bought at Walmart, before we left Atlanta and began our trip.

"We can't pour all this down the drain," Jo declared.

"And we don't want to leave it and risk corrupting or getting someone who cleans up our room into trouble for toting it home or chugging it down on the job, right?"

"I'm impressed we have leftovers after ten days. We've been good girls. What do you want first, Bailey's or a beer?"

I'm not sure when that evening got away from me, but when I opened my eyes the next morning, it turns out I was the naïve one. Before that night, I've never been able to get to 'really drunk' because my body ejected excess alcohol. I figured I couldn't get drunk.

Jo was already in the bathroom by the time I woke, so I took advantage of the extra moments to snuggle under the covers before rising. There it was.

"Have you seen the trash can out here?" I call out. Overflowing with empties, it teetered against the far wall past the end of our beds. I can see it without lifting my head.

"We're not wasters." Jo peeked her head around the corner, her toothbrush protruding from her mouth. Propped on my elbows to expand my vantage point, I assess the damage.

"We polished off four shots in that bottle of tequila we dragged through three states, a third of a bottle of Bailey's, two Yuengling ales, two bottles of Blue Moon."

"And," Jo interrupts, as she launches a paper airplane at me. I unfold the checkout bill and wonder if the Marriott team member snickered when they slid it beneath our door this morning.

"We ran up an eighty-dollar bar bill?" I think I whimpered when I finished that question. "You need to drink cheaper tequila, girlfriend. Three shots of 1800 Silver with grapefruit juice in two drinks?"

"Yeah? Well you took your second and third shots of Hennessey on the rocks." Jo's laugh borders on her warrior whoop.

"Why drown perfectly good bourbon in soda? Good damned thing we ate a greasy meal before we did this."

"We did it over six hours. Bless our fast metabolisms. We processed food and liquor admirably."

My phone popped to life when I snagged it off the nightstand to turn off the alarm before it went off. "Oh noooo...." I drawled out. "I sent an "I want you, all of you," text to Daniel at 11:23 pm last night." It's a mistake to smack my forehead as I make that announcement. It dislodged an enormous rock that banged painfully between my ears.

"I told Gerry I wanna fuck him inside and out." Jo hollers from the bathroom over the sound of running water and follows it with a disgusted gag.

"Leave it to you to out sext me, even in a drunken stupor."

"We need governors on our iPhones." The dry cough that has plagued Jo the entire trip erupts again.

"Triggered by a breathalyzer. If we blow more than a .04 they shut down," I add.

"Would be worth millions. Get one of your grandsons on it, will ya?"

"What the hell?" I lament as I yank my pillows against the headboard and sit up. "There's sand in my bed."

"Corn chip crumbs. Bag tore when I ripped it outta your fists last night."

"I ate corn chips?" It was becoming clearer my memory had gaps.

"Faster than a squirrel scarfs pine nuts."

"Swell. I'll see those on my hips day after tomorrow."

"Could've been worse. Had to plant my foot in your chest to get 'em away or you'd have finished the whole damned bag."

"I want to take it back." I'm wincing now.

"Can't. You evidently crushed the spilled ones to crumbs."

"Not the chips. I want to retract my sext and my pride. What in the hell was I thinking?"

"I want to snatch mine back, too. When I'm drunk, I don't want to just have sex with Gerry, I love the golf, fixing dinner together, snuggling on the couch when we watch TV. Why do I only want that stuff, want the relationship I had with David, when I'm trashed? Because I sure as hell don't want it now."

"One, because Gerry may be all those things once in a while, but he's also an asshole that disappears for days, shows up like 'what? I'm here now?' He lies about stupid stuff, and some damned big stuff. That shit aside, I think you suppress the want for the good stuff when you're sober, Jo. You want to love and be loved. We both do."

I hear Jo's toothbrush scrubbing again. It was a two-round brush morning. Would be for me, too. She spits and lets out a long lung-emptying "Aww. A dragon shit in my mouth."

"That dragon passed out behind the mirror over here. Bastard had diarrhea of the mouth last night, and he's a patriot to boot. My eyes are red, white and blue." I leaned towards the mirror over the desk, and peeled my lower lids down.

"Feels like my eyelids are coated in corn chip crumbs. Are you almost out of there? I need a shower to wash off the stink of that damned dragon."

I'm glad Jo and her dragon shifted us off the melancholy express. We take turns at the wheel. I reached around the bathroom door and held out a bottle of water to Jo.

"Here's to slayin' that flippin' dragon." I take a long drink from my own bottle of water, then rifle through my carry-on bag. "If I can't find the Excedrin, I'll have to hang onto that bastard's tail and let him drag me home."

"You're driving, once we head out of Phoenix."

"Shit."

"Exactly," she snapped. It was going to be a long two-plus hour drive up to Flagstaff in late afternoon.

Jo finally vacates the bathroom. I adjust the water temp for my shower to just below scalding. It gives me chill bumps when I first step in, then pounds gratefully on my neck and head. Feels so good.

I rarely let things go without beating them to a pulp. My sext to Daniel was no exception. While putting on my makeup the topic erupted again.

"My text trashed my pride."

"Yeah?" Jo scoffed. "Well mine revived a dead fucking horse. Now I'll have to drop that son of a bitch again."

"I'll load for you."

Being alone is not the nature of our species, it requires adjustments, attitude changes, and a solid self-image. We're working on it.

I lifted my chin as I brushed on my mascara. "I need to nurse the shitty feeling of humiliation at home when I'm alone, not now. I swore I'd never let it near me again. When he dropped me at the airport to intercept you, I said and meant goodbye. I was classy. Last night, I was not. Period. I screwed it up."

"He's been calling you every couple of days through our entire trip. What the hell's that?"

"Not sure, I'm new at this, remember? Reminds me too much of Brad balancing between me and his gal pals for me to stick around for Daniel's crumbs."

"So, what are you going to do?" Jo asked.

"I don't know. Delete his contact info? Block his number? Pretend it never happened? What the hell, I'll figure it out when I get home."

What I intended to do when I got home was pour a glass of wine, take it down into my backyard where there were no fences or boundaries, only a view of old and distant mountains. I'd wander among the pines that have survived wind, weather, and wounds inflicted when our house was built. *My house*, I mentally correct. Not '*our*' house. This takes time, learning to be a 'just me'.

I'll take a few quiet moments to wrap my mind around Daniel's demise, as part of my life, anyway. I have a swelling sense of relief to end the complications and questions that have surrounded my relationship with him, but I already cherish the memories of my first affair. Will I want or need to cry, or just turn my back and walk silently away?

Walking away is important. I will not do it at a run. No more running.

CHAPTER 22

Does 'Why' Matter?

As I reflect on that intoxicated last night in Atlanta, I don't have a clue what I don't remember. Dangerous territory I need to avoid revisiting. A simple suffix can transform the intoxicating allure of a passionate affair to intoxicated, ego-wounding stupidity. My drunken text to Daniel declaring my lust had already scraped my fragile ego. He was my first affair. I was ready to pay up and move on. The cute thumbs up emoji and a wink he responded with spoke volumes without saying a word. I wonder if he uttered the word shit when he hit the send tab.

New relationships are very confusing once sex is involved. To experience the arousal of attraction, my response to being touched, held and wanted, yet keep my heart a safe distance, and my mind in the moment alone, not allow the possibilities to tantalize me, is like walking a tight rope in high wind. To say nothing of staying disease free. But…this is dating and it's perhaps the most unnatural thing I've ever done.

I wanted to close the chapter on Daniel. It was a good chapter intense with passion, great sex, the grip of his hand on my shoulder as we walked through the marina. For a little while I belonged to someone, even if he was temporary.

Brad emblazoned the player's instructional manual on my head and heart, rotating through affairs like a jukebox on a packed night. Good thing I've kept my emotional self on the shelf this time around. Well almost. I had one foot in 'Maybe Everland', but I didn't have any weight on it.

I didn't want to hear from Daniel again, but the day after I got home to Flagstaff, he called. For a man who can travel for three weeks across Europe with only a carry-on, I discovered Daniel didn't just have luggage from the past. He had a cargo trunk.

We did the casual chit chat for a few minutes, but his distance and my sodden sext clashed like symbols in the background. I finally took a firm breath and blurted it out.

"I have a question Daniel, and decided to simply ask you. What happened? We had snappy, edgy texts and conversations every day until about halfway through your trip to Europe. Then your texts became newsy, 'I went here, saw this.' It was never the same when we've been together, either. What changed?"

"Well…" he drew out. Sighed. I could hear the high-speed hum of grey matter calculating a response. "We had incredible sex for hours, every day we were together. The chemistry we have is rare, you know?" I could see him shrug over the air waves as he continued. "But I've been dating this gal for about six months. She was supposed to go to Cabo with me, but we had an argument and sort of broke up. That's why I was kind of bummed out when I met you at the beach party."

He was bummed out the night he planted his huge hands and lifted me to kiss him?

I resist the urge to define 'sort of broke up' by the man who went three times the first night we were together, but instead, I simply uttered, "Uh-huh."

"That's why my friend Dan went along. He wanted to go marlin fishing. Anyway," Daniel quickly gains momentum. "I've known her for years. She's best friends with my best friend's wife, only lives twenty minutes away. She wants to work it out. Everyone wants us to work it out." Then he trips, but too late to catch himself. "Younger women can be tough."

I'm relieved he is honest with me, finally. I know why he just sounded defensive. I held my laugh down to a soft chuckle. It was the best I could do.

"She says she wants to slow down at work. To spend time with me, but if she doesn't, I'm done. I…"

"If it doesn't work out between you two, you wanted to keep me in the wings?"

"I really do like you, think we could…"

"Well, we can't," I manage, as my chuckle resurfaces. "I'm glad we met, Daniel. Glad my first affair was with a nice man and excellent lover. You were good for me." My smile as I say this is genuine. I squeeze my shoulders toward my ears, and roll my neck. The tingle links me to passionate moments with him, and I want to hug the man that invented Viagra.

Through my kitchen window, I see Jo pull into my driveway. I volunteered to make stir fry, she was bringing salad and wine.

"You're great," Daniel said. "You were good for me, too. I want to stay in touch, see how you're doing. Is that okay, if we stay in touch?"

"Sure. That would be great."

"If this doesn't work out with her, I'd like to see you again."

"I wish you the best, Daniel. I really do."

"But…"

He starts to say something else, but I'm ready to fire up the wok, end this chapter, start dinner, tell Jo the mystery is solved, and embrace the relief of resolution.

"Take care, Daniel."

Jo and I dipped our fingers in the lids of a couple of sauces, deciding on Szechwan and a Thai Peanut sauce. She commandeers the spatula as I chop and add in chicken and vegetables.

"I told you in Cabo," she said after a sigh of regret. "He probably had a life back in Atlanta, and you rocked his little world."

"I'd do it again in a nanosecond. No regrets, not even the lie when I said, 'Sure, stay in touch, that would be great." I toss my hands in the air and make a clown face; high brows, exaggerated grin.

"Whoa, watch the knife, sister," Jo says, even though my blade isn't within a foot of her.

"So," I say, reaching to tap our bottles of Corona Light in a toast. "This journey along the relationship trail appears to reveal that there are no right answers, direct routes or perhaps even definite destinations…but there are patterns."

I slid beneath my warm covers that night, content. I won't grieve for Daniel, not for something this fleeting, but I will take a moment to watch it slip away, open my fingers and let it go. I don't want to lose the part of me that can feel. Just in case.

Just in case...love does find me one day.

CHAPTER 23

Darkness and the Devil Within

I talked to my middle son, Ben, this morning and told him about the demise of my relationship with Daniel.

"I'll probably spend the rest of my life single." I'm aware this is a catch phrase cast in hope of snagging positive reinforcement. It didn't stop me.

He tries to console me, with a "No you won't, mom."

My chin lifts a tad. My slight smile is soft and unbidden.

"Single isn't all bad. I won't risk spending the last years of my life nursing an invalid. No more 'for better or worse, in sickness and in health' for me. If a guy in my life gets sick, I'll call his kids."

My mind has worked overtime to craft reasons I'm better off single. Wounded ego treatment.

"Wow!" Ben exclaims. "You're absolutely right. I never thought about it before!" The revelation excites him. "You dodged one hell of a bullet. You've taken care of kids, grandkids, dad, and your mom all your adult life. Now you can do what you want."

"Yes, Sir. I'm at the top of that responsibility chain and have a hunch I better get my balance, because I'll stay here. Add another dandy attribute to my dating profile, right?" It's nice to end conversations with my sons upbeat and full of adventure. Sometimes I am both. Sometimes I slip.

Since leaving Brad, this ride of rediscovery I'm on is a roller coaster, but not an amusement park ride we hop on for thrills. In bad-relationship roller coasters, the pulls up hill are tough work, not a lean-back-in-your-seat free ride. The downhills vary in grade, speed, and intensity. At their worst, I feel too much; my heartbeat in my ears, my nose damp, tears puddling and then tracing down my cheeks. It's really weird, because my hands are icy cold when I wipe the tears away. Breathing is key here. Three deep breaths signal your body to relax, fight the fight or flight rush. It helps.

Tonight, I make popcorn on the stovetop, open a Diet Coke, tuck my feet underneath me, and settle on the couch. I'm back to watching *Outlander*. Sex, violence. Violent sex. My body responds easily. Too easily, damn it. I don't imagine the thought of dead rats would counteract my desire to feel the grip of passion, hot breath on my neck, the weight and scent of a passionate man.

I walk up seven stone steps from the great room to the kitchen for a glass of water in my warm Ugg slippers. The silence quakes me.

I am alone. May always be. Most of the time this is okay, but just now, I wonder if that is my mask, and the quake of silence is the reality. Do I mask loneliness with a gut-it-out determination to brave the world single?

I have no man to call, no man that wants to touch, hold, or make love to me. The drawer in my closet holds relief, cold and unfeeling, yet it peaks sensations until my body undulates in release. I am driven not to ignore my swollen sensitivity. Allow it to finally fade, as though it doesn't matter. As though I don't matter. For long, blood-rushing moments, blissful relief blinds me to the ache of loneliness, of fear, of not being wanted. The tightness in my chest lifts as my back arches.

But there is a price for this. When it subsides, I'm still alone, no one to reach for, to hold or be held by, and it begins. My chest quivers as I inhale a ragged breath. Tears like these sob aloud. I clutch my arms across my chest, draw my knees up tightly as I roll to my side. I can't stop it. Shouldn't try. I know to suppress this will bring the weight back between my breasts. Why tonight? I haven't cried like this since the day my mother died. Not for Brad, never for Daniel. What is happening to me? Am I finally going to fall apart?

The ache of desire, of unmet needs, is a very real part of living alone. A consequence of leaving your mate that needs to be factored into your final decision to stay or go. Nature has an agenda; unrequited desires don't simply disappear. This is a natural response you don't want to smother, be ashamed of, or withhold.

Hours later I lay huddled into myself on my bed in Flagstaff. After popcorn chased by the episode of *Outlander,* I'm wet-eyed and wide awake. Out of nowhere Brad's face, his vacant eyes, fill the darkness behind my clenched eyelids. I pierce the deafening silence. My voice.

"I hate you. I hate you. I hate you. I HATE you!" I say this aloud too many times, until I no longer wish to hear the rage vomiting from my mouth, over and over like dry heaves when there is nothing left to expel.

I've used pansy phrases like, 'I resent him. He disgusts me. He pisses me off'; I've called him a bastard. But I've never admitted to hatred. It is a dark word I never wanted to utter, let alone feel, but I do both. At this moment, I don't hate myself for it either. My jaw muscles ache when I clench my molars.

So much of the time, I struggle to keep the brakes on my emotions. I know suppression is corrosive, but so is being out of control. Afraid I won't be able to pull myself back together, I'm terrified of the barbed wire. I'm more terrified of that than I am of being alone. I don't remember when sleep came, but when I woke the next morning, even though I felt like I'd been beaten up, my resolve had returned.

I brush my teeth and hair with authority. I'm stronger. Strong enough to boot up my computer and tell you the truth about last night, not to whine, but to prepare you. I think this must be how it works, the same way you have to work muscle to fatigue, break it down, to build it up. Gain strength. Mind and body aren't always one, but they are linked.

This morning I am more confident than ever that I did the right thing when I left my husband and stepped into this unknown. I'm tough enough, and damn well worth it.

I climb back into that roller coaster, confident that the ups and downs will begin to level out. If not, I already have calluses from hanging on, so what the hell.

CHAPTER 24

Being NICE. :-(

Time marches on, despite me. I simply try to keep up and stay informed. Morning coffee presents the perfect opportunity to peruse emails. Searching the internet allows me to explore whatever comes to mind.

I read an article this morning that being too nice to a guy, too worried about how he feels, what he wants, is a turnoff to him. I reflect on Andrew, my oldest son's new relationship and his old one, and wonder if this could be an active element. When he dates the really nice women who are pretty, accomplished, easy to get along with, and who offer no conflict, at first he loves it. But this always fades to complacency. He's way more attracted to high-energy, free spirited, hard-to-handle women. Their swing from erotic to exotic to bitch keeps him dizzy. I think it's also more exhilarating than a placid walk in the park on a sunny day.

I call Jo to run this concept by her and we realize it is playing an element in her re-hook up with Gerry, initiated by her drunk dial our last night in Atlanta.

"I never shut a guy down like I have Gerry. Told him he's a pain in the ass, don't call me again, and for a long while he won't. Then up pops a 'How ya doin'?' text, and I answer the son of a bitch. We go a few more rounds of food, drinks and hot sex, then he disappears. I get pissed. Tell him off."

"Maybe he, or men in general, just want what they can't have. Love the chase. Get bored with the party after the hunt. We walk on eggshells..."

"You might, but I don't," Jo broke in.

"Well, I've got enough eggshells imbedded in my feet it's a wonder that my shoes fit. You didn't let me finish, and I think I may have figured it out. What we do wrong is let them catch us. When they're little they play tag. They grow up and chase golf balls, any kind of balls. The tension as cars chase one another around a high-speed track. They hunt, catch fish..."

"And chase women," Jo interrupted again. "I think you're on to something." We both bust out laughing. Could it be that basic?

"Does that mean if a woman wants to be wanted, she has to stay on the run?"

"Like a fox and hound hunt, right? Why they call us foxy and we call them dogs." Jo managed while laughing.

"Scares me that it might be the best part of any relationship. I'd like to get away from all of it for a while. Take a break. Work on my golf game."

What I really want to do is turn my thoughts off and on at will. They're a constant hum in the background.

I wonder if other people live with a voice in their head. I hear them say, "I *think* to myself," but *my* thoughts articulate. Right now, 'You have to learn to be single before you can make space for a man in your life' blares loud and insistent through the gooey grey matter behind my eyes. Blurs the shit out of my vision. Distorts everything.

I want to be touched, held and made love to. How do I get that, at a high-speed run? How can I gag that bitchy voice in my head?

I know. I know. Meditation is mind taming. I need the discipline to sit with my discursive thoughts and I commit to begin with a twenty-minute guided meditation every day. It's a start that certainly can't hurt. This monkey mind has gotten out of control.

Fine. That night I did twenty minutes to Deepak Chopra's affirmation meditation. I got a leash on the monkey mind, but the little bastard strains so hard to flee, climb, and hop around that he's choking, coughing, and giving me the evil eye over his shoulder. Wow. Everywhere I turn I learn I have a lot more work to do, so I may as well get at it.

I boot up my computer and open Ourtime.com. Maybe, just maybe there's someone reaching out? Sure enough, a man viewed my profile and left a message. Unfortunately, he turned out to be a guy I would finger print and have tracked instead of date. Shit.

But, in the beginning, Excop911 sent me a smile, a flirt.

Nice.

When I opened my messages to see what he said, his face popped up seven times in a row, consuming the entire screen page. He'd 'liked' seven of my ten photos.

Okay, I give the guy a break for enthusiasm and open his profile. I'm curious.

Not bad looking at all. I read on.

He lives in the woods just outside Flagstaff. I immediately think of B. J. and his pal Dick. One woodsy woody I never want to see again, but this fellow is an ex-cop, published author. Nice, again.

He gave the title of his book in his profile, and its rating on Amazon. I looked it up, read the first few teaser pages. I'm impressed and begin looking forward to meeting him. Before I reply to his message, I want to finish reading his profile.

Suddenly he's not so nice. If Excop911 was a tactical expert with the L. A. Police Force before retirement, he did not learn the art of tact or subtlety with women.

"I am looking for an attractive woman. Sexy (A MUST)."

That's bad, but not horrible. Perhaps I've become jaded by lousy profiles over the past six months. My first thought is that he's still up and at it. Good to know.

But the line that immediately follows zings my gut instincts. *Run far and fast away from this dude.*

So, the entire line read, "I am looking for an attractive woman. Sexy (A MUST). No inhibitions. Open to anything."

Seriously? I hope he has his wallet loaded and out of his pants before he tosses them in a corner, because he needs a cheap room and a woman who charges by the hour.

I can't resist replying to him, in the name of research and all, right? His profile first mentioned the book he wrote about bad cops, so I started there.

"I found your book on Amazon. It looks interesting. Got five stars. Congratulations. Your bio on Ourtime.com was fascinating, until I reach the part about 'sexy (A MUST) No inhibitions. Open to anything.' This smacks of 50 Shades of kink, and would be better placed in the personals of the L. A. Times. Got me on the run. Sorry."

I didn't expect a reply after a shut down like that. Surprised me again.

"I can see how that might be misinterpreted. By no inhibitions and open to anything I meant not afraid to hike or go white-water rafting. I'm a really nice guy. Why don't we meet for coffee, say at Barnes & Noble on Milton?"

I hate to be treated like I'm stupid. Okay. I've been more than stupid a few times, but this guy thinks women are stupid enough to want to show him how sexy they are, at risk of whatever the hell he has in mind. I want to pop him in the nose and haven't laid eyes on him yet.

He's a published writer, and uses 'no inhibitions' to mean open to outdoor activities and adventure? He just lied his ass off.

Daniel had lots of experience, unleashed my playful side. It was great, but there was never a moment I felt unsafe. Excop911 needs to be browsing hookers with badass pimps to protect them.

What if I decided to believe him, which I won't, but for conversation's sake give him a chance. We meet for coffee, then dinner. Date a bit. Then we have sex one time, maybe ten times. I would always be afraid that one position, action, or reaction might trigger something I absolutely don't want. But by then, I'd be in no position to stop him.

At that point, I imagine him tightening the wrist straps and saying, "You read my bio, bitch. I want a woman with no inhibitions. Open to anything. You signed on for free meals and pansy ass sex long enough. Shut the fuck up and do what I tell you."

"But you said that was about white-water rafting and adventure."

"And you're a dumb shit. Now spread those cheeks."

Get my drift? The bad bio guarantees I'm a no show, now or ever, for Excop911. Door closed. If he is simply a nice guy that just screwed up? Well, we both missed out.

CHAPTER 25

Kicking My Own Ass Now

For better or worse, life distracts us. When my son Ben walked Houston through my front door, it sucked all thought of Brad into a dark corner, out of sight and mind. But I need to back up for a moment and explain why I hadn't seen Houston in such a long time and what was so very wrong.

Seven months after I first left Brad, Ben, my middle son, moved into a small house, on a fenced-in wooded acre, ten miles outside of Prescott, Arizona. Once you turn off the main road, he has neighbors scattered along the half-mile of gravel road that winds to his property, but you'd need a pretty good arm to throw a rock to any of their houses.

He needed a place outside city limits without building permit restrictions, a county property on which he could build his wood shop. He has a real talent for designing and building custom wood furniture and is gaining quite a reputation in the area. Through spring and summer, Prescott holds art and craft shows in town square nearly every weekend and the town draws people from all parts of the state.

Sober for six years by then, Ben was building a new life he could share with his two sons on odd weekends, over their holiday breaks from school, and stretches during summer. But in the beginning, Ben was alone in his new home, a lot. He needed Houston, what he and I call 'our therapy dog', more than I did.

It was the beginning of the first summer after I left Brad. Too restless to be home much, I went to the driving range or practice greens. I signed up for ladies' golf activities, and Houston spent too much time alone, so his going to Ben's was good for all three of us.

Ben and I have co-parented Houston since he was ten weeks old, so he's rather like a child of divorce that grew up living with both parents, but not at the same time or in the same place. He loves Ben's acre plus, fenced lot, and the doggie door that gives him total freedom.

When he's with me in Flagstaff, I take him for long walks where we pass other dogs and there are plenty of trees to mark, but he has to be on leash to be outside. I can't help but notice wet runs on tree bark when he pees. But at Ben's house, though the two of them are glued together, they respect one another's privacy. Ben shuts the bathroom door behind him and he doesn't follow Houston from tree to tree.

The morning Houston vomited and then curled up behind Ben's claw foot bath tub, Ben called me.

"Probably ate something in the yard," Ben said, and I concurred. He chews on pine cones, and loves wood, bark and all. We were wrong.

Ben didn't follow Houston from tree to tree, so he had no way of knowing he wasn't urinating when he lifted his leg. The day after Houston first vomited, Ben took him to the emergency vet in Prescott. She drained his bladder. The ultrasound revealed it to be as big as a small watermelon.

"His prostate is enlarged and cutting off his urine flow," she explained. "We'll give him a steroid shot to reduce the inflammation, but he needs to be neutered. You should get him to his regular vet within three or four days."

I do understand the obsession to sterilize strays, to reduce the flood of homeless dogs and cats from being euthanized. But Houston wasn't a stray. From the moment Ben and I first held him, we wanted to have one of his pups to hold when he grew old. Dogs his size have short life spans, often less than ten years. Though we contribute to homeless children, and some of us adopt, it doesn't stop us from wanting children of our own.

I'm not blaming the veterinarian. The ultrasound showed the size of his bladder, but it did not reveal the tiny bladder stone, the size of a pea that plugged his urethra. In actuality, they'd rammed a catheter over the bladder stone lodged in his urethra. They also put him on Bactrim, an antibiotic notorious for flaring the pancreas, and added the steroid shot with the same reputation, to shrink the prostate, which wasn't a factor as it turned out.

"He needs to see the vet here in Flagstaff. She's given him all his puppy vaccinations, and really likes our big guy," I told Ben.

That Monday morning, two days later, is when Ben walked Houston through my front door, and all thoughts of Brad fled face first into a corner like a naughty child in a time out. Within ten minutes Houston was in the back seat of my car. I called Dr. Brennan's office, the vet in Flagstaff, and told them we were on our way.

Veterinarian's offices always have doors they disappear through when your pet is really sick, and waiting rooms with nothing to do but fiddle with your phone or leaf through a magazine. But it's tough to concentrate or focus. Eventually I was called into one of the examination rooms to meet with Dr. Brennen. Houston wasn't with her when she came in.

"He's the most stoic dog I've ever seen. I'm sorry, but he's much sicker than he appeared when you brought him in. His veins are the size of a ten-pound cat's, not a hundred forty-pound dog's. We finally had to lance his jugular to get an IV in. He needs to go to an emergency vet in the valley. I can't give him the care he needs here."

After a battery of tests at the emergency veterinarian's in the valley, Houston had surgery to remove the bladder stone. He seemed to rally; appetite back, gulping water. Three days later, I brought him home, thinking the near miss of losing him was over.

Our second day at home, I couldn't find him when I got up in the morning. I searched the house and finally found him throwing up in my laundry room. We again rushed to the local veterinarian's office, and were on our way back to the emergency vet in the valley shortly after noon. I just made that morning sound easier than it was. There was a flat tire from a screw in the parking lot and my stomach had begun to mirror Houston's.

It was nearly three in the afternoon when we pulled into the emergency vet in Gilbert. Two young assistants met me in the parking lot with a lead and a gurney Houston refused. At this point if he wanted to do it on his own, he was entitled to try.

His stomach was painfully distended with fluid. He yelped when he stepped out of my car but walked into the vet's office under his own steam. Within moments I was left in the waiting room as he disappeared down the hallway. Technicians said they'd let me know as soon as they knew anything.

I didn't see any puppies in for shots, only weary faces on both pets and the people who loved them. One man stroked the head of his black Labrador, then ran a hand under his dog's gray chin whiskers.

"I call him my new Toyota," he chuckled. "Could have bought a new car with the money I've spent on vet bills, but he's worth it." He hugged the dog hard. Something told me it was not going well.

I was pretty sure I was going to have to make a life or death decision for Houston, whatever the diagnosis. I'd called Jason to see if he could come, but he was at the grinding shop, working against a deadline. Andrew had Emily, my eight-year-old granddaughter and she didn't need to be here. Ben was back in Prescott with his boys, his girlfriend, and her daughter.

I figure at this point I could be the Lone Ranger if I had a badge and silver bullets. I open Safari and look up Webster's synonyms for "alone". They sum it up pretty well: solitary, by oneself, solely, and no one else, and nothing else. Why would I even look up the definition of alone at a time like this?

I dink around with my phone while I wait for them to call me back to see Houston and hear test results. Emails can be land mines I can't handle right now. Solitaire is too slow. I can't concentrate on a book. So, free association with my mixed-up mind occupies me. My default at the moment is a pity party. Both Houston and I get to blow out candles on that cake today.

I fiddled with Facebook, watched videos of step-by-step recipes, then there they were. A picture of Brad and his girlfriend, Hannah. I scrolled down to see who posted it. Cindy.

She is Brad's best friend's wife, an anchor in the old guard. She has told me that she tells Hannah she's my friend first. If anything, I wish she had said she is *also* my friend. I know she's trying to make me feel important to her, but at the moment, I'm sure that's not why she was compelled to slap a shot of Brad with his arm snugged around Hannah on Facebook for me and our mutual friends. They were at a table in my favorite Encinitas restaurant, with Cindy and Ron.

I don't know if any time would have been a good time for me to see that post, but that afternoon in the waiting room, wondering whether I'd ever bring Houston home again, was not good. Maybe everyone figures I need to get over it.

They don't see me out with new friends. I golf, laugh, rock to live bands at the Museum Club. Dance, travel, read, work. I am healing, building a new life. But when I see them it's like stepping through the gates of a time machine. I'm uprooted. I don't belong anymore. Despair has given way to getting angry a lot more quickly than it ever did.

That proverbial last straw keeps regenerating, showing up in the damnedest places, more brittle each time. I stew and reason that it's okay for Cindy to post the photo. Why do I even care? Why does it feel like a smack in the face from their smiling faces?

I'm finally called back to an exam room. I pace as I wait for Houston and the Doctor in Exam Room Three. Stacy, the technician looking after him today, walks him inside. His tail does a double wag before it drops and tucks under. I sit on the floor and stretch my legs out as he lumbers toward me. He lays down with effort and drops the weight of his head in my lap. We wait for the Doctor to come in.

"We've done blood work, urine samples, imaging, ultrasound, x-ray with dyes, and we still don't know what's wrong. He won't eat or drink, is on injections to prevent nausea, fluid is building painful pressure in his abdominal cavity, and he gets weaker by the moment, Mrs. Delon."

For a flash of a second I want to tell her I'm not Mrs. Delon anymore. Well, I am, but don't want to be, but I don't care. I have to digest what she's telling me.

"There's so much fluid in his abdominal cavity we don't know if the bladder is leaking, or what else may be going on. Maybe an abscess. Going in surgically is the only way we can know for sure."

"What are his chances of surviving another surgery?"

"Honestly?" she cocked her head and shrugged at the same time.

I hate any news delivery that ends in a question.

"He's been on continuous IV fluids, so he's hydrated, but we don't know what's wrong, fifty-fifty would be an optimistic estimate of his survival."

The rush of memories. His puppy breath. Him skidding around the dining room table glancing over his shoulder to make sure I'm still playing chase. The times I burrowed my face in his neck, when holding him was all that held me together. The prospect of losing Houston rushed hard and fast. I wonder if they expect me to ask them to put him down. It is probably the humane thing to do. My face started to ache again.

"I want a few moments alone with him before I decide."

After the door closed, I took his huge head in my hand and looked in his eyes. He was too tired to look away. God, even his broad mastiff head was shrunken and bony.

I suck up tears, but my jaw quivers, as I plead, "I can't lose another thing. Not so soon after...after my mother. Not you, too. Please." I press my forehead against his for a long moment, then finally pull back and look into his eyes.

"Do you want another chance, Big Guy? Are you willing to fight?"

He didn't blink or break eye contact, but stretched his neck to poke his dry, warm nose on mine. He'd fight for both of us. Live or die, our spirits rallied.

"Give him your best shot, doctor," I said, with a confidence that defied logic. "He's going to defy the odds and make it." Sometimes saying things, positive, strong things, helps, even if you have no reason to believe them, but want it bad enough to try.

After they led him out, I had hours to await his fate. It would be 6:00 p.m. before they had him prepped and ready for the three-hour surgery. I hadn't eaten today, but consumed enough coffee to keep me awake for a month. I left Houston in hands more capable than mine and drove a few miles to Keegan's Grill to force myself to eat something and to succumb to a glass of pinot noir.

By the time I pulled into the parking lot, Brad and Hannah's faces, imprinted in my mind, are the distraction from worry about Houston. I feel like a ping pong ball batted between paddles like the one my mother used to spank me with when I was bad. Don't worry, I'm not scarred. She didn't do it that hard, or that often, but I hated it just the same.

The proverbial last straw had snapped in half. Again. I turned off the radio, and called Cindy on her cell.

We do the usual, hi, how ya been chit-chat for a few moments before I get to the reason I called.

"I just saw your post on Facebook. It's the first time I've seen Hannah. It's a visual I've intentionally avoided."

The rush of defensiveness in Cindy's voice is unmistakable. Strong as an air bubble rising from the depths of a tank of black grease. She expected this.

"Ron asked me if I was sure I wanted to post it, and I said yes. I have every right to post pictures of myself and my husband so our friends can see what we're up to and who we're with."

"Absolutely. You have every right to post whatever you want, Cindy." My words and whisper attitude in their monotone. I dull them with effort. At least I try. "And I have the right to unfriend you on Facebook so I don't have to follow Brad and his girlfriend on adventures with you. He and I are still in fragile settlement negotiations. Explosive, actually. And beyond that, I haven't officially filed for divorce because I've tried to protect relationships with the banks, business, our employees and my son's who've invested their careers in the family business. Then you post that picture for me, your three hundred other friends on a social network, and all of their friends it reaches out to when they hit the 'like' or 'comment' tabs?"

"I didn't think about that."

"I did."

"I didn't ask Brad if I should post it. It was insensitive and I apologize."

The apology isn't sturdy enough to cover the insensitivity or the lie. Of course, she asked Brad if she could post it. I can just hear his arrogant, "Why not?"

It reminded me of a conversation I had with my counselor not long after I left him.

"If I'm right," she'd said, "you landed a huge blow to Brad's ego when you left him, and wouldn't get back in line and come home. It fits the pattern for him to move on very quickly, flaunt his new girlfriends in front of family and friends. It basically says, *you didn't mean enough to me to mourn. I'm doing just fine without you.* In fact, if he truly follows the pattern, he'll talk her up to everyone as the greatest woman ever born. So much more accomplished, better and nicer than you ever were." He's more than followed the pattern. Brad was never one to do things a little bit.

As I sit in Keegan Grill's parking lot and listen to Cindy rattle on about how she values my friendship so much more than Hannah's, I want to disconnect. Not hear any more.

I need to figure out how to separate myself without making enemies of old friends that I'll see around Forest Hillside. I can hear my heart beat. I wipe my nose with the back of my hand, so I don't sniff and give myself away.

The regenerating damned last straw is in a shredded pile at my feet this time. It's tinder, and the friction I feel between Cindy, Brad, and his girlfriend, fires it up. I pitch my shit sweeping broom into the flames and don't step back. Let the son of a bitch singe every inch of me. I don't want to miss the lick of a single flame.

Suddenly Cindy's voice stirs me back to reality.

"I'm so sorry, Alex. I'm glad you told me it upset you. Our friendship is strong enough we can talk about things like this. It was insensitive and I am sorry."

I can't bring myself to say, that it's okay. Smoke from my shit-sweeping broom blaze is burning my eyes. Damn it.

"Let's get together for Mimosas when I get up to Flagstaff," Cindy continues. "We need a girl's night out."

"I'm sure we'll run into each other when you're up there. Tell the gang I said hello." Click.

I know I need to resolve why the picture of Brad and Hannah bothers me. Why the fact that Cindy posted it made me angry with her. I don't want him, cringe at the thought of him touching me. So why?

You have no idea how much I wish I'd really understood then about narcissism, codependence, and the fucking lever.

I stared vacantly across Keegan's asphalt parking lot that first week of June, seventeen months after I left Brad for the last time. Waves of heat emanate from the blistering blacktop, visible only because they distort a six-inch blanket of air. I'm stunned that movement gives substance to and distorts the invisible space.

I'm stunned that my mind shifted to air and asphalt, blanking out thoughts all on its own. Meditation residue? Without thought, my mind is set free and that's damned dangerous these days. My quiet mind lasted all of a nanosecond before it reeled me through a time warp, back ten years. WTF?

I recognize that this is a moment of insight. Know they hit like a bolt of lightning. This is my third time to experience such a sudden realization, and it isn't a pleasant one. It's awful.

That bitch in my head is brutally insistent. Stern. Scolding. And in first person.

I'm a hypocrite. I am. This is a life lesson smack between my eyes. I had done worse to my son, Jason, than Cindy's post did to me, and at the time, I felt magnanimous about it. When my son divorced I made a decision to be kind, not hateful to his ex. The way my mother would want me to be. Forgiving.

Oh my gosh. Cindy is a paragon compared to me.

Jason divorced the mother of his two sons for reasons similar to mine.

I wanted to stay close to my grandsons. She has a wonderful family. So...I maintained a close relationship with her. Even took her to visit Bonnie and Willie in Sandusky, Ohio two years in a row. I made DVD's of the trip. The boys couldn't wait to play it for their dad, so he could watch them fishing, on the playground, jumping off the back of the boat into Lake Erie. His ex was with us all the way.

Why did I have to turn my back on their mother? I reasoned. *I didn't divorce her*, I'd arrogantly proclaimed. Wow. Is this what 'getting a dose of my own medicine' is like? Karma in a crap fight?

Yup! I just swallowed an entire bottle of Castor Oil and shit all over myself. I got pissy with Cindy and she didn't do half what I did to my son. A person I'd take a bullet for. WTF am I doing? Who in the hell do I think I am?

The worst part? I didn't get it then, but I do now. That bolt of insight makes me see that what I did to Jason must have hurt way worse than what Cindy did.

But I'm still pissed at her. Is my heart so full of fury there's no room for reason?

Knowledge, realization, can evidently be intellectually accepted without grazing the emotions. What I needed now was physical. Food, water, and wine, not necessarily in that order.

Keegan's is an Irish Pub. Lots of warm woods, dim lights, and lively conversation. I don't want to sit at a table alone. I learned early on that it is much more fun to sit at the bar. Besides, I like the bitter aroma of beer and whiskey. I order the Mediterranean hummus plate with fresh vegetables and a glass of Duck Pond pinot noir.

I put my elbows on the edge of the bar and inhale the dry-fruity scent before I sip my wine. I'm sick of me at this point. Houston's fighting for his life and I still act so broken-hearted over my shredded marriage that I bleed all over the floor, stand in the puddle, make a mess, and track it everywhere when I try to wipe it up. What in the hell is wrong with me? I don't want anything to do with Brad.

How do I get rid of my rage and resentment at him? Or relinquish the loss of the life I'd worked my whole life for? I was making great progress, laughing a lot, traveling, enjoying friends, family when they came to Flagstaff or I went to the valley. Then something like that picture on Facebook plopped me on my ass.

Was I lying to myself that I was doing better? No. I am better. But it is a process. Will I ever be numbed to all this? If I had a man in my life, would it be easier? Yes, probably, but that's not what I want.

I intend to master myself, my emotions, and find balance on my own. Life will always have its ups and downs. My balance is better. Core strength, right?

I intend to be proud of myself, not to prove Brad wrong, but for me.

CHAPTER 26

He Isn't Just a Dog?

I need to be tough as well as balanced when I go back to in the veterinarian's office after Houston's surgery. They left a light on by the back door. Hopeful for good news, braced for bad, I tapped on it at 8:30 p.m., but he was still in surgery. The night technician led me to the all-too-familiar waiting room.

Houston was in surgery for three hours. The culprit is the most inflamed and angry pancreas the surgeons had ever seen. The prognosis is not good. Evidently the prior surgery disturbed the organ. The strong antibiotics trashed his digestive system. The steroid shot didn't help, and the pancreas waged war. Inflamed and angry, the organ produces enzymes it ingests... to eat itself alive. A cannibal organ lives within us.

He'd developed a suspicious contempt for the day staff that poked him with shots, IV's, and made him move when he wanted to do anything but. The little night nurse took him under her wing. She'd let him out of his kennel when the rest of the staff left and he slept under her desk, his head on her feet. When she went into the lunch room, she offered him a slice of deli turkey. He ate it, and the tides turned.

I took him home to Flagstaff after three nights recuperation in the hospital, without much encouragement. "He'll make it, or he won't. Let us know how he does," they said.

For four days, I attempt to disguise antibiotics and pain pills with peanut butter pill pockets. It is awful. Houston burrows between the wall and the toilet to escape my ministrations.

"If you don't take your medicine, you'll die." This time the dirty look he gives me is unmistakable.

His breeder, Pat, called to check on him.

"I'm having a devil of a time getting his meds down him. I don't want him to wrestle or run away and hurt himself, but he has to take them. He hates me." I describe my efforts and she chuckles softly.

"Stuff the pills in a chunk of cream cheese and he'll wolf them down like a piece of candy. They love cream cheese."

Unbelievable. This information should be posted on every veterinarian's wall around the world, because it worked every time. Houston pops pills with the ease of an addict, as long as they're wrapped in cream cheese.

The antibiotics require probiotics to keep from trashing his tummy again and the pain meds back up his bowels. I wonder if I'm helping him live or prolonging his suffering. Damn it.

"We've come this far, big guy. We're gonna see it through."

I tell my sons I'm cautiously optimistic he'll recover. And that's more enthusiastic than I feel.

CHAPTER 27

Our Fourth Son

I need to back up and fill in some intentional blanks. My middle son, Ben, has been sober for over six years. I call Ben's 'under-the-influence' self our fourth son. He did the work, wanted to begin again, too. Clean slate. I'm with him. Letting go of the unchangeable past is vital. It's also easier when there's nothing you want to do more than forget and put it behind you.

New friends, community, and life don't need a profile of Ben's past struggles and transgressions. They'll never know what a triumph these past six years have been for him.

When Ben crawls into the bottom of a bottle, my son disappears. Is possessed. No greater good will be served by sharing the details of decades of alcohol and drug addiction. The toll it takes on the addict and those that love them is profound.

He's highly intelligent. Except for his ex-wife, I'm the last person Ben wants to suspect he is again out of control and under the influence around his boys. During their divorce, he was in full addict mode. I ensured he did not get custody of his sons. He called me on the phone and told me he hated me more than he's ever hated anyone.

"Someday when you're clear headed and sober, you'll thank me for taking care of your sons when you weren't in able to do it."

That day, he ended that conversation with a vicious, "Fuck you!"

A year into his sobriety he took my chin in his hand. Tears brimmed his lower lids. "I want to thank you for taking care of my boys and to apologize for what I said to you." We hugged till both our shoulders were damp.

This morning, I'm glad I'm near my phone when it rings. I'm bad about leaving it around the house. A sprint to the ring is part of my workout routine. I rarely wear pants with pockets, and most fabrics are too soft to support a clip on.

I'm rattling on. Stalling. I don't want to tell you about the call from my thirteen-year-old grandson, Luke, this morning. But I need to tell you so you can understand the size and force of quakes building into the tsunami that roiled toward me.

"Gramma? Gramma?" Luke is sobbing. Frantic. A thirteen-year-old on the brink of hysteria.

"Luke, slow down. I'm right here. What's the matter?" My stomach drops beneath the soles of my shoes. I walk out to the kitchen patio, because Colby, his older brother is sitting on the floor feeding boiled chicken to Houston, piece by piece. He won't eat on his own yet.

"Dad's passed out on the floor under the stairs. He won't wake up." Sob. Sob. "I love him." The sobs raise the pitch of his voice high and heartbreaking. "I love my dad. I'll never see him again if my mom finds out. He hid my phone away. I found it though. Promise you won't tell my mom. Dad said I'll never see him again if I call her."

I take a deeply audible breath. Calm. I intend to stay calm. Solid. Luke is my only concern at this moment.

"Where are you, Luke? At the house?"

"No," he gulps, then sobs. "I'm at the bottom of the hill, at your mountain house."

Brad wants this house in the Bradshaws and the acreage, in our settlement. The land holds relics and history of turn of the century gold miners, a bustling town whose remains are within sight of our great room porch. It's only twenty minutes from Ben's place. What in the hell are they doing up there? Why aren't they home?

The house sits atop a sheer granite cliff in the rugged Bradshaw Mountains north of Phoenix. At nearly seven thousand feet elevation, the winters are brutally cold, but summer's a welcome respite from the desert heat just two hours away. Pine, scrub oak, cedar, and alligator juniper are green year-round and coddle the house and hillsides like a prickly blanket. This morning it is a very long two hours away from both Phoenix and Flagstaff, and from both Luke's mother and me.

I know the steep, over half-mile of winding gravel road from the house to the bottom of the lot that Luke has just traversed. I imagine him slipping on gravel, bleary eyed, rushing down and away from the house and his father. My fourth son.

If I scream the word "fuck" at this moment, it will be so bloodcurdlingly loud I'll shred my vocal cords. Stay calm. Another deep breath. I soften my voice. Put a confidence in it I do not feel.

"I'm proud of you, Luke. You did exactly the right thing."

"I'm goin' back to the house. I want my computer and my stuff." Anger has quelled his sobs. Good for him.

"We'll get all your stuff later. Right now, I want you to walk across the road, to the house down by the creek. You remember Mr. Carlson's house, don't you?"

"Ya." He chirps like a small-frightened bird again.

"Okay. Now stay on the phone with me. Walk down and knock on the door."

I hear gravel crunch under his shoes, finally his rap on the wooden screen door. There is no answer. Luke is crying over and over, "I love my dad. I'm never gonna see him again. I love him."

Son of a bitch! I want to tear through the woods screaming my lungs out.

"It's okay, Sunshine. He's asleep and we need to take care of you right now. It's what he'd want you to do. You're going to be fine. Now I want you to sit down on the porch. Lean back against the house. Take some deep breaths. Okay? Can you do that for me?"

The porch faces towards the creek, away from the road. Luke isn't visible as long as he stays there. I dial his mother on the house phone. My relationship with her was shattered four years ago when Brad and I helped Ben win back joint custody of the boys. That's too long a story to tell here, but he'd been sober two years and they needed him.

"Jess," I say. "You need to go get Luke right now. He's at the Carlson's house, across the road from the mountain house. The one down by the creek with the apple trees."

"What's wrong? What happened?"

"He's safe. Just go get him, Jess. I have another call to make. Go get Luke *now.*"

"Okay." We both know she's two hours away, assuming she doesn't hit traffic or road construction. I know that's too long. I can only imagine what's going through Jess's mind, but I'd bet she buckled her seat belt within thirty seconds. She has issues. We have issues. But she loves those boys. Ben loves them too, but it isn't enough. Not now.

Enough of the destructive addict-alcoholic shit. Too much.

Colby is two years older than Luke. He's been with me all week, to help with Houston when I brought him home from surgery. Colby's eyes don't hold the questions they should as he listens to my side of the conversation with his mom. They do cradle tears. He must have known or strongly suspected his father was drinking again. They've been in Prescott the past month with Ben.

"Talk to your brother while I make another call. It's going to be okay, Colby. You're both going to be okay." I hand him my cell phone. I want to say more, but as the Mayer sheriff's office answers on my house phone, I step back outside to the kitchen patio and close the door.

"I need the sheriff to go get my grandson. Now. Right now." I give them directions. Jess's phone number. Colby is talking calmly to Luke. They are amazing boys.

I want to know what set Ben off again. How long has it been going on? I didn't know. In hindsight, I wonder if it began with over-the-counter meds: Benadryl, sleeping pills. He has vicious allergies. Did this escalate to anti-depression or anti-anxiety prescriptions from doctors who didn't understand they were treating an addict?

He loves his sons completely. He knows that if he drinks, he'll lose the right to see them. Were there drugs? Did they become difficult to obtain? When Ben resorts to liquor to do the job, I know oblivion is the destination. Luke said there were bottles of wine all over the floor. Brad and Hannah must have left wine there, at the house. Brad drinks expensive Scotch, too.

Johnny Walker Blue is brown, and lethal to an active alcoholic. Shit.

Brad and I have dived over that cliff to get Ben. We've been scraped and dragged over it. Have thrown ropes to rehabs, bailed him out, refused to bail him out. Talked, reasoned, reached out, turned our backs in despair. Neither Brad nor I are quitters. Until now. Ben's brain is broken. I'm not going anywhere near that cliff this time. Buddhists would define any attempt at this point as 'idiot compassion'.

Often times, it's so hard to know when an addict or alcoholic is sliding back into the abyss. They're masters at concealing addict behavior, making excuses of extreme allergies, fatigue, the flu, stress ulcers. My mom, his grandmother, died. His dad and I are getting a divorce. His new girlfriend's ex was an alcoholic, so she can't know about his past. I have a hunch he stopped going to meetings, working his program, to hide the demons that can devour him.

Don't add to his stress with accusations or observations that can jeopardize time with his boys. They need him. The journey back into the bottom of a bottle doesn't take long for an ex-addict or alcoholic of Ben's degree. His descent will be faster and the landing harder than ever before. Fatal? Very probably. I need to numb out. I have a well-worn path to follow.

The sheriff has all the information he needs: a description of Luke, the color and kind of clothes he's wearing. I know I have to call Brad. Strangely, I want to call him. Will sharing the burden with him help? If he yells in a rage, I'll hang up.

Brad doesn't rage. I imagine his head dropping back as a puff of air whispers, "Fuck."

We both thought Ben had made it, that the disappointment and despair of drunks and addiction were behind us. I echo Brad as softly. Go figure, we're allies on this battlefield. We can both whisper 'fuck,' and not at each other. I know he and I will do whatever we have to do to protect Luke and Colby.

Colby and Luke, fifteen and thirteen, are seasoned sons of an alcoholic. Brad and I are veterans, too. We carry deep scars from the legions of this dark side of humanity.

"You did the only thing you could do, Alex."

His support at this moment means more than he will ever know. I can't find numb. Begin to stumble, but can't fall or falter. Being needed at times like this holds me together.

Barbed wire. Fucking barbed wire.

"Colby's here. Do you want to talk to him?"

"Yes. Of course, I do." Brad doesn't say this with contempt, but with heart.

Brad and I will never be 'together' again, but at this moment we are working together, putting our family first. And it is at this moment that I realize that the bond we share as family – not as husband and wife, but as family – will never be broken. Those we both love are links that bind us.

CHAPTER 28

Social Suicide

I admit to being in a funk for a few weeks after Ben's dive to the bottom of yet another bottle. This morning I'm grateful for the six sober years we had together. I saw my son, his bright blue eyes, genuine smile, and warm heart. What blinks back through the ass end of a liquor bottle is distorted, beyond my reach and my reserves.

"Lose the worries, Ali," Jo urges. "They're a waste of precious time. Meet you at the driving range in thirty."

"Just what I need to cheer me up, a couple of shank shots."

"Knock it off. You never play or have time to practice. Hit the hell out of a few golf balls. Works for me. Might help you loosen up. You're so damned tight."

"According to Daniel, being damned tight is a good thing." This is one of those moments I catch myself laughing.

"Ewww." Evidently Jo doesn't think it's as funny as I did. "Your shoulders and hips are too tight, sweetheart. Not that. God. Too much information."

By now I have to dab my eyes dry from laughing. How is it that both joy and pain produce tears?

Jo's a championship golfer. It's her passion. For me it's a painful way to make friends and get out of the house.

For me today, the driving range is brutal. I'm getting more terrified by the minute of the three-day tournament next week. Why did I ever sign up for it?

"Hurts like hell." Jo grips her shoulder, rolls her neck and scoots another ball into position with the head of her club.

"Stop swinging so damned hard," I scold.

"I'm not."

"You just blew a seven wood past my driver. Go sit down and rest the shoulder. This is humiliating enough."

"I'm going to Prescott tomorrow to see Karen. I think she can help me swing so I don't hurt so damned bad."

Karen was the women's golf pro at Forest Hillside for years. Dynamic, efficient, and energizing the women's group like never before. She intimidated the shit out of the male pros who had to hustle to keep up. To compensate her they offered only seasonal employment, no benefits, no raise in responsibility or pay. They won. She's now director of golf at a prestigious course in Prescott: half our size, less chance of recognition, but free to be. Quite a number of women make the trek to Prescott for tournaments Karen sets up, for lessons, and simply to visit with a terrific lady we miss.

Jo called me at nearly eight the next night while she was driving back from Prescott.

"I thought you were staying the night at Karen's," I said.

"I just want to get home," she said.

I wonder if she wants to get home to Gerry, or for Gerry to know she's in the neighborhood and perhaps behave. Trust is a bitch. Her instincts are keen, I fear.

Slamming brakes squeal and growl at the same time as they burn rubber. An unmistakable sound.

"Jo! What happened!"

"Fuck! I just bumped an elk calf. Holy shit! There's a herd of fifty of 'em spilling ditch to ditch across the road."

"You okay? No airbag face plant?"

"Nope. Whoa." She gushes with an exhale. I imagine her arms outstretched, gripping the steering wheel, full push-up position.

"They're in velvet. You should see how thick their antlers are."

"Get your car moving before you get hit from behind. Call me when you get home."

"No, wait. I called to give you a laugh. Just let me catch my breath. I can't go anywhere until they're off the road. Maybe my headlights will keep someone else from hitting them."

"Okay, I'm not going to laugh when you tell me Karen helped you hit the ball twice as far as you did yesterday and it was so simple. Just a little fix. I'll throw my clubs in the driveway and run over them."

"No, silly. While Karen and I were at dinner I got a text message from Bill Brady."

This does make me laugh aloud. First, because every time I hear his name, the chorus to *Won't You Come Home Bill Bailey* gets stuck in my head. Somehow rhymes for me. Second, Billy boy goes through single women in Forest Hillside like a college frat brat on a binge.

"Yeah. Here it is," Jo confirms. "Enjoyed seeing you today, exclamation point, exclamation point. Really like what you've done to your hair, exclam." At this point, she chuckled. "I've been in Prescott all day. I didn't see Bill Brady anywhere."

I laugh louder now. "*I* saw him today. Had Houston out in the yard when this guy in a red shirt, white shorts and cap waves, arms overhead and hollers hello from the sixteen-tee box. I holler back, 'Who is it?' He answered, but with the wind I couldn't hear, so Houston and I walked toward the tee box. Houston let Bill pet him. Go figure. I wished him happy birthday. Told him I saw it on Facebook. He asked if we were friends on F. B. I reminded him he sent me a friend request after I nearly hit him with a golf ball on the chipping green."

"The bastard has us mixed up!" Jo hoots.

"You can show the message to Gerry. Have a few more laughs."

"You know I will."

"We're both evil. You know this guy is social suicide, right? Besides, I don't think I can handle a hand that's been on the boobs and in the crotches of Sally, Mary, Jennifer and how many more?"

"He gets around alright. I wondered when he'd get around to you."

I was curious as hell about how Jo would answer Bill's text message. The two of us had met Brady on the driving range a few weeks ago. Six-foot-two, broad shoulders, square jaw. Not all men deserve the reputation of being a player, but this guy does, at a glance.

I swung my club across my body instead of towards my target and pulled a chip shot to the left. Way left. My ball almost hit the man. We chatted. He joined Jo and me in a putting contest. Used his wedge instead of his putter, "To make it fair," he said.

After Jo annihilated him she left the range to meet Gerry and I bit my lip to keep from smiling. Bill gave me some putting tips. I teased that it was close to decision time for me.

"If my game doesn't improve I'll give up golf and head to the Caribbean."

"They serve a drink there call Sex on the Beach," he snapped back. A quick glance at each other for both of us. First thing that came to my mind was, that if I'm going to have sex on the beach, I want to be on top, which signaled me it was time to go home before I bumbled my way into a mess. That wasn't an "I'd like to take you out and get to know you" crack. It was an "I'd like to get in your pants" smart crack. Again I wondered, was it a test to see how I'd react, the way I'd wondered about the picture of Orifice Annie at the bar that night.

When Jo got home from her 'nearly crippling a baby elk' mishap, she returned his message. "I've been in Prescott all day. Didn't see ya. I think you have me mixed up with Alex Delon, but kudos to a man that notices a woman's hair."

The next morning, I receive an iMessage from the infamous Mr. Brady.

"I now remember we met at the practice range. That's when I sent you a 'friend' request." Could he get any drier?

I waited a day then replied. "Aww…Just when I want to be unforgettable…LOL. Am gearing up for the Blazing July Tournament. The Caribbean is calling me…golf's running a turtle pace second." I'm new to Facebook and text messages, so I can only hope I'm not posting to the public here.

His next message asked if I'd seriously trade Flagstaff for a foreign beach and then asked if he and his female terrier, Betsy, could join Houston and me on a walk.

"Flag is home but I need an escape plan when winter's bite is too relentless or my golf game requires more humility than I can muster. Houston is an intact male so Betsy's status is a consideration. Houston loves to play. He's four full weeks post-surgery and doing beyond great, so should be fine to romp with a new friend." I'm clearly out of my mind.

Betsy and Houston don't bother with intros or slow sniffs. They take one look at one another and take off at a play, spin, hop pace. She's smart enough to realize that small spaces under chairs or the table center are great to hide and catch her breath. I wonder if she's ever seen a dog Houston's size. Bill had asked about walking them together.

Walk? Within three minutes, Houston, my ever-intact man-dog, has a scoot-hump move I'd never seen before. My kitchen deck teeters between a PG-13 and R-rated performance.

Nice. Real nice, Houston. This doesn't make for long awkward moments with a man I barely know? Betsy runs under Houston's belly without ducking, thank goodness, or Houston's efforts might prevail. Then Bill can call the cops and claim statutory rape. Betsy's a year-old pup with an oral fixation. She chews Houston's jowls and anything she finds on the floor. My house is not puppy proof.

While Bill and I sip tequila on the back deck, Betsy hocks up unidentifiable debris padded in a pile of Houston's dry dog food beside my chair. Clearly, I should have closed the pantry door where I keep his food and water dishes. Houston eats on demand and never over eats, but this little gal has no such restraint. I'm amazed that her tummy could even hold that much dog food. I get a plastic bag and a roll of paper towels for Bill, who insists on cleaning it up. That's when it happens.

Squatted beside my chair he leans in and kisses me. Damnit. A bag of vomit at his feet and he's still incredibly romantic and proficient. Maybe the surprise factor made it better?

Why didn't Brad ever learn to kiss like this? I don't think he wanted to learn. Too intimate for him. I wonder if he kissed his girlfriends. There I go again, pumping that fucking lever.

Daniel and Bill evidently both took lessons or got lessons and now gave lessons to me on a very erotic art. So tender, yet they radiate the strain of leashed passion. A coincidence they're both six-foot-two with sultry blue eyes?

What in the hell am I doing here?

Considering social suicide with the patio lights on, the bitch in my head answers.

"Have some fun!" Jo had chided, when I told her he was coming over to dog walk. "What in the hell do you care what anyone else thinks? You haven't been laid in so long pheromones cling to you like a cloud."

"That's my aura," I whisper teasingly.

"That's 'fuck me blind' mist."

She has a point about it having been so very long. It had been over three months since I left Daniel in Atlanta and nothing since. I'm single. I don't need a relationship. I want sex and I imagine a player like Bill Brady's got game. I think this obsession with sex is part of my transition from married to single. This little goody two shoes, faithful to the end wife is due a little wild-side entertainment.

My imagination doesn't disappoint. He has moves alright. Pulls me up into his arms, and kisses me right out of my flip flops. Barefoot and on tip-toe I kiss him back. His open palms wander down my side, move up and down over the curve of my waist, in and across my tummy. More than suggestive, but well above getting-out-of-hand territory.

At the moment, I should be thinking passionate thoughts. How tender his kiss. The soft yet firm the grip of his huge hands. Should I let him make love to me? All the rules say sex on the first date stamps you a tramp. Give me a break for even contemplating it. My first thought was the old cliché about a bird in the hand, but I didn't intend to put my reputation in his hands this damned fast.

I don't want a relationship with a player either. Another player. I want to be touched, kissed, held, and ache to feel the pulse and pressure of a man inside me. Damn. How exciting and liberating is this?

Then practicality surfaces. I'm still in my golf clothes, sans the sweaty sneakers I ditched for a pair of flip flops. I need a shower, leg shave, and wax. Am I actually considering getting naked with a man that I'll see in the clubhouse, on the range, at Friday Night Skins? Lock me up now.

"Nope," I smile and place my palms on Bill's massive chest to create distance. "You're not getting laid tonight, pal." This is fun. I can tease and talk smack to him. We're both single. No expectations. No eggshells.

With Brad, sex was rough and rowdy, but the only time I recall that he liked to kiss was at the drive-in theatre before we married, when we weren't having sex. Even then, I don't remember being kissed like this guy or Daniel. I've never felt a man's mouth so soft and hungry. It's strange to think about how much I loved sex with Brad, without the passion. We both learned to play and perform in a purely physical environment. I responded to Brad's targeted approach easily and often.

But then my body responded to Daniel's passion in a wet and wild way. I'm responding to Bill tonight. Yet Brad provided multiple finales I have yet to achieve since him. The son of a bitch. Did he just know how, where, and what pressure to use to trigger me using over forty-seven years of practice? Or was it because I truly loved him?

I think that with Daniel, my mind was so cluttered with pressure to provide a screaming, final act to meet his heated requests that the curtain dropped on my head and smothered me. I'm not a screamer. I haven't told you I faked it over and time again with him after our first times together.

As I reread what I just typed, I decided to get up from my computer, wander around on my kitchen patio, to wonder why I'd left that out. Did I want my affair with Daniel to sound better than it was? Or was the way he held and kissed me enough? The weight of him, his touch, scent, his mouth, that he wanted me was more than enough, I think.

Then I wonder, why do I bother, through this entire book, trying to figure out why someone else said or did something, when I can't tell what motivated me to long for sex riddled with fake orgasms? I was definitely aroused. Excited. But my thoughts buzzed like static. Am I taking too long? Why am I taking so long? I never take this long. What if it doesn't happen? Do I confess? Will it ruin it for him? It is not good to confess that all the pieces are there, but you can't put the puzzle together. Not to a man in the moment. Screw it. Fake it, relax and have fun.

I'd rarely had the problem with Brad, even though I wasn't as passionately aroused as with Daniel. Bottom line is, Daniel didn't need to know, so I faked it, and kept my mouth shut, even to you.

Already my mind and muscles tense in Bill's arms. Will he know how to do whatever in the hell it was that Brad did? Will I need to fake it? I decide I don't care. If his equipment is adequate and I'm pretty damned sure it is, there are a number of positions in which I can bring enough intense internal crescendos to more than satisfy. I'm betting the man has not garnered the 'player status' he's known for by being a three-minute flash to the finish.

I need to transition from Brad. Learn a new game on a new field. Another aspect of life in which I must learn to relax, let the tension and need to control myself melt. The voice in my head chides, *You need to figure out why you're attracted to players. They're unreliable bastards, but good in bed. Are you that shallow?* I tune her out. I try to at least, as I think, *evidently.*

I don't falter about the 'not tonight,' unshowered, unshaven, though. I reiterate "You're not getting laid tonight. No," aloud, with a smile, but with finality. Bill Brady then asks if he can take me to dinner after another dog walk 'attempt' tomorrow night. Guess he figures he needs to incorporate a more conventional approach to get between my sheets.

Persistence just might prevail, I think, as I contemplate social suicide.

CHAPTER 29

In The Meantime...

I woke in the middle of the night and wondered what in the hell am I doing? I went from a lifetime of monogamy, on my side at least, to careening full speed, taking curves on two wheels? I have to wonder if that means I'm on a downhill track, or simply have the pedal to the metal on a new fun track? Either way, I'm out of my element. Determined to adjust. Adapting is one of my specialties. There has to be an upside to codependence once in a while.

I admit to a little flutter realizing Mr. Persistent will be here to take me to dinner in a few short hours. We pinky swore discretion, but that's a crap shoot. Forest Hillside rivals a Peyton Place of busy noses and whispered gossip. Do I want to be one of his minions?

Hmm. Perhaps make him one of mine? That makes it more palatable. The only other men who've made advances here are married. I'm going to have Jo give me lessons on a good right hook. Not really, but it would feel damned good. When married men make advances, I wonder how often it works for them. Do they always get shut down, or do many other women want to play married tag?

Not every date will lead to romance. I'm going to a benefit dinner Sunday night with Ted. He, Jo, and I refer to ourselves as the Three Musketeers. In his mid-eighties, he's twenty years older than either of us, but friendship doesn't have age boundaries. Ted misses going to the symphony. He and his wife had season tickets, so when he asks one of us if we'd like to go, we flip a coin and he has a date. We wag a few tongues when we go out with Ted on our own, but all the more fun for the three of us. We don't care. When we give him a rough time about dating younger, he puts an arm around both of us and laughs.

The three of us converged on being single from different paths. They both lost their spouses to long illnesses and all that encompasses. I know exactly where I left mine, and why, but if we were used cars on the market, their grills would be polished to a sheen. Emotionally speaking, I'd be the one with a cracked windshield, faulty brakes, and busted tail lights in the back row.

I inserted a space between the paragraph above, because after I wrote and then reread it, I took a break. As a rule, I avoid looking into the mirror unless I'm doing my hair or makeup, and I rarely make eye contact with my reflection.

Making eye contact with ourselves in the mirror can be the equivalent of mainlining truth serum. Defenses dissolve like torn curtains to reveal harsh realities about ourselves, our situation, or others when we look ourselves in the eye. Those harsh realizations demand choices be made to do this, change that.

I'm not sure why I looked into my eyes while drying my hands. I know better, especially when I'm working and don't want to be distracted. Perhaps my subconscious knew I needed to take a good look at myself at that particular moment.

Jo and Ted have been single longer, had more time for the repair shop, but they've both been to hell and back. Ted took care of his wife through fifteen years of Alzheimer's, and Jo's husband was an invalid for five years before he died. When she gets down about something, she often talks about David. The last seconds of his life he opened his hand. When she gripped her palm against his, he pulled her close.

"Thank you, baby, for taking such good care of me. I'll love you forever. Already have." His last effort and breath was for her.

I got teary when she told me about it. It's moments like those that I slip on my pink-pity-party dress and feel cheated. Both Jo and Ted were loved by the loves of their life.

Why not me?

Truth serum flooded through me. It had been my job to fix my relationship. Keep my family together. My mother said so. Did it herself. Tried to, anyway.

Codependency is an excessive emotional, physical, and psychological reliance upon a relationship that is dysfunctional. But I wasn't just crazy. He was the love of my life and remembering the good stuff is easier than facing the truth behind the bad.

"There were years Brad and I were twenty-five dollars a month above break even and our check book hovered near the poverty level. My mom and sisters would show up and happen to have a grocery bag with a pound of ground beef, perhaps a gallon of milk with them. Nowadays they tease about the care packages they brought to us. Sunday after church we went to Brad's parents for real, not-canned ham or roast beef, with potatoes and gravy. It was a treat," I told Jo one night at dinner.

"Brenda told me about that the last time she was up here," Jo said. "There had to be some good things, Allie. Reasons you loved him."

"There were. The good part of those early years is that we needed each other."

"For a story that we know has a shit ending, you've got an awfully content smile right now."

"I remember a Sunday when Brad needed to study for finals. We lived in our first house, on an access road beside McKellips. Andrew was a toddler and kept pestering him. Brad finally tied a rope to Andrew's four-wheeled Snoopy Dog, put Andrew on it. Brad stretched out on his stomach, his book on the floor in front of him, and read while he launched Andrew down the hall with his foot, then dragged him slowly back with the rope. Over and over. Tile floors weren't all bad."

"So, Brad wasn't always an asshole." Jo conceded as much as confirmed to herself.

I don't trust my voice to answer, 'No, he wasn't,' so I just shake my head and press my lips together.

"There was a time he said he didn't sleep unless I was in bed beside him. Strange that I have to dredge memories of a time he did love me out of so much muck." I have to be fair to him, even now. "His goal, his obsession was success. He valued his employees."

"Sure," Jo popped back. "They were revenue producers."

"It was more than that. He succeeded by making a success of losing stores. Men who'd hung their heads at district meetings strutted in as top of the heap profit makers by the time Brad left. He mattered to them. A lot. I imagine my pride in him was part of my hook, too."

"I imagine you're right," Jo said.

I don't like the word codependency, but at this point I own it. I can't bribe the bitch to shut up either. She doesn't take checks, cash, or credit cards. Is essential. Material. Not materialistic, but deeply rooted.

Becoming codependent reminds me of the way a plant will bend, then eventually grow crooked trying to reach sunlight. The longer it is deprived, the more desperate it becomes to survive. Codependency is gradual process driven by deprivation and need, not desires or wants. It's part of the mind fuck. You think if you only try harder, they'll try harder, too. It doesn't work that way. Generally, it's the exact opposite. They see you as needy, therefore less desirable. I didn't know or understand, but I'm learning, and that's a good thing. So, I'm not as nice, but more desirable? What I have to do, is learn to value myself.

It's also good that the sad, sorry-for-myself moments wash over me, then recede like ocean waves rearranging the sand on shore, filling the holes, smoothing the surface. I tell you about them so you don't feel so alone, or bad about yourself when it happens to you. It's part of the process.

If you keep your heart open, you'll cycle through regret, sadness, desperation, loneliness, anger, and even moments of despair. It's okay. Be brave enough to stay open, to feel and love. Don't sweep that away with the eggshells.

So far, Jo and Ted haven't kicked me off the used car lot. In fact, they've become the closest friends I've ever had.

I'm there for them, too. We all have moments. It's part of life. We laugh a lot. An even better part. The three of us can and do talk about nearly anything. No one gets to cop out, without getting called out. The bonds of trust between us set us free to be.

I think that is the key I've learned from their friendship, about friendship. Don't confine your friends to ones that revolve around your significant other's circle. I know I was entitled to friends of my own, but didn't stand up for myself. When Brad threw tools and a temper tantrum because friends of mine dropped by unannounced one afternoon, I chose the easy solution and saw that it never happened again.

Would it have changed our relationship, my life, if I had challenged his mind and manners? It might have changed me for the better. But I believed in keeping the peace, so I walked gingerly on eggshells with a soft tread, and I sucked it up.

It's a shoulda, coulda, woulda reflection, and suddenly I smiled at my own reflection again. Right into my eyes. There's much to look forward to, when I stop looking back.

CHAPTER 30

Mind Game Therapy

Monday night I have a first date with a tall, dark-skinned, handsome man, or so my oldest son's girlfriend tells me. He is a client of the law firm she works for and when she asked if she could give him my phone number, I said, "Sure." I love that she's comfortable enough to set me up on my first blind date. I'm more worried about disappointing her than him. This girl could be Andrew's wife and my daughter-in-law one day.

I pondered what to wear. Classic? Country Club casual? Sass it up with a funky belt and jewelry? I finally decided on a combination that included a pair of skinny jeans, tucked in powder blue blouse, a silver-chain belt, and strappy sandals with a one-inch heel. I felt like a lady, with a little pizazz.

Picking the right clothing for the place or occasion is important, as much to make you feel comfortable as to make a good impression. Perhaps more. Be yourself, no matter what, but be versatile, too. If cargo pants and a T-shirt or denim are your ultra-casual look, great. I love my skinny jeans, but can dress them up or down.

Sometimes it's good to ask if there is a dress code. And don't whine if there is one. What you wear is an expression of your individuality and versatility. It can demonstrate that you're not afraid to step out of your jeans and into a pair of slacks, or vice versa. It expresses your dimension, shows strength of character, confidence, and being real keeps you from tripping over your own feet.

Along with my pending dinner with Mr. Blind Date, the day after Labor Day a man I've been in online contact with through Elite Singles is coming to Flagstaff to meet me. A man I refer to as Georgia. Again, I've found myself thinking of and referring to internet individuals by their locale. Helps me keep them straight in my mind, especially since two thirds of them on date sites seem to be named Jerry.

It's no joke. You need a method to keep them straight. You need to remember who you told what to, so you don't repeat yourself, or chat with them like they know something about you that you told the other person, not them. Consider it mind game therapy. I've come to realize it's a place for singles to have other singles with whom they can communicate and share. Even if we never meet in person, I've developed friendships and look forward to hearing from some of them.

Georgia wants to ride the railway to the Grand Canyon and asked if he can buy two tickets. Lots of firsts for me. Confusion and fear that I'm messing up dating around; but Jo and Debra, my dating coach, are in the bleachers, cheering me on. When I gave my dating coach a quick rundown, expressed my fear of being labeled a slut, or worse, feeling like one, her email provided direction I dare trust. At least I'll fake it till I make it.

"Kind of fun, all this going on, don't you think?" Debra's email begins. "In general, you do not need to wrap anything up in a perfect scenario. Regardless of their feelings, you have not made a commitment to anyone and do not need to, ever, unless you want to. You also don't need to tell them everything you are doing. Let club playboy be smitten and enjoy your time with him. Get more smitten yourself if your feelings lead you there. But until you are both saying 'Hey, let's make a commitment' and define what that is, and both are all in, it isn't there. And move forward with Grand Canyon plans. No commitment to him either, besides Grand Canyon plans. When you know you want to see just one and when you can feel secure that they are able to commit to you and give you what you need, that is the time to put all the cards on the table. I think it usually takes more time spent together to know those things with confidence. Hope this helps."

Help? I feel like I just deplaned in a foreign country and culture that empowers women without disempowering men. Delusional or real? The ground quakes, but the sun is shining.

Married to single is a huge shift. A game changer bigger than Bridge to Rugby, rowing to white water rafting. Most singles I talk to say they hate dating, are ready to settle down. I'm new in the trenches, and at the moment I'm wondering, *what's not to like*? Variety. Freedom. Adventure. Did I mention Freedom? It's a little like trying on shoes. Walking up and down the aisles to see how they feel. But then the next day? I might not want to shop, especially for shoes. It's raining, the winds of change rip through my space. It goes like that, at this point in my dating career, at least.

The Elite Singles date site isn't as prolific as Our Time.com, but there's less riffraff to filter through. I try not to peek at their photos before I read their profiles, but let's face it. Their profile on my computer screen doesn't hint of after shave or resonate a masculine voice or posture. I need a visual.

Internet dating is different than a personal introduction. One thing for sure, beards are evidently in for the over sixty crowd. I get a lot of long-bearded men sending smiles and flirts. Totally bald is not rare or unattractive, either.

My profile picture on both sites is one Jo took on our first Cabo adventure last January. It's sassy me.

We were at a beach store. While she was trying on swim suits, I plucked up a pink fedora that matched my blouse, adjusted the small-brim mobster hat at an angle, and couldn't resist it. Not for five dollars.

No new swimsuit for Jo, but one new hat later for me, we made our way to Sammy Hagar's Cabo Wabo Cantina, a hot spot of live music, dancing, drinks, food, and fun. After a bucket of two-for-one Coronas, two bottles each, Jo and I sing to the music and dance with our waiter. After two buckets, she takes my profile picture. I decide I need to drink more often before photo ops.

When the man I call Georgia first contacted me through Elite Singles, it all started with "Love your hat." I liked my genuinely happy smile.

I'm not just running wild. I evaluate. Measure. Dare I say, judge the men who breeze through my dating circle.

I've dubbed Bill Brady Mr. Persistent. Since he has a house here in Forest

Hillside, it's a dead give-a-way if I call him by locale. He has a lot of things here: a stellar golf game, great eyes, a bratty little dog he uses as date bait when he walks her through the community, and a particular persona.

I think of him as a playground dater. You remember the kid that would swing, laugh, and visit with someone, hop off and run to the teeter totter with another, then rush to block the bottom of the swing, and tease someone new, but you never saw them walk home with anyone. They didn't pick, in public. He's that guy, complete with a wandering eye.

I played in the three-day Blazing July Golf Tournament. In retrospect, I should have run over my golf clubs or my foot instead, but the lunches, cocktail parties, and friends that are part of it lured me in and were a ton of fun. Two teams tied for first place, so it was drinks all around in to-go cups before they head to the tee box for the first playoff hole. The rest of us gather around the first green to watch them come in. These gals are real golfers. Serious ones, and fun to watch.

Bill Brady had been moving through the crowd of mostly women specta-tors like that kid on the playground. I didn't know he was beside me, until he spoke.

"I love the matching outfits those gals have," he said, nodding towards a twenty-something woman ready to putt for first place. "Wow. Look at the legs on that one." He's kibitzing while watching the Blazing July tourna-ment champs. I'm evaluating, measuring, judging Mr. Persistent. The litera-ture about narcissism addresses this behavior; calls it triangulation. Talking about, praising other women to create insecurity so you'll try harder to please them because, after all, there's competition. Brad did it, too when he talked up his gal pals. He used to introduce them to me while he was having an affair with them. I have to wonder what they thought of that. Wow. It's startling to see the patterns; like there's a playbook, but I don't think there is. Maybe there is a master's guide to manipulation; but then, business training on motivational skills would teach the basics. Do I need to stop dating busi-nessmen and look for plumbers and contractors?

Today, it's as though Bill wants me to know he's chosen to stand beside me, but by commenting on the great legs on the green, doesn't want me to feel too special. Mission accomplished. He just moved himself deeper into 'disposable territory'.

Back to Mr. Blind Date. Andrew's girlfriend set me up with a phone call from a man she knows through work. "He's really nice, and nice looking." I could hear the smile in her voice.

I took the phone on the kitchen patio when he called to introduce himself and ask me to dinner. We talked for nearly an hour. I'm not a phone person, so the conversation was engaging until he blundered.

"Just tell me if you have nice legs," he says.

I want to respond, "Tell me you don't have a pot belly, jowls, or erectile dysfunction." You have no idea how badly I wanted to do that, but I behaved myself. He'd tattle to Andrew's girlfriend, without telling my side of the story.

"If we meet for dinner Monday night, you can make that call," I answer, instead. I was going to be in the valley for a meeting with Brad, so the timing was good.

What is it with these guys? Daniel, my first real affair, had a foot fetish, sent me FMP's, otherwise known as 'Fuck Me Pumps'. He also sent thigh-highs because he liked the feel of them against his hips and thighs when we were tangled together.

At Daniel's direction, I learned how to dress for that first revealing moment. It was a valuable learning experience I've incorporated ever since. Getting naked for the first time with a new man is enough to cause an anxiety attack. Victoria's Secret is better than a shield. Armor up with lingerie and when you take it off, do it slowly.

Better yet, tell them to do it.

CHAPTER 31

Bait and Switch Bullshit

My first behind-the-scenes encounter with Bill Brady happened approximately twenty-four hours and one dinner after our first kiss on my patio beside a mound of puppy puke.

I'm trying to reconcile with being single, but I miss sex. I'm in no way ready for a full-blown relationship so have decided I'm either celibate or I learn to enjoy casual sex. It worked with Daniel, for sure. I have no idea how I'm going to feel about this guy later, but nature is pounding at my bedroom door. Hard. Loud.

I answered it wearing a black shelf bra, black thigh-highs with lace tops, a naughty black thong, and braced my extended arm on the door frame to keep from falling on my face. I winked and smiled, let him know I was having fun. Ready to play. As I said before, five-inch Stilettos are hazardous on thick carpet or flagstone. I had nowhere to go, so tried to slip seductively out of them once the original presentation was complete.

"Wait!" Brady exhaled. "Don't move!" His bolt for my kitchen was a sight I hope to forget. When he walked back into my bedroom, I couldn't believe he'd brought a pro camera in his duffle.

"Put that thing down this instant. You're on Facebook, for crying out loud," I emphasized. "No way are you taking a lingerie picture of me." I can't help but wonder if he keeps an album of conquests or 'accidentally' flashes a photo on his phone when he's with his guy friends.

If he heard "No, absolutely not," once, he heard it no less than five times before he gave in, gave up, reached out, and pulled me into his arms. Good thing, because I was ready to robe-up and send him out the front door. Luckily, he redeemed himself.

Turns out I was right about Mr. Persistent's equipment. Impressive. Responsive. I get why the ladies gravitate towards this man. Then he kisses me and I have no regrets about this moment in time. It's better than the first time on the patio and it's been a long time since I've been held with the promise of so much more. Daniel would be proud I didn't waste the gifts of slinky lingerie he inspired or the FMP's he sent me.

We take our time touching, kissing, exploring. He brought a candle and Kama Sutra oil in his dandy little bag. It enhances the feel of his hands on my skin as he massages my shoulders, back and hips. The guy has done this before. Watched a video? Porn? Knows what he likes? What I'll like? I try to stop analyzing the pressure of his palms as they glide over my body on a film of fragrant oil. The tingle of his fingertips stroking my stomach. Okay. I'm ready to get serious, shouldn't want to rush this, but ache for more.

It has been over three months, and that was a long time for me before my single status. By this point in my life, sex is second nature. Soon we both relax, begin to move and respond to one another.

Good sex mingles tastes and textures. Reminds me of a moist chocolate donut with frosting and sprinkles. You can lick the frosting, savor the sugar and cocoa as it melts in your mouth, then play with the sprinkles on your tongue. Or…you can tease with your teeth before you take a bite of the firm, frosted-sprinkled treat and enjoy an explosion of flavors and textures at once. The warmth of a kiss, while hands grip your hair or roam your skin, as heat moves and tingles inside you. Hmmm. This is more than I have missed.

Finally spent, he wants to cuddle. Is this guy for real? Cuddling is still a new frontier for me, but I mold myself inside him, lay my head in the nook of his arm. Do he and Daniel really like this or are they determined to offer the whole package to their women? Brady is different than Daniel. Foreign to Brad. A fantasy of mine. I think Brady has the moves down. I realize I used to pretend Brad couldn't keep his hands off me, wanted me, just me, when I was near climax. There should be an Oscar for performances not only in bed, but also in our heads. That's probably why all systems were go with Brad. Oscar Award mind fucks. I was both the performer and audience.

This club playboy is not my guy. I have a list of reasons why he's not my guy for the long term. I don't care what my dating coach says about casual sex. Suddenly I tense. Wonder what in the hell am I doing. This is a damned difficult position to enjoy and at the same time remain detached. Then as suddenly, I relax again, because it's a little like suspending your disbelief to really get into and enjoy a movie; even science fiction or time travel. We all know they're actors with other lives, that there's a real world out there, but for the moment, in the moment, we pretend.

The voice in my head isn't a bitch tonight. Her whisper is soft and sultry. She likes this, wants me to stop analyzing and simply enjoy it. I don't want to fall asleep and miss this, but my muscles untangle, no longer wet sheets twisted and wrung into ropes. Amazing how easy it is to breathe deep.

Just when I snug in and feel comfy, "Great timing, right?" The sultry voice in my head can't leave well enough alone for long. She now has a scolding edge. I talked to Mr. Blind Date for over an hour last night. I'm meeting him for dinner Monday night in the valley. Famine to feast. Desert to rain forest. A duck out of water or maybe on the ocean paddling around with a variety of creatures that can devour it if it doesn't pay attention.

Date two men at once? Three if I count the dinner Sunday night with Ted. Four, with Georgia. Who does this? How do they remember what they said to which one? Will anyone be my guy? Will I become poison if it gets out?

Georgia, the widower, is in the lead. He sent me a book about beginning again, accountability, living and loving life, called *The Traveler's Gift*. The next day a DVD of *Seven Days in Utopia*, a golf movie about hope and heart landed on my doorstep. He's an Ancestry.com member and disciple that has compiled my family's history beyond what I ever was told or found out. My hairdresser says that's stalker crazy. I want to believe he wants to impress me with something he's good at. And he has a talent for genealogy research.

Evidently my paternal great grandparents were on the 1871 Census in Quebec. French Canadian. I knew there was a link, just didn't know it was so close. Georgia mentioned that he'd followed their heritage trail back to France. Last night he asked if I'd ever read *The Five Languages of Love*. I won't be surprised to find a copy on my doorstep. He's not the wealthiest or even the most handsome, but he's got heart. I read a review of the book. It's about the touch as well as the language of love. How to make it last. The pack is trailing so far behind this guy I've never met, they're nearly invisible in his cloud of dust.

Can I live with myself if I hurt a man like him? Pretty arrogant to think he'd care about me enough that I would, or could.

As though my question caught a breeze that carried it across the country, the next day he sends an email that begins, "I had a dream last night."

It was one hell of a dream.

"I saw my wife, reached out and touched, held, and kissed her. I asked if she was okay. Happy. She said it was trying. Because I had spoiled her so, it was hard. Then she was gone, and I collapsed in tears. My daughter thinks I need grief counseling that I never did."

He wants to know what I think, if I have any idea what the dream could mean. I don't say this, but I suspect that Georgia is so snared in the past, the pain and loss of his wife, I'm nothing but a distraction. Someone he tripped over while on the run.

I reached out to him, as I pushed him an arm's length away.

"Your daughter sounds very wise. Resolving loss in one's heart and thoughts is a process. It takes work to move through well-defined steps and support that grief counseling offers. I don't know about the dream, Gary. Perhaps you want to continue to take care of her, to be there for her, so she cannot be fine and happy where she is, and not need you. Perhaps it's simply a resurfacing of the feelings you had before she passed away in pain and distress. Caregivers, as you were, have to sacrifice themselves and cope with the helplessness of watching one they love, suffer and pass. It's not easy to shift your focus, begin to take care of yourself, believe you're worth it, that you deserve a life going forward. It can be a breakthrough moment for many. Depression, anger, fear of what to do with ourselves, our time, and emotions loses ground when one is 'no longer needed'. These things cloud the sense of self, peace, and joy in the future."

As I write to him, I realize this tender man in pain is not ready to move on yet. I was a caregiver in my old life: wife, mom, grandma, daughter. Everyone else's issues and needs took priority over my own or the weight of guilt straddled my shoulders. I wasn't a paragon or saint. I was a high functioning codependent.

Now I want to run, play, make love, visit, laugh with a man. I don't want to nurse one through the loss of his beloved. Selfish? It's my 'break the codependent cycle' frame of mind. No apology or regrets, but the voice in my head has questions and she's relentless.

Are you afraid of a man capable of complete commitment? Would you feel smothered? Do you like the chase? Are you afraid sex would be boring? Do you need to seriously consider committing yourself to an institution for the mentally fucked up?

My dating world has become insanely crazy, a whirlwind of activity. I am fumbling my way through, one day, one date, one fun tumble at a time, into the great unknown. Definitely need to ditch the Stilettos and get my running shoes on to keep up. It is exciting, scary, and about damned flippin' time. Besides, running is good exercise, right?

CHAPTER 32

Business…Anything but Usual

After I left home the first time, Brad wanted us to go to counseling. Becky Barry wasn't a typical counselor. Her website revealed a workbook approach to resolution, not a "He said, she did, what do we do now?" referee. Questions focus on the individual, not their spouse. What did I envision my life being? What did I feel capable of achieving or changing in my current circumstance? That sort of thing for both of us to answer.

Brad didn't surprise me. In a nutshell, if I would stop questioning him, stop talking to him, be upbeat and cheerful no matter what he did, I wouldn't irritate the shit out of him.

"You wanted me at home with our boys, in the office, and eventually free to travel, not signed up for college classes when you want to take a winter trip to the Caribbean. Any of that ring a bell?" I asked.

He countered with his all too familiar refrain by now. He earned all the money. He was accomplished, successful. He worked out regularly. He had friends to fill his time before it was time for TV and sleep.

He was the perfect profile for Narcissistic Personality Disorder: egotistically perfect tunnel vision. I resonated the fed up, passive-aggressive codependent whose workouts were limited to clenching my jaws and scrubbing my lips together. I did workout, but it wasn't worth pointing out. The more I listened to him rant during our counseling sessions, the further away from him I intended to stay.

Resolution. It's a dandy word.

Our only common ground was an active sex life. Becky tried to focus on it as a core strength to build on. "Some couples have no strengths to build on, so this is good. We can start here."

"No, Becky, we can't." I finally spoke up. "He exchanges intimate emails, sexual remarks with someone we work with, yet says they're just good friends. Then he tells you I don't understand friendship because I don't have any friends. I don't understand his affairs, so I need professional help." *Entitlement is a real fucking bitch, right?* I think, but don't verbalize.

Becky is also a licensed mediator and this becomes invaluable. Somehow, she is able to discount his tempers, my codependent behavior, and advocate for each of us when appropriate. Brad and I finalized the division of personal assets in her office.

It was a far cry from our first settlement mediation at the end of May and reminds me we've made progress. Up till then, our mediation sessions have been about business and often included our oldest and youngest sons, Andrew and Jason, as we move to restructure management of the family companies to which they've devoted their careers. Mediation is an interesting process capable of many variations.

The day of our first personal property division session, only Brad and I were going to mediation. When it was over, I was going to our youngest son's house to celebrate his birthday. I wanted to do the meeting by conference call but Brad insisted we meet in person. I wondered why until about ten minutes in. His eruption rocked near ten on the Richter scale. Epic, even for Brad. A heat seeking missile targeted me. Did he need to clear the air? Get this shit off his chest? Retaliate because we were finally down to dollars and cents?

Money. Half. He would only be half as rich, because of me.

I started to write his actual dialogue here but deleted it. He's since apologized for the outburst that threw me back into the abyss for a few weeks. I wasn't strong enough to hold on when the hatred in his words, voice, and eyes boiled across the conference table at me. When he finally slapped his papers together and stormed out the door, my heart pounded, I caught myself holding my breath, and my eyes stung when I blinked.

I'm still too vulnerable for this. He had been my hero. I built him up, winched him onto a pedestal so he could be all and everything. High-functioning codependent that I am, I was an artisan.

By the time I left Becky's office and got in my car, I had to grip the steering wheel and concentrate. "Breathe. Breathe deeper. I can't. I...I... can't. Stop this! You're having a panic attack! Don't you dare let it get out of control. Now slow down. Focus. Breathe. Okay. Okay."

What rattled me wasn't Brad's temper. I was used to his explosions. This time what had erupted was a violent, living contempt for me. I shudder realizing he has hated me for how long? Probably decades.

I've loved a man who hates me. I know. All the literature says a narcissist isn't capable of real intimacy. They can value a partner that makes them look good, fills their needs, but could never love them. It didn't seem possible. I didn't want to believe it was true. Could be. Ever was. Always was. Always will be.

I need to stop thinking. Concentrate on the radio, the lyrics to, of all songs, *Let Her Go*, by Passenger. "You only know you love her when you let her go." I change stations.

Audible breaths help until I open the car door to heave the contents of my stomach onto stained asphalt. I swallow against it. Son of a bitch. He can't do this to me anymore. I've been mad at him before, even felt the fury of hatred, but never have I accepted the depth of his hatred for me. Stand up to a narcissist and be ready when the mask comes off.

I wish I could tell you I experienced a sudden shift that night. That I was able to step into my son's kitchen and open the gate to the love I have for him. To walk in the arena of celebration, remember the moment I first saw his face, all the smiles and wonderful things that are my youngest son. Instead, I wanted to run into the night screaming.

My life. My entire adult life I lied to myself. He couldn't love me. He isn't capable. Brad's behavior towards me fits within the spectrum of NPD. The repercussions of an abusive childhood attached to some volatile genetic threads. Does it only display itself towards a spouse or partner? Do they select a single target? Or not so closely tied to others, are they able to maintain their game face more easily?

Cheer up, Alex the voice in my head scolds. Put on a face. Celebrate your son's birthday. He doesn't deserve to have you ruin it with your shit. Brad won't be here.

I think about that voice and know I'm not crazy. Whether we think of it as our conscience or the voice of common sense, people have acknowledged it since the beginning.

Rumi, an 11th century Persian poet wrote, "There is a voice that doesn't use words. Listen."

I decide it's time I name mine, this creature made of grey matter that gives voice from the recesses of what and who I am.

From now on I'll call her Grey. Damn it, I wish she agreed that I'm tougher than this these days. I just need time to regroup.

This time, regrouping doesn't take the 'berate myself, pull up my big girl panties, and deal with it' routine. On the drive to Jason's house, my fuse finally flares into the arsenal of my heart. Who knew I'd packed so many grains of gunpowder in it over all these years? I don't know what to do with the explosive fury Brad ignited, but I'm a fast learner.

That may be one of the biggest whoppers you've ever told yourself, Grey snapped, but I was on memory tear and barely heard her at the time.

He did it all? He gave me everything I have? Like hell he did.

Evidently the absentee father was so wrapped up in himself, in the job, that he never realized I washed the car, shuttled kids to events, ball games, friends' houses, school, helped with homework, cooked, grocery shopped, cleaned the pool, made events and holiday parties happen without any help from him. Hell. He was late to Christmas Eve nearly every year because the golf course played slow. I now wonder if he was late because he needed to tag up with a girlfriend on Christmas Eve. He never saw me in the office all those years, either. He didn't appreciate or even acknowledge that I cleared his plate so all he had to do was work and play golf. I'm on a rant here. I wonder if having sex with me while he was having affairs made them more exciting? What a stud, right?

At Jason's house, I try valiantly to soften the hardened grimace. I fake a smile and hope I pull it off. Damn Brad. That son of a bitch. Grey is vocal and getting violent: *When will you stop letting him control you and your emotions? Step up and own yourself,* she rages.

When? Good question. Brad ditched his subtle approach to devaluing me with things like telling me his gal pal is just a little muscle, disciplined, got her MBA, and has garnered his respect and admiration, in contrast to me. If I were more organized, the grandkids wouldn't lose the remote in the couch cushions or leave an empty toilet paper roll. I'll spare us both the long litany of inadequacies he fires like bullets from a Gatling gun.

Before I left him, I really enjoyed the times Brad left Flagstaff to go to our house in the Bradshaw Mountains to work on the mine. He realized every little boy's dream of owning and operating a backhoe, track hoe, dump truck, and gold mining equipment. He's been an amateur miner for over six years.

"I'll come with you this weekend," I offered, one Saturday afternoon. We were growing further apart by the day. We needed time together, not apart. Stupid thought, in retrospect.

Ludicrous, Grey chimes in. She's getting way too bitchy.

"Thanks, but I need to unwind," Brad had answered. "Have some peace. Time just to myself, but I'll take Houston with me."

My radar went up as I packaged meals, coffee, incidentals he might be out of up there.

"To have peace you need to be away from me?"

"You always overdramatize everything. I want time that I don't have to talk or interact. Downtime. It has nothing to do with you. I want to be alone."

The only way for me to know for sure if he's actually alone up there is to show up well after dark. Then what? If he's alone, I'll feel like a sneaky jerk. If he's not, how fast could I get out of there?

Houston, the most emotional dog we've ever had, doesn't do well without Ben or me in the vicinity. Brad woke the next morning to explosive diarrhea splattered in front of three exit doors of our mountain house. No need to expound on Brad's explosion. He told me he cleaned it up himself. Then a week later he tells me 'she' (his work wife) used the house for the weekend, and cleaned all the carpets for him.

"She is playing house, in my house, Brad."

"She's looking for a high-country cabin to use on weekends and I told her she should look around up there. She'd know somebody in the neighborhood, instead of going off all alone."

"Would you actually go that far? Be that blatant?"

God, do I feel like an idiot recounting pathetic me, as I write this. Grey reminds me that I said I was a fast learner, but if I bought that bullshit I was dumb as a stump. It's like she has a death grip on this powerful flashlight, and shines it in the dark recesses where I hide memories that hurt.

She's right to remind me I need to speed up my learning curve. This was one of those times I knew he was having an affair but didn't have any solid evidence to counter his denials and attacks yet.

"Nothing's enough for you, is it?" he counters angrily. "She does a nice thing and you twist it up in your dirty little mind."

Justification and control. Corrosion.

You have no idea how many times I've replayed his words and his attacks in my mind.

Reruns running through your mind are part of the process of getting your grubby little hands off the lever. Rattling the cage door and picking at the lock.

Not long after his blow up in mediation the day of our youngest son's birthday, I took a stand. It was past time, and a sign I was healing. Codependent no more. Stupid in retrospect, because I had no way to enforce it if he refused and I'd have had to swallow the defeat. I did it anyway.

I'd seen the golf roster and sure enough, Brad was signed up for the Senior Club Championship at Forest Hillside. I was certain he and his new girlfriend, not the work wife I left him for, would stay with Ron and Cindy for the three-day weekend of festivities and competition, the way we used to before we bought our house here.

I felt invaded. They'd be at the clubhouse for meals, festivities, among my new friends, as well as our old group of friends. He had kept our dream house in Phoenix; the house, land and mine in the Bradshaw Mountains; bought himself a ritzy condo on the waterfront in Tempe. Now he got to be here too?

Strange, but I didn't deliberate or analyze how I felt. It was crystal clear as I called him on my cell phone.

"I looked at the roster and see you've signed up for the Senior Club Championship next weekend."

"Yes, I did." Brad hates to be questioned, and I'm the only who does that. He's on the defensive.

"This is my home. Since we're still officially married, it isn't good for you to be up here. Your girlfriend evidently has no problem living with a married man, but men up here aren't okay with dating a married woman whose husband is sitting at the next table. I have a right to start over and don't need you in the foursome with a man who may want to ask me out on a date."

"I'll cancel out right now." There is no kindness or understanding in words clearly spoken through clenched teeth. He resonates contempt he used to mask most of the time.

"Thank you." I couldn't force him to cancel, but am proud I asked, and glad he did.

"Once our divorce is final, I'm buying a house up there."

"Not much you do surprises me anymore."

I still have a tendency to over-explain to justify a position or value during our subsequent mediations, but I am getting better. The settlement agreement we finalized is a triumph for both Brad and me and for the process of mediation. We agreed on assigned values, and designated who gets what. He even relinquished his membership in Forest Hillside. I am now the primary member, and I like it, even though I expect my haven will be short-lived.

He apologized several times for his behavior in the mediation session the day of Jason's birthday. Crumbs of a morsel sometimes fall from the shoot. In subsequent sessions, he went out of his way to compensate. I wonder if he backpedaled because he was afraid of losing our sons' support on the business side? Could his moods genuinely shift thoughts and perceptions that dramatically? From hatred to tolerance?

Grey actually smacked me in the head. Did she have a pellet gun in there?

I don't come to realize until much later, that these shifts from kind to cruel are all part of the NPD cycle to keep us engaged. For him, it is all about winning. He lost me. Lost nearly half his wealth. My boundaries are like red flags to an angry bull. His happy, 'look how great I'm doing' face is to one-up me. Let the world know he's better off. Worth what it cost him to get rid of me.

Stay buckled up at this point. At the flash of a red flag, that bull's nostrils will flair, he'll paw the pavement with fury and charge.

Between the first mediation meeting and what I thought was our final settlement, my mother died, Houston survived two surgeries, nearly died, and our middle son, Ben, face-planted on the recovery trail. The wheels fell off the wagon Ben had been on. Brad and I stood shoulder to shoulder. Does adversity forge reluctant alliances? I could go on and on. Analyzing too much is not an attribute, especially since 'why' rarely matters.

With our settlement agreement signed, Brad told me he wants to be friends. "We have all those years together, and our family."

Perhaps one day. It took me nearly two weeks to climb out of the abyss after that first mediation meeting. Once I finally squared my shoulders, I can proudly tell you, I'm stronger. Through the process, I had to own up to and vent a vat of suppressed rage. I had to do it in an echo chamber, just Grey and me. I'm learning.

What I've finally realized is that I need to stop being angry with myself.

CHAPTER 33

Act Like a Man?

Yesterday Bill, Mr. Persistent, wanted to meet me at the driving range at around five p.m.

"Don't worry about it. I help lots of women with their golf swing." He proceeds to name a number of my friends he's coached, some married, some single. We'll be safe from the gossip chain in Forest Hillside.

Grey chides me: Don't ask if he's had affairs with any of them. None of your business. Remember, the dating coach's advice works both ways.

He's a scratch golfer and, I hear, a good teacher. Jo tells me to take advantage. "Let him help you with your swing. It'll be good."

It's Thursday. Bill has a noon tee time, done by four or so; will go home, let Betsy out, then will call. "We'll meet at the back range around five," he said.

It was a sound plan, only he didn't call. At five thirty, Ted called. His son is in town. Jo told him she'd go out to dinner and have a shot or two of tequila to put the demise of her relationship with Gerry in perspective. She broke up with him less than a week ago.

I do a happy dance behind her back. She wants a drink.

"Can we pick you up at six fifteen?" Ted asks me.

"If I can make it, I'll meet you in town." I haven't told him I've been seeing Bill. Discretion? Partially.

I know there have been lightning delays and rain on the course, that Bill won't finish his round at four, but he has a phone. He can text that he'll either be late or will need to take a rain check. No problem.

But, no communication *is* a problem. I refuse to call or text him an "Are we still on for tonight?" I feel really stupid because I made dinner. Roasted a tri-tip in green-chili enchilada sauce, have all the trimmings. Corn on the cob. Thought it would be fun, pay back for the golf lesson he gave me.

By six p.m., it felt like waiting for Brad to call. I'm done waiting, and call Ted. "Can you still pick me up at six fifteen?" When I get in the back seat of his car, I slide my phone to silent and drop it in my purse.

Reentering the dating scene is like walking along an unfamiliar trail because it is new, but then you begin to recognize the pieces of gravel that suddenly invade your shoes. It feels like coagulated eggshells. When you stop, bend over to empty your shoes and brush the bottoms of your feet, all of a sudden you are in too-familiar territory. I bolted.

Ted, his son, Jo, and I have a great time at Picasso's, a local Italian restaurant that serves outstanding salads, thin crust-organic pizza and an array of heartier entrees. Ted's son has his father's sharp wit and sense of humor. An hour after they drop Jo and me off at our homes, I call Jo and tell her about my no-show, no-call or-text, Bill Brady event.

"I don't want to think I'm jaded, but this is such Brad behavior. Instead of a thirty-second call, they just go silent."

"I know. Gerry did the same thing. Think it comes with the hairy testicles?"

"If it were that simple, I'd have them blindfolded, tied down and pluck my little heart out. Problem is, I think this is the perfect opportunity for me to break it off with him. I like the sex. It's not mind-blowing, but it's good. I'm at least sane enough not to fall head over heels for someone who gets around as much as Bill does, even after he told me he finally wants to settle down. Find the love of his life. Oh wait," I chirp. "He told me Patti had been the love of his life. What a year does to his recollection of romance, right?"

"Maybe he *is* ready to settle down. It could happen." Jo is playing devil's advocate here.

"I'm jaded, remember. But if I break it off because he stood me up without a call or text, he can take the rap. I get out of it and I'm off scot-free."

"Check between your legs to see if you've grown a pair. That's guy-think."

"I know. Liberating as hell, too."

After we hang up, I check my recent calls.

Damn it. I did miss a call from Bill at seven, while I was at the restaurant talking, laughing, and having a great time with genuine friends. It's now nine thirty. I'm glad it's too late to consider calling him back.

This morning I wake to a text from Bill. "*R U up?*" Where was that text finger yesterday afternoon, pal?

I send back a thumbs-up emoji, and immediately regret it. Have no desire to call or talk to him. If I ignore him long enough, will he just go away without me having to say anything? Is Jo right? Am I starting to act like a man? Is being single and having casual sex about disconnecting? Being unaccountable? Blame shifting? Or are these gender-unspecific defense mechanisms? I know better because I know a number of women who are players. I've felt sorry for their husbands. I smack the heel of my hand on my forehead at the absurdity of that thought. I felt sorry for a girlfriend's husband when she treated him like shit and didn't equate his situation to my own. Another of my dumbshit moments.

Back to Bill. I forgot my phone was still on silent. He called after I sent the thumbs up emoji. I missed it. So now he texts a paragraph about how golf was weather-delayed. Did I see that he called me last night?

"I saw that you called at seven, two hours of no-show too late," I mumble to my phone, as though it cares.

The text continues: "Do you want to meet at the range today around two? We'll give it another try?"

"I'm meeting Jo at the range at three, before the Skins Game."

"I don't know if that is a yes or a no," he fires back.

"That would be a no. Too much range time before play isn't good."

"I'm playing tonight, too. I'll see you there." He signs off.

I am overusing the thumbs up, but send another anyway.

Jo and I have decided we should use our relationship as a benchmark from now on. It's easy. There's no insecurity, no competition. If Gerry showed up for a romp and she cancelled plans with me, no problem. In Cabo, she did laundry while I romped with Daniel. No problem.

One thing we do is communicate, not leave the other hanging.

The Skins game is better than real golf. For me, it's a fun free-for-all. On Friday nights at the Pine Golf Course, they label each cart with team names, and line them up, ready to head out onto the course at four p.m. sharp. The ladies start on hole number three, the men on the first tee. It has sprinkled off and on enough that my hair falls straight, too damp to touch with a comb. The spring in Jo's natural curls tightens, shortens and escapes her ball cap like froth boiling from under a pot lid.

The lightning siren signals no play on the sister course, the Estate, just as the head pro tells us to take off on the Pine Course. The lightning system automatically detects danger and sounds a "get off the course and under cover" alarm.

Seriously? Jo and I exchange a toothy Clarabelle grin before she tromps on the gas pedal.

"What the hell. We're on rubber tires. Impervious to lightning," she says.

"Until we pull a metal club out of our bag and swing it overhead while standing on an elevated tee in damp grass," I point out.

"Let's try and get at least one hole in, to make the round count towards the final," the head pro hollers as carts splash past him.

Everyone is surprised that the group finishes all seven holes. The sky isn't clear, but the late afternoon sun sparkles through wisps instead of a layer of dirty-linen clouds. Carol, my conscience on my first trip to Cabo, is a fair-weather golfer, didn't play, texted she'd saved us a table for the after-party. She's at an eight-top with two couples.

I want to clout her for the mixed company that will curtail our usual banter, but decide to tame down and smile as I order a glass of Decoy pinot noir.

As Jo and I sit down, I wonder if Carol is on her second vodka, water, ice, with a twist of orange. Her eyes spark with mischief that suggests it isn't her first. I got to know Carol a bit when she joined Jo, Chrissy, and me for a few days in Cabo last January.

Jo and I declare that we're starving.

"I always have a piece of toast and peanut butter before I come up here for cocktails," Carol explains. "It's too early for me to eat dinner. You two go ahead."

Jo and I excuse ourselves and go through the line of steamers hiding heavy hors d'oeuvres. As I sit down with a plate of fried chicken sliders, ranch dressing, and chipotle potato salad, my jaw drops before I have to quickly recover my composure. Carol is into a full rendition of the first night she arrived in Cabo and she's gone too far to rein her back without causing a scene that would only end in more gossip later. Jo gives me a WTF poke in the ribs.

I know the prelude to Carol's story. I'd listened as she told her story of my debacle to Chrissy, when she arrived in Cabo the day after.

The evening started when Jo, Carol, and I had taken a cab to a restaurant touted as a favorite of the locals in Cabo. Carol had stepped out of the cab, took one look around at the melamine tables, plastic chairs and said, "No. No. No. I'm not going to eat here. I'll get another cab and we'll go to the Office. It's on the beach. You'll love it." She did, and we did.

Afterwards, the three of us went to Cabo Wabo Cantina. Daniel and I had cooked up a surprise for Carol. Jo was our cohort in crime. When the dance band kicked up at 10:00 p.m. Daniel was going to walk up to the table where we sat, grab me in a John Wayne move, plant a kiss on me, and sweep me onto the dance floor. Carol wouldn't know I knew him. All the subterfuge would be so worth the look I expected to see on her face. Problem was, she'd been traveling all day, was tired, and at 9:00 wanted to go back to the room.

I tried to reach Daniel to cancel, but couldn't, so announced that I wanted to hang out a while. Maybe dance a little. We assured Carol it was safe because Cabo Wabo had uniformed security outside that hailed cabs, listed our destination on a clipboard, and sent us off. Jo knew Daniel was coming, or she would likely have pitched a fit. I also sent her a thumbs-up emoji when he arrived. We stay tagged. Safer for both of us. In retrospect, I should have told Carol, but didn't. The guilt of omission is generally better than a lie, but can feel slimy as the head of an oily mushroom when you have to chew on the consequences.

Back to the Friday night Skins Game, the table in the bar, and Carol's double vodka rendition to a mixed group. She was shaking her finger at me at a point.

It was after she and Jo went to bed, back in the condo that night, that the trouble started. Not really trouble at all, until she talks about it. Here. In Forest Hillside. At a table with a board member, his chatty wife, and a couple I don't know.

"Yes," Carol emphasizes, as I snap open my napkin. "I woke up at two in the morning, terrified. I shook Jo and told her Alexandra isn't here. Should we go look for her?"

"No. Go back to sleep. She's fine." I imagine Jo pulling the covers over her head when she says this.

"Then at three and again four o'clock, I checked, and Alex still isn't home," Carol rants. She was evidently doing a roving bed check, because my room was on the other end of the condo.

I want to slink under the table and crawl away on hands and knees. It's too late to stop her vodka-fueled momentum. Truth is, I got to the condo at two a.m. She's embellishing. Correcting her won't sound anything but lame.

"She was with..." She turns and squints at me. I'm sitting right beside her. "What was his name?"

"My name's Mud if you finish your story," I whisper.

"Oh, it's fine. Nobody cares. It's a fun story. What *was* his name?"

"Daniel." I shrug as I give Jo a helpless eye roll and sigh. She shakes her head. I guarantee this isn't Carol's first time telling this story. To lie and deny will be worse for me. Not only will I be a trollop, I'll lose my integrity.

Carol proceeds to explain that I was with this man that she, when she finally met him, didn't like. "Remember that awful table he saved for us, right in front of the speakers that next night?"

"I left that party and went back to the condo with you, Jo, and Chrissy that night." I said, trying to salvage a shred of my dignity by this time.

"Of course, you did. It was a girl's trip. You belonged with us. Not him."

"Where did you meet him?" the board member's wife wants to know.

Okay. At this point I'm in, so I let a smile lift my cheeks and chin.

"At a beach party. I'd been on my own for over a year. I was in Mexico for two fun-filled weeks. He was a nice guy. I have no regrets. None at all." With that, I force a fork full of potato salad in my mouth and chew in a very ladylike manner.

"Who was he?" the board member asks. Great, now I'm explaining my affair to a man? In public?

I want to shout, "It's none of your flippin' business," but bold up, guns blazing. "He was a Top Gun pilot, a Naval Commander, and is a retired 747 Captain." If I'm going down, I intend to do it with a hot guy, full throttle. Topic closed all around. Whew.

Jo and I no more finish our food than Bill Brady decides to brave our table and breech our 'discretion pinky swear' treaty. Jo and I exchange a snap glance before she twists sideways, links her elbow over the back of her chair, turns toward him, and dominates his attention. He follows her lead and acts as though he dropped by to see her. They chat about golf, her game, his chip shot struggles. I interject a comment here and there, but also chat with Carol. Turn my back to him, which I want to do after his no show last night, anyway.

Tongues around here don't wag. They slurp gossip and will undoubtedly drool about the club playboy showering his attention on our table. Shit.

Then he glances down his left shoulder at me. "Yeah, lightning delayed the round I played with a course rater from *Sports Illustrated* yesterday. I was supposed to meet up with a friend, but couldn't even call because I'd left my phone in the car."

Jo pretends to scratch the top of her ear as she bends her head toward Brady, to keep from projecting her voice. "Think your friend wanted to scalp you *then*? You're on a fast track to bald, buddy."

I look past Jo's shoulder and see the leader of a lady's clique at the end of the bar, chatting away while glancing our way. Double shit. Each blink indicates a blip on her radar.

"Is that lightning?" I point out the window. "Or did I see the flash of a blade?" My eyes speak clearly when they narrow and my right brow pitches. They said it was time for him to leave.

I have no intention of going into combat with that group of women at the bar and for some reason, he commands their attention. He announced it was time he got home to his dog. After an appropriate pause, I intended to go home, too.

But...Bill couldn't have reached his car in the parking lot before a text pops on my phone. Thank goodness, the phone is sitting on my right, near Jo, not on Carol's side.

"Wanna have hot sex tonight?"

Jo and I both burst out laughing.

"He left his phone in the car, right?" Jo said.

I shrug.

I slide my phone in my purse. But not before I send one more thumbs up. It's a dandy little emoji.

CHAPTER 34

To Stand Up and Be Me

The Alpha of the lady's golf clique has an inordinate interest in Bill Bailey and I'm beginning to understand what his legend is made of. On my way home from the golf course I text, *"I'll leave the garage door open. Bring Betsy and we'll make it a double date. Houston will love it. Thirty minutes lead time good?"*

"There in thirty. Don't shower."

I had imagined my soft damp skin slipping on fish net thigh highs, black lace panties and a naughty black bra before he arrived; that's why I needed half an hour. I wonder why he wants me not-so-fresh off the golf course until he walks through the door, flashes a seductive half smile as he brandishes a very nice bottle of red wine in one hand and bubble bath in the other. It's boy bubble bath. Blue, not pink.

So, he wants to take his time. Play. Hmm. My head cocks slightly, I return his slow wink, half smile, and trace his body with my eyes, before meeting his with intent. To fill my tub with ultra-warm water nearly drains the water heater, but I do it without hesitation. I turn the Sonos speaker system on. Music from the Annie Lennox station I built on Pandora: *Annie*, The Canadian Tenors, Josh Groban, Maroon 5, The Republic, Enigma, breeze through the house. I even threw in Andy Grammar's snappy country-paced songs, and love the variety.

I think Bill Brady is more excited than I am about the Sonos system.

He loves the music, knows the artists, the year each song came out, when and where he was at the time. Mr. Persistent is gaining dimension. When I finally turn off the faucets, delicate bubbles frost water invitingly. I take the hem of my blouse, ready to lift it over my head, but his hand's still holding mine.

"Let me undress you." He lifts my golf shirt up. Instead of freeing my arms and uncovering my head, I feel warm breath and his soft mouth brush my stomach and move slowly up between my breasts to my neck. I don't tell myself to breathe deeply; it just happens, because what he's doing is erotic as hell.

He holds my hand as we step naked into the water and slip beneath the bubbles. I tap my palm on the whirlpool jet controls and the water boils around us. Sensations from the steamy water, the touch of his hands, of his body on mine, the vanilla scent of bubble bath, the pressure of the pulsating jets, make being in the moment easy. I close my eyes to block out visual distractions.

I had no idea the jets would whip the bubble bath suds into a stiff meringue, but we play with it like a couple of kids. I pat suds on his cheeks, he mounds them on my breasts, then forms and draws them to enviable shape before blowing them away and tasting. When we finally stand up, we both burst into fits of laughter. We look like a couple of Pillsbury Dough Boys, sans the chef's hats. We dust each other off, laughing, patting bubbles, until he suddenly pulls me into his arms, hard against his scorching skin, and gets serious.

I'm not telling you this to add a seductive sex scene, but to explain that sex, sensation, touch, and laughter have come into my new life as never before. It feels as though my old wounds are nearly healed. I want to open my arms, mind, heart, and free myself of the bonds of inhibitions that snaked through the barbed wire that ensnared me like parasite vines that suck the life out of vibrant trees.

After an hour, he calls an intermission. "But we aren't finished," I almost plead.

"No, we aren't, but I bet that even when your ex was in his teens, he needed a break after an hour."

Ohh. True to his word, after a breather, he revs up in rare style. Dynamic finale for both of us. I wonder what in the hell I'm doing as I lie in Bill's arms, spent, satisfied, content. I keep stressing 'Friends with Benefits,' and doubt this snuggling is something pals do after sex. I like it too much to bolt out of bed into the chilly air.

The Sherwood Forest Trumpet sounds an incoming text from my phone on the nightstand. I reach for it and grab the glasses beside it. It's from Jo. She stayed at the clubhouse to visit with Carol once Carol finally decided it was time to eat.

"Chief engineer of the gossip train just came over to the table, said she thinks Bill might like me. She saw him nudge my hip with his knee. She poked her knee in my ass to demonstrate. Yikes!"

Bill appears as confused as I am. Well, that's not entirely fair. I probably understand jealous-female behavior a bit better than he ever could. Maybe. After all, he's been single for a quarter century, so you never can tell what he's gleaned in the process.

"It seems evident that Sandy has an active obsession with our club playboy," I said.

"I don't want anything to do with her. I don't like being called the club playboy either."

"Well, you need to own that one, bud," I wisecrack back.

The ramifications of all this are yet to be seen. I've never hung out with groups of girls or women. Wasn't particularly sensitive to peer pressure, even as a kid. But Forest Hillside is a close community. To join in the activities, you interact with the group.

I've got Jo. She's solid. Taking one for the team at the moment, since Sandy thinks Bill's got her in his sights. Then there's Carol. She has a tender heart and strong faith, but I am beginning to realize she's been so prim, proper, and restrained for decades no one sees the spirit she reins in. Carol wants to race on the track with Jo and me, and I have a hunch if she turns loose, her gait will be long, smooth, and damned fast. Carol's been divorced twice, is now a widowed single, and hasn't been interested in dating. Tonight's dissertation about Cabo Dan established that Jo and I have to put her on a need-to-know basis as far as our dating activities are concerned. Possibly gag her until she gets her stride.

If news about mine and Bill's tryst gets out, will I be envied, shunned, ostracized, or what? I need to be prepared for all of the above. I won't lie and sacrifice my integrity. I can call foul, announce that a question is inappropriate. No one's business. Perhaps I might instead add intrigue with a silent wink and a smile. No denial or confirmation.

Bill doesn't want intrusion into his personal life, especially in the public arena. He's either covering his fragile ego or covering his tracks.

Married, my place as Brad's wife possessed structure, clear expectations of rules for my behavior. Being single is a new adventure with mind-boggling options. Monogamy isn't a requirement. Multiple partners? Ditto dating? Sex without love or commitment is a tender trap. My mother never prepared me for this learn-as-I-go program.

I'd be lying to you if I denied that the options, independence, and intrigue of dating isn't empowering as hell.

Adrenaline is a dangerous drug.

All-natural napalm.

CHAPTER 35

Who, What, Where, When, and How

W ho am I? What do I want? Where am I going? When will I get there? How will I know when I've arrived? All valid questions. Damnit, I wish I had the answers.

I walked Houston for an hour. Topics race like Indy cars for position. Thoughts of Ben, hope he will surface, shed the addiction. What if he doesn't, with a new baby on the way? Brad, our old life. Will I be alone like this forever? Do I want someone in my space? Can casual sex be enough? When will I cross the age that I won't look or feel sexual anymore?

The carburetor sticks and one thought floods with emotional fuel. Chokes out. Another spins out of control and I snap myself back to the present moment where I need to be, and smile inside and out as Houston trots, sniffs, whizzes every thirty feet. He's a miracle of survival, good surgeons, and lots of protein. Friends tell me their dogs eat dog food. I look at Houston and see a carnivore. Meat is a mainstay after his massive weight loss. I cook for the dog. Go figure.

I need to figure all this out, do laundry, iron a few things but I am restless. When I was ten, I wondered *what* I would become but it never occurred to me I'd wonder *who*. I didn't know I could disappear. I am a daughter, sister, wife, mother, grandmother, aunt, and also a mother-in-law. Generic labels.

Every woman is someone's daughter. Yet without the labels I had no identity. I was only what I am to them. An actor on stage when I had a role to play and always busy, I never ran out of scripts. There you have it. A pretty inclusive description of a codependent. Then, I moved two plus hours away to ferret out who I am, off stage.

Jo is at a golf get-together for a tournament on Monday that I'm not good enough to play in. I'm not sorry. No pressure for me on Monday.

Still, I'm restless and can use a decent meal. I call Ted and ask if he wants to meet me at the clubhouse for burger night. He's a great date, one of the nicest people I've ever met. I'm killing time until I leave to meet him at six thirty. He was in his grubbies and needed an hour to spruce up.

Validating myself seems to be a lifelong mission. There wasn't enough of me to go around for Brad. As for Ben? I read volumes on the nature of addiction, went to meetings with and without him, and to enough counseling sessions to learn how to help him, stop helping him, start helping myself, to have paid for one dandy vacation. I'm not telling you I did everything right, I did plenty wrong, but I tried my heart out, and loved him enough to keep going back for more. Whatever drives him is beyond my reach when that 90-proof monkey jumps on his back.

So, back to the who, what, when, where, and how.

What criteria do I use to evaluate myself?

It depends. I suppose I start by turning on overhead lights and checking my reflection in the mirror before I go out. I do this even before I walk the damned dog. I wear makeup to the gym; in fact, I don't answer the door without makeup. Neither did my mother. Ever. That offers a bit of insight. Self-conscious? Ya think? I look for approval or disapproval in the eyes of others. Brad. My mother, just to begin with. Through this process of introspection, I'm coming to know my mother better all the time.

She was truly kind, but in the last year before she died, she shared truths about my father's infidelities, her father's leather razor strap and the marks it left on her, even as a teenager, for having a stain on the back of her skirt from her period, or just in case she wasn't telling the truth. My mother wouldn't have lied to save herself.

All the years I tried to emulate her, measured myself by her, yet never measured up, I thought she was so completely kind she was above getting mad. Forgave everything. Always ferreted out the good, even in some damned dark souls.

She was and did all those things, but along the way, she crafted a mask. Mastered suppression of hurt, anger, and fear. She smiled, but rarely laughed. Even. Predictable. Controlled. I now know she'd numbed out. She ruled her emotions by anesthetizing them.

I didn't evaluate myself. I let other people do it for me. I was a comparison junkie.

I'm tired of being so shallow, being dependent on uncontrollable people, situations, their foggy perceptions, and just plain shit. I need enough self-worth to value my opinion of myself. I'd like to have my nineteen-year-old body back, too. If I'm making a wish list, why not make it a good one?

I'm glad to be meeting Ted for dinner in twenty minutes. He's real. He is a man that matters. He won't fly in and out of my life on a whim, or because a short skirt with big tits struts by. Hell, I'd cheer him on if he did. Our relationship isn't sexual, it's more than that. It's heart to heart. Soul to soul.

Nearly twenty years my senior, even in his mid-eighties he defies the image of being old. Sure, he once walked a bit faster, climbed trees, and ran bases, but not much beyond pace marks his age.

A retired corporate attorney, he has a sharp, analytical mind, clear values, intimidating morals and loyalty. Jo and her husband David were close friends of Ted and his wife Lena. They were a fun foursome on the golf course and socialized together until Alzheimer's crept into the creases of Lena's mind and replaced her memories with blank spaces and sadness.

Life-altering diseases not only affect the individual, they stain and strain the lives of those who love them. Ted retired to take care of Lena. After twelve years, Jo told me she had really pushed him to find a place for Lena to live. Lena had become paranoid, sometimes violent, and he needed to have his life back.

"You were taking care of David at the same time, weren't you?" I'd asked, though I knew the answer. David was two years older than Ted, survived heart surgery, but major complications rendered him an invalid. Jo discounts what she went through as his caretaker.

"He was the child I never had." She'd stiffened, scrubbed her lips and shifted the conversation back to Ted and Lena.

"Ted's wife became an angry stranger," Jo had told me. "Alzheimer's is insidious. The woman he loved didn't just fade away. An angry shrew took possession of her. Like something out of the *Exorcist*, but there wasn't a ritual out there to save her."

"Alzheimer's and infidelity have something in common," I said. "Reminds me of one of those quotes I saw on Facebook. It said, "The hardest thing you'll ever do is grieve for the loss of someone who's still alive." At least Lena didn't hurt Ted on purpose.

Ted finally moved Lena into a beautiful Sedona setting for the last three years of her life. Even during the fifteen years of her illness, he remained faithful to the love of his life. He might be the first man I've known that is capable of such kindness, caring, and commitment. It wasn't because he isn't interested in sex. He is seriously on the make, move, prowl, and ready for action these days. Go Ted.

I would have taken care of Brad for better or worse, but I possess no desire to make that kind of sacrifice for a man now. I wince as I admit this to myself, because behind my blue eyes is damage I hope I can buff out over time. Right now, I'm not the kind of person I once was, or that I hope to find.

Wow. When I began this chapter, intent of figuring out who I am, where I want to go, I expected my responses to clear the fog, elicit a sense of triumph, a pride in myself that I've come so far. How did I end up with moist eyes and a burning desire to toss towels over every mirror in my house, so I can hide?

Shit.

People tell me how courageous I was to finally leave Brad. They have no idea what a coward I've become.

CHAPTER 36

Stall, Teeter, and Fall

After my first sexual encounter as a single left a shit taste in my mouth, I started this book to create a navigational guide to late date dating. I did not begin this to resurrect the idiot who loved Brad, no matter what, for way over thirty years too long. I wanted to learn how to be safe in this new world of dating, which either leads to sex or 'see ya later', and share it with you.

Then, at some point, I wanted to reach out about more than safe sex. I spent decades in a lonely, emotionally-barren, degrading marriage, playing the role of his happy wife. Some, because I was afraid to leave the life I knew, to become single. Some, because I believed it was my fault that he didn't care about me. I shouldn't need to be loved. He said so often enough. Then said he did love me, just often enough to insure my connection to that damned lever.

I know there are a lot of you out there wrestling with the same bitter-sweet situations, when loving them isn't enough to save the relationship that is killing you, one lie, put-down, and infidelity at a time.

When I left him, it was not the first time it had come down to survival. Him or me. Don't discount emotional carnage. Physical abuse shows. Can put you in a hospital, or worse. Emotional abuse corrodes you, like injected acid. It too can be deadly.

I'm holding out a glimmer of hope that resurrecting my journals, the mess I was twenty-eight years ago, is going to show both of us how far I've come.

I should probably write down "I've come a long way", and tape it to my desk to remind me as I take the steps into the past this morning. Shit.

I can do this.

I only hope it helps someone out there realize they aren't alone. That their journey is not over because they've stayed. That if they've stayed, they are still strong enough to survive.

I was in my thirties the first time our marriage fell apart. It's not the first time I was lonely. It's the first time I realized he didn't want to salvage our relationship. He wanted someone else. There's probably some psychological reason why I want to block out that time. God, how I wish I'd never said anything about it to Jo. Shit. I'm hedging. Again. But she keeps harping.

One evening in late summer, nearly two years after I left Brad the second time, Jo and I had left my house, walked and played holes sixteen through eighteen, ended up at the clubhouse, found our rockers and the fire pit waiting.

We only talk about light and fun stuff, tease and laugh on the golf course. It's important to keep some places and activities sacred. Safe places away from the roar of the past or fears of the future, but once we sat down in the rockers, there were no rules of engagement.

I knew it was coming. She'd caught me in an off moment late yesterday when she called to see if I wanted to play three holes tonight.

"What are you up to?" she'd asked.

"Wallowing. Do you realize that twenty years ago David was a controlling shit to you, so you left him, went back to the valley, bought a gay dating service, and had a torrid "Bridges of Madison County" love affair with a man young enough to be his grandson for two years before you went back to him?"

"I do," she said suspiciously. "So, what in the hell were you doing? Because you're wallowing in something shitty."

"Me?" I shot back without shouting. "I was rolling kids out of bed to get ready for school, dropping twenty pounds in six weeks, wondering how in the hell I was going to get Brad to tell me why he left, who he left me for, and what the hell he was doing driving strippers home from our house. Three years later I finally filed for divorce, took him back and stayed another twenty-five years. That's what *I* was doing."

ALEX NICOLLET DELON

"Have you been drinking?"

"Not yet."

"Well I don't know what riled all this to the surface but Gerry's due here in fifteen minutes, I need a shower, but after we golf three holes tomorrow you're going tell me what in the hell happened thirty years ago and why it's got you so pissed today."

"Maybe."

"Fuck that. You'll fess up. We'll tee off sixteen at five. See you then."

Once we'd settled in front of the fire pit the next night Jo didn't ask nicely. As soon as we ordered a glass of wine she harped.

"And by the way, don't drop a bomb like that fifteen minutes before I'm getting drop-in company again. I want to know what in the hell happened thirty years ago. Strippers? Seriously? Where has this been? You knew he was fooling around, finally filed for divorce, but then went back? What were you thinking? What drove you to leave this time, when you stayed then? Don't wallow in it. You're not a wallower; just dredge it up, and spit it out. Then you can gargle."

"Shhh," I scolded. "Keep your voice down."

"Only if you cough it up. I had that CT scan this morning, a therapy appointment, and it's been bugging me all day."

"How did the CT go? I'm sorry I forgot to ask."

She furrowed her brows, scrunched her lips together and bored a hole in me with those grey-blue eyes. We both knew she wouldn't have the results for a day or two.

"It all started yesterday with a plastic ball marker. A red one I got at Kapalua on Maui in 1984 or '85. A stupid, red, plastic, butterfly, ball marker." I'd played golf that day, rode in a cart with my best friend Rachel, but any memory of her snaps to the scene in her kitchen when I confronted her about sleeping with Brad. I didn't do that until I knew for sure.

I gave Jo the highlights.

"People need to understand more about you than what they see now, Allie. To know this goes back to when your kids were still home, when not only your husband, but your best friend…Holy shit, Alex. You need to put this in the book."

212

"I don't want to." My cheeks pooched in a straight lip-line smile.

"If you want the readers to identify with you, you can't lie to them. Give them half a story. They'll read about the great stuff you two have collected and figure so what, he had a girlfriend or two in his sixties. What the hell."

"You haven't read the book, but you have a point."

As we finished our second glass of wine I told her I'd pull the journals down again, but admitted I'd rather run through the clubhouse naked.

"Let's plan a ritual for when I'm done with this book. I want to burn the journals and dance around the flames under a full moon."

"We'll do it." She scrubbed her knuckles on top of my head and we both headed home.

I may not wallow, but this ritual of resurrecting the past is a dark art. Last night I made the decision to do it, but wanted fortification. Validation. After Jo and I left the clubhouse and the fire pit behind, I called Bill Brady from my car.

He somehow sensed my melancholy, said to leave the door unlocked. He'd be there in half an hour. Instead of being rowdy and playful, he was strong, passionate, and didn't ask questions. I slid quietly out of bed after making love. He stirred, but went back to sleep. As I pulled my tie-dyed T-shirt over my head, it reminded me of the stains from the past that would never wash out. Forgetting is generally a matter of being distracted. Never remembering is the bitch.

Once in the kitchen, a distance from Bill, I put my face in my hands and wondered if numb will ever wear off. I like him. Enjoy the sex. But my heart doesn't stir when I hear his voice or feel his touch the way it did with Brad. If Bill left or had another woman, I'd miss the sex.

The next morning, I woke with resolve to do what I told Jo I would. Write this stuff down. I want to get this over with. Bill always leaves before sun up. I'm sure he's afraid someone will see him pull out of my garage and back up my driveway. I'm no better than he is. We're both in it for the sex.

I scrub my teeth, walk Houston, so I won't feel guilty ignoring him while I work through this.

I walk into my closet but can't reach the blue notebook that contains my journals from 1984 to 1989, not even on tip toe; so, I hop and poke my fingertips against the binding. Knock down three other books to get it, but what the hell.

I wonder if I'll be able to hit a golf ball this afternoon when Jo comes to reel me in. I talked to her this morning, told her I was ready to plunge myself into the mother of abysses, and reading, even touching the pages of my journals would do just that. I said that to her first, because I didn't want to hear another, "You need to write this shit down," speech. Shit is exactly what it is. The kind that has a rancid odor and stains.

Instead of arguing with Jo, I'm arguing with myself. Using this manuscript as a sounding board. How nuts is that? I'll go you one better. Going back and reliving a five year stretch in my thirties when I fell apart, lost twenty pounds in six weeks, rarely slept or cared, finally filed for divorce, but went back to Brad in the end, smacks of insanity. Again. I get a lot of those smacks it seems.

"I'll come get you at five," Jo said, before we hung up this morning. "We'll play holes sixteen, seventeen and eighteen, end up at the clubhouse again. Write your heart out. You fall into the hole too far to climb out, I'll come get your ass. No worries."

The lifeline she threw gave me confidence there would be a better end to this day. Because I didn't know I was wrong about that, I didn't tiptoe or trip. I plunged all the way to the rocky bottom and landed on my hands and knees.

I'd told Jo a lot of what happened, but not what I allowed it to do to me.

Touching the notebook, the pages of lined yellow tablet paper I'd put the heel of my hand on as I wrote, stirs me. I can feel her. Myself, that many years ago. I should have burned this journal page by page, long ago. Maybe I'd do that when I finish.

The ritual fire we'd talked about, full moon and all.

I put the blue book on the kitchen counter. Stare at it. Walk past it to fold a load of laundry. Feed Houston. Go to the bathroom. I make a pot of cinnamon hot tea, then a cup of coffee while my tea steeps. Fuck.

I decide to detach and to dissect why I didn't just get pissed as hell, throw Brad out on his ass when he wanted other women more than he wanted me. Maybe that will get me started. I'm tempted to put on rubber gloves before I touch those pages again. Shit.

I need to break myself down to manageable parts and motivation from a clinical perspective. Create a distance, so I don't have to feel my way back to those years. So, here goes the clinical researcher side of me. Abstract... existing in thought, but not having a physical or concrete connection. I need a few paragraphs of this to bolster up.

Joseph Wolpe, a South African psychiatrist, thinks he developed a form of counter conditioning called *systematic desensitization*. I have a news flash: Women have known about and experienced it since the beginning of time. We don't coin psychology terms. We simply know that over time, we'll get used to it, whatever *it* is. If we experience rejection, fear, abandonment, are yelled at, devalued, lied to, cheated on enough times, a large number of us will eventually numb out. My mother and I are a testament to this. So is my middle sister, Brenda. Sort of.

Is it stupidity that we don't run, hide, or retaliate, or is it a defense mechanism? A means of survival? Of protecting our young? If we numb out long enough, do we stop loving, stop caring if he comes home smelling like KY jelly or a strange perfume? Do we simply salt a bowl of fresh popcorn, unwrap a Hershey's bar, and change the channel to something he wants to watch? Who or what have we become when we only cry when we're alone?

I'm on the mission I committed to. I dredge through sheet after sheet of lined yellow paper that makes up my journals. Sometimes I wrote in pencil, other times printed in ink, and wonder if that means something. A pattern emerges, a repetition as I read these undelivered letters to Brad.

"You don't love me, but reconsider, because I love you enough for both of us. For our boys."

No kidding. Like loving me or not was something he could reconsider, the way he'd weigh the choice between a Ford or a Chevy. It isn't a decision, it's a feeling; but I wrote things like that, over and over. As I reread those pages, I was so glad I had the sense never to let Brad read any of them. I run across names I've long forgotten. Some of his other women. Something in the center of my chest tightens into a ball when I read about Christie, Rachel, Lynn, Elaine.

I knew, but he told me I was crazy, suspicious, jealous... I skip around. Only read segments of the journals.

Enough. Too much. I make myself keep going, because this is the last fucking time I want to touch these pages. I start over. Turn them one by one.

My journals began in 1984. We'd been back in the valley and in business for seven years. Money was tight, the business growing, the economy uncertain. As the decade progressed the nation was in the throes of the Savings and Loan debacle. Our business could go under from one or two bad months because the banks repossessed more property than they renewed commercial loans.

The office was in our house. Brad was a master of managing expenses, adhering to budgets which weren't labored analysis statements back then. The budget was how much money was in the bank. Period. Brad said, "The business can't afford to pay a bookkeeper, so you're it." After eleven years with Goodyear, he knew how to do the paperwork but said he didn't have time to teach me as he plopped his college accounting book on the corner of the table for me to go through. As a side note, one of Brad's reliable characteristics is looking at nearly any project, even ones he's going to tackle, with distorted estimates on time. What takes four hours, he announces is less than a one-hour project. The bookkeeping was no exception.

At first, I kept books manually on green ledger pages that I put in a notebook, much like the one my journal pages are in. I taught myself to use a ten key without looking because I got dizzy looking back and forth. After dinner, homework, showers for the boys, I spent time with Brad. When he went to sleep, I often went back into my office to try and catch up.

One of the nights I was working late—three o'clock in the morning late—Brad straddled the doorway, arms on either side to brace himself. Ebenezer's squinty eyes. Hostile.

"What the fuck do you do all day?" he sneered. "If you were more productive and motivated, you'd get this shit done during the day."

I wanted to yell, "Are you shitting me? I make breakfast, pack lunches, do laundry, shuttle the boys to school, ball practices, go to their games, make dinner, answer phones, track or file sales and payroll tax forms, payables, keep over two hundred and fifty thousand in receivables updated when the average ticket is less than three hundred dollars. Hand write month end statements, and talk myself through journal entries on the learn-as-I-go program."

Instead of yelling, defending myself, retaliating, kicking him in the balls, or clobbering him with my calculator, I bolted to my feet, flew past him, ran out the front door, climbed in the back of his El Camino sitting in the driveway, clutched my arms across myself to stay warm, and bawled until I was too exhausted to cry another tear.

The next morning, I made a stand. Gave him two weeks to hire a bookkeeper. I need you to know I wasn't a total wimp. I just never made a stand that won Brad's respect, or mine. Interesting how that works. Unless I got his approval, even I wasn't proud of what I did.

I call this *reflective vision*; I saw myself through his eyes, not my own. I now think of the plant that bends, crawls, reaches for the light it needs to survive. I went back into the office many times over the years when the books got tangled up. So, though I did stand up, I also dusted myself off, thought maybe the next time would be different, then got back in line.

The bookkeeper he hired didn't work out. He enclosed our back patio, we moved it back into the house for a number of years, and I faced my first computer...the Apple 2e. I think it's still in a storage room somewhere, software and all. At least it was when I left.

This morning, armed with a fresh cup of coffee, I flipped pages with the eraser end of my pencil. A dozen pages later I put my coffee down and ran my fingers through my hair, temples to crown, as I read about the day in 1986 when Margo told me what her husband told her, about the party at my house a few days before. She was a woman I golfed with who was the wife of one of Brad's friends.

I'd gone to my sister's one night when there had been a guy's party at our house. The boys were spending the night at friend's houses. Brad volunteered to host. Someone was turning forty, or getting married. I don't remember. I do remember there were strippers and the plumb feather I found on my bedroom floor.

The next day, Margo told me, "Mark said Brad drove the stripper home."

I imagined the stripper's head in his lap. Am sure she liked his new shiny-black Corvette. Hope she choked herself on the gear shift, but if she'd choked, I knew it would have been on something else.

Brad was sitting on the couch when I told him what Margo said and asked for the truth. What happened when he drove the stripper home? I wanted to hear him admit it. He pulled off his flip flops. Threw them past me, across the room. I dodged them as they flung toward me, then again as they ricocheted off the wall.

"What the fuck is Mark doing, telling his wife shit like that? The son of a bitch knows better. I'll deal with him tomorrow." No apology. No explanation. Admission in the form of aggression.

Brad.

In my journal I recounted the action, but not my reaction. I don't remember how we ended the conversation, or if I slept that night. I know I didn't leave.

On page after page I tell Brad I love him, but finally…eventually let one sentence fill an entire page.

"I don't want to stay in our marriage the way it is."

Another quarter inch of pages of my journal later I wrote, "There's a part of me that hates you because you hurt me worse than anything in my life ever has. But I hate the part of me that loves you, in spite of it, even more."

This is a dangerous place to be…hating yourself for loving them, no matter what.

Brad didn't know what he wanted. Out of our marriage. At first, I am certain a part of it was my best friend, Rachel, then there was a woman that went along as a cook on a horseback trip he and five or six of his friends took through Wyoming. Our advertising representative for the newspaper. At home, his tempers and fury raged like those of an animal caught in a trap. He told our friends I was a needy mess. He didn't confess his part in it, but he was right. Sort of.

I was broken. I'd never weathered adversity like this before. If I could, I'd mandate classes for at least high school students, to learn coping skills. By then, most of us need them anyways.

Not even barbed wire held me together back then. I tried to convince him he wanted, needed me. Was making a mistake. I declared my intention to fight for him, until one day when I stepped out of the shower.

My naked reflection in the mirror jolted me the way a head-on collision would have pitched me through a windshield. My hip bones and ribs protruded. I was twenty-five pounds below my size-four solid weight. This was my first moment of insight and it hit with the impact of a lightning strike. If I was going to survive this, I had to step up and take care of myself, and my sons.

The next morning, after years of him not knowing what he wanted, Brad and I had a strangely tender scene. He'd moved in and out about four times.

"It's over, isn't it?" I asked, as we stood in our bathroom, of all places.

He nodded.

"Then we need to end it before we end up hating each other."

"I can't do it. Do you think you can?" he asked.

"Yes. I'll file for divorce." I walked out the door, and made my way to the back yard. I didn't want to watch him leave that final time.

I dangled my feet in the pool, gripped the sides of the cool deck and thought how easy it would be to simply slip under the water and take a few deep breaths.

If I could have left my boys, if I'm ruthlessly honest, I might have.

I will always remember that afternoon, before the boys got home from school. My sister Brenda found me crumpled on the corner of my bed.

Resolve comes and goes. It's like trying to pull free from a long strip of flypaper. Get a hold of one corner, and before you pull free, another part sticks, so you put a foot on it, and it sticks to your shoe. It's like that...I want to say at first, but it can be like that for a long time.

Brenda took a wide stance, crossed her arms and glared down her nose at me.

"You need to get your shit together, Allie. Mom sent me to check on you. She's afraid you're going to do something stupid."

"Leave me alone," I whispered in a monotone, as empty of emotion as I felt. I wanted to get my shit together, I just didn't know how. Did she really think criticizing and bullying me would help? I can attest today that it didn't. Well, maybe it did, because it made me mad and anger makes you tough. Did me. I got my teeth into that damned flypaper, chewed, spit and kept on going. Sort of. At least I continued to progress.

There are shelters for women physically abused, which can do only so much to protect and retrain them, and only for so long. But what about those of us in defeating relationships where we're neglected, devalued, lied to, cheated on, and grow to feel we deserve even less?

Over years of conditioning, we become prisoners of this relationship war. We wonder whether there is sanctuary or desolation beyond the walls of our confinement. We stand and gaze into the vast unknown, pace back and forth, but don't step through the open gates. Why? Why the hell not?

We think through the consequences, test the invisible barrier from time to time. Wonder to ourselves, how many lives will my selfish desire to escape impact? Will my heart and soul suffer more from the guilt of consequences I cause my kids to suffer if I leave, tear our family apart, splinter holidays and celebrations; or can I adapt, endure and make our lives the best I can?

Then here comes the clincher. It eventually comes down to this.

Am I worth salvaging?

Or worth more as a sacrifice?

CHAPTER 37

A Moment of Insight

It was late in the day when I reread those last two lines; am I worth salvaging, or worth more as a sacrifice? It's like asking yourself if you'd rather be shot in the right foot, or the left.

Stand up, say I'm leaving, no matter what the consequences, or who I hurt. Or sit down, shut up, suck it up, and be a martyr.

I guess I've completed the circuit, because I'd taken the shut up and suck it up option for years. But in the end, I stood up and walked out and ended it.

The day I'd worked on this segment was the second day in a row Jo showed up at five p.m. sharp. I should have put on my watch, set an alarm or looked at a damned clock. I'm not dressed, so get myself together in a rush. She hits the ball so much further than I do, it's humiliating, yet at the same time I'm proud of her. She's one hell of a golfer. It's good to be outside and not alone. We dissect our swing, look for balls, talk golf, make jokes. I'll stress again that it's important to save some place or activity as a refuge.

People at the clubhouse often watch golfers coming up hole eighteen toward the clubhouse. It's a long, uphill par five with a wicked green guarded by kidney shaped sand traps. I duffed my approach shot, but made a great chip. Rolled within three feet of the pin, but rimmed the cup for a bogie. Jo was on in three and birdied with a one putt.

"How's your shoulder?" I asked.

"It hurts like a son of a bitch." She's worn out from the pain that's been chronic since she had shoulder surgery last December. The real bitch is that they've pretty well decided the problem is in her neck. She probably shouldn't have had the surgery. The pain is a small part of this for Jo. Since David died, golf was more than a pastime, it was her identity. Where she shined.

I'm glad that the wooden rockers by the fire pit are empty again, when we finally reach the clubhouse. We order Steamers from Angela at the bar. They're a treat of frothed milk, coffee, Bailey's, Frangelico, and Kahlua, and were so damned hot I burned my tongue.

Once we were settled, drinks in hand, feet up on the fire pit, Jo asked, "So how did the rip your-heart-out writing project go today?"

"Have you ever looked at an old picture of yourself, gangly, shitty hair trend of the day, still flat chested, with knobby knees, and wanted to tear it up?"

"I get it. Going back is a bitch. Describe your worst photo." She knows metaphoric me, that the pictures of me are in my mind, intangible, yet full-color.

"I told Brad I wasn't asking for a commitment that he loved me, just reassurance that he cared enough about me to try. I did this shit for years."

I'm proud of Jo for not responding. What can she say?

"Did I tell you about the time Brad went to Los Angeles for four days, at the same time my best friend, Rachel, went there to meet an old relative? She and I had been best friends and golf partners for nine years. She'd never mentioned a relative in Los Angeles."

"What did he go for?"

"I don't remember. I didn't know where he was staying. Neither of them called."

"Did you ever confront your best friend? Ask if she was fucking your husband?"

"She got pissed. Denied it. Said she couldn't be around me when I was such a mess."

"You let her live?"

"I'm disgusted with myself. Seriously wanted to puke before you came over, but figured, why waste a nice glass of merlot, right?"

"You had a glass of wine before I got there tonight?" Jo asks.

"Lower your eyebrows. I stopped with one."

I stared down the lush fairway, the blades of grass fine, tender, yet sturdy. I'm told it takes them twenty seconds for the greens to recover from golfer's cleats. They do rebound, spring back and bristle. I needed to rebound.

The pines became dual sided; sparkling on the setting sun side. On the near side, they reached out across the fairway with shadowed hands towards the east.

"I used to imagine Brad with another woman. One who had never changed a dirty diaper, mopped spit up off her blouse, or dressed to the nines for a party, trying to make sure there was no dog hair or traces of children's sticky fingers on her clothes. I didn't know who she'd be, but I hated her.

"If Brad and I had divorced, the court would have made me let them go. I know he doesn't cook and am pretty sure she wouldn't need to bother with much beyond a blow job. How much pizza could they eat?"

Jo rappels down the cliff to get me in silence. She knows that to reach me, she has to give me room and time to talk, then she'll pull me up. She also senses I need time to regroup. I don't want to cry here in front of strangers or a friend that doesn't know what I've been wallowing in today. The ability to reach back and relive may help in the long run, but it can fuck up a nice evening in a hurry.

"Brad and I were separated for six months. The last two months, all he wanted to do was come home. He wanted to take me to dinner. To a movie. Date nights. He came over unannounced one afternoon, sat at the kitchen table, took my hands in his, and told me he needed to come home. Didn't know what was happening to him, but he couldn't focus during meetings, couldn't concentrate on work, couldn't sleep. Needed to come home.

I wanted to tell him it was his turn, but just shook my head, walked into the bedroom and shut the door. I couldn't get past all the lies, betrayal, contempt, tempers. I was a safe distance and I needed to stay there."

I lifted my chin and smiled at the memory. I had been strong. At least for a while.

"So, what in the hell changed your mind?" Jo asked.

I glanced at Jo, then back down the shadowy fairway. "It was four a.m.,

February 4ᵗʰ, 1989. I was asleep when the phone rang. Ran to the bathroom to answer it."

Jo flashes a sidelong squint I caught, out of the corner of my eye.

"It was nearly thirty years ago. We didn't have portable phones. I had one put in beside the bath tub in the master," I explain and shrug.

"What about a phone in the bedroom?"

"It was on his side of the bed," I said, turning to face her. "Are you going to let me finish this?"

"Sorry. Was it Brad calling? Something happened to him and you rushed to his side, right?" She slopped her own drink with the hand sweeping gesture of me running to Brad's rescue.

I closed my eyes, shook my head, and took a sip of my Steamer.

"It was my oldest sister, Karen. I'll never forget the shrill pitch of her voice.

"'Dad had a heart attack. He's on the way to Desert Samaritan now. I think it's bad, Allie.' I threw on some clothes, but before I left for the hospital, I called Brad. He'd been close to my dad."

"So, he came to get you?" Jo asked.

"No," I half smiled as I shook my head again. "He told me to call him when I knew something. He'd be in the office all morning."

"Asshole."

"How you can make me laugh at a moment like this, I don't know." I shook my head in disbelief this time.

"When I walked through the emergency room doors, Brad was the first one I saw. He'd beat me there. Took me in his arms. When he gripped the back of my head, pressed it against his chest, I knew. My stomach dropped like a million-ton anchor."

I took a deep breath, audible on inhale and exhale. A second time.

"Brad told me we were all too late. He'd died in the ambulance."

My nose stuffed up as I told Jo about the morning my dad died. I hadn't talked to him in nearly two weeks. I'd been hiding out at home then. Didn't want to talk to anybody but the kids, unless I needed to.

I sniffed. Rubbed the corner of my right eye as though it itched, and then stared down the fairway again, seeing only the past.

"I think Brad was always sorry we were separated, and he hadn't seen my dad in months before he died. My dad told me he thought I was crazy for not wanting Brad to come home. He called one afternoon and was hot. "What's wrong with you, Alexandra? He's a good provider, doesn't beat you, and comes home every night."

"Sweet. Grade A qualifications for a husband," Jo said.

"My dad's father died before he was born in 1918. He was the youngest of twelve. I think he used a different scale to qualify himself as a good husband, too. I knew he'd catted around, as my mom put it but didn't know how profoundly it affected her until a month or so before she died last March. She'd told my niece and Ben about a day when she was pregnant with me. She'd taken both my sister's hands, stood on the shore of Lake Minnetonka and thought about walking out too far. Do you think Melanie from *Gone with the Wind* ever thought about suicide?"

I glanced at Jo, but the look of pity in her eyes made me turn away.

"The day after my dad died Brad told me he was going to come home and take care of me. Be the husband and father he hadn't been." I debated with myself as I stared down the fairway. Sure, I was lonely now too, but it was better than lonely beside Brad wondering where he'd been. Who he'd been with. Why he'd turned his back to me. Had I done the textbook thing? Married a man like my father? I didn't want to be mad at my dad. For all that he hurt my mother, my father was a good dad and I loved him.

The pine needles that sparkle like shafts of crystal in the setting sun, the voices of others in the clubhouse around us, the now warm drink in my hand, all disappear. My sight and senses are lost in that moment, as I stood in the harsh-bright hallway of Desert Samaritan Hospital, nearly three decades ago.

"It was my mother's birthday." I said, glancing at Jo. "He died on her birthday. Bless her heart, she wanted to go home. I slept on my Dad's side of their bed that night. Held her hand. Brad stayed at home with our sons. Never left."

CHAPTER 38

Clandestine 101

Now that you know where I've been, let's get back to where I'm going. This is lots more fun. So is Bill Brady. Who knew the shit sweeping broom I'd used to clean up crap in mine and Brad's relationship had a relative? I call her Sadie. I adopted her for times like this, when I need to sweep the past away, give myself a clean space to start over. I can pick and choose what to sweep and what to keep, but when it came to keeping our affair private, it became tough to distinguish secrets from lies. The longer I pretended I wasn't doing things I was doing, the more it bugged me.

When I was nine I'd had a brush with telling a secret that my oldest sister called tattling. Sometimes the past is worth revisiting, to reinforce lessons I learned. On a sweaty-summer night in Minneapolis, Karen decided I needed a couple of hands-on lessons about secrets. Good thing I have thick hair, because I lost a wad of it when she caught me that night.

Karen was sixteen. I was nine and to her, I was a pain in the ass she either had to babysit, or chase outside when she wanted to talk on the phone. That particular night she didn't know I was in the laundry room getting a pair of socks out of the drier, when she led Jack Foster down the basement steps. He sank into a deeper-than-forest-green chair with swirls of texture in the fabric. I never liked that chair. It looked like somebody scribbled on it, tried, but couldn't make it black. It nearly swallowed him. Karen sank onto his lap and they kissed with their mouths open. Yuck. At least that's what I thought at the time.

I crept on all fours up the steps to keep them from creaking, but the door was closed. I sat down on third stair from the top, in the shadows, and peeked into the basement family room. Okay, I was spying.

At nine, I wondered how they breathed during what seemed like a ten-minute lip lock. His hands moved up and down her back, then one went under her blouse. Suddenly, he tangled his fingers in her hair and took a vice grip on the back on Karen's head. I didn't care if the steps and the door did creak. I hopped up and opened it. Mom needed to know. Karen could suffer oxygen deprivation. That's what had happened when Johnny Rector fell through the ice the previous spring. He didn't freeze to death. He couldn't breathe. They didn't find his body for a month.

Mom was not happy. She made a lot of noise when she marched down the steps. As soon as Jack Foster was gone, mom shook her finger at Karen and grounded her for a month. I almost rounded the corner to the kitchen, fully intent on high-tailing it out the back door, when Karen caught me by my hair. Then she repeatedly thumped me on the head, where no bruise would show, with the knuckle of her third finger. I saw stars.

Lesson about keeping her secret and my mouth shut, learned. I'd let her suffocate next time.

An afternoon in September, nearly two years after I left Brad, I discovered another thing about secrets. Keeping them also has consequences. I discovered a few things about myself too.

Bill Brady and I pretended not to recognize one another or say much more than hello when we saw each other in Forest Hillside, or in the bar after Friday Skins. I teased and talked more to the bartender and only to Bill when we were in a group. Never one on one. But Bill isn't shy about us having lunch or dinner together in Flagstaff restaurants.

My wife training all the years with Brad didn't include how to orchestrate clandestine meetings. From what Bill has told me about his affairs during the years he was unhappily married, he and Brad could compare notes. Teach a class. How to Bamboozle Your Spouse 101. The rush of banging another man's wife was mentioned.

When I think about it, it's no wonder Brad was so stressed out. Cheating requires planning. Organization. Coordination. A backup plan or story, in case you're seen by someone you know, or who knows your spouse.

One afternoon, Brad was seen coming out of the Grace Inn, that local hotel near Café Boa, by one of our son's friends who was a teenager, not a tattle tale. While taking a cookie out of the jar on my kitchen counter Jason's friend said, "Hey, I was at that Arco station today, and saw Mr. Delon walking out of the Grace Inn."

"At lunchtime?" I asked. There was a restaurant in the hotel.

"Nope. About an hour ago."

"How's the cookie?" I asked, forcing a smile, and a change in the conversation. I intended to ask Brad about it, but wasn't hoping to hear any tawdry true confession. I wanted him to have a good explanation, so I could forget about it.

Brad had game plays, tactics to turn any accusations about his extracurricular activities into an apology from me for even asking. One of his primary plays was to never take the one down, defensive position. No matter what. Instead, get outraged. Pissed, that your integrity or activities have been questioned. Have a good excuse crafted and handy, so you can pull it out of your ass in a hurry.

"I was planning your birthday party. Looked into having it at the hotel. Now, we'll just have it here at home. This minute," he seethed with a sneer, while poking his index finger at my face, "I shouldn't even bother giving you a party."

It was my fortieth birthday, five months after my father died, and Brad had moved back home.

CHAPTER 39

Back Pockets and Closets

Twenty-eight years later, I found myself single, out with a single man, and sneaking around like a pair having an affair so we would not be a topic of gossip in our golf club.

"What if we run into someone from Forest Hillside when we're in town?" I asked.

"We go to out of the way places."

"So, I'm in your back pocket?" I asked. "The kind of thing you keep close, but out of sight?"

"Only if I can snuggle into your back pocket, near that tight ass of yours."

I can't help but laugh.

You wanted it this way, Grey reminded me, and rightly so. If Brady and I date publicly in the kingdom of Forest Hillside, we're both off the market. *Or*, Grey chimed in again, *you could multi-date in the open. Problem is, that would make you a tramp and him a stud.* I wondered if this was one reason people used drugs…to gag the voice in their heads. I'd like to stuff a sock down Grey's throat sometimes. Like that moment.

Besides, I thought, (I do actually initiate thoughts of my own, while Grey crosses her arms and pouts), this is how I weigh options. Make decisions. I argue with Grey in run-on sentences.

If Bill and I become a public item, announce that we cared about one another, then each of us risks being humiliated, dumped, rejected, in front of everyone we knew. *Being single can be lonely. Being in a relationship, can be risky to my ego and heart,* I thought, but Grey countered.

Being in a relationship with enough distance to protect your ego and heart is like going to church and wondering why you're there. If it's only to stay out of the rain, go to a bar. Have a drink. Get a buzz. Get to know the bartender. If you want to be touched, get a massage. Matthew at Massage Envy has great hands. Soft touch. Warm towels. She's chatty and bossy as hell.

I wondered if I was getting the hang of casual dating or was I replaying my relationship with Brad? Willing to settle for being desired, but not wanted enough. What I couldn't do was lie to Bill. I do believe in karma.

Late September is officially fall in Flagstaff. The sun sets before dinner is ready. Rises late. And my relationship with Bill Brady has grown intimate over the past few months. Sex is definitely intimate, but sleeping together incorporates caring and comfort into carnal activity. He sped his car into my garage and then slept over. A lot.

One evening we soaked in a hot bath, washed each other's backs, then let our touches linger, explore. The sensation of steamy water brings tingling chills as I pull my hair up and let the water envelop me all the way to my chin. His hands brush my skin softly enough to tickle, but firmly enough to make me exhilarate in the rush. The wet hair on his chest is silky beneath my open palms. The same light touch. I still ached, as the flu bug my granddaughter left me over Labor Day hangs on. I'm tired, but too stirred by his touch and feel to resist melting into his kiss.

I manage to focus on this, the moments it takes to make love. It's as though the softer our kiss, the deeper it reaches inside me. I let myself ride these waves with abandon, but when it's over, he needs to lie without covers. He's a space heater; still warm from our hot bath and the heat of passion.

I can hear Bill breathe while he sleeps. Soft, content breaths. He's in my bed, but not beside me. Early morning darkness stretches rudely between us. Who decided king-sized beds should span seven feet from side to side? Someone that wanted room to romp, then spread out, or simply have distance in the dark? I open my eyes. I don't want to disturb him, but cannot lay still beneath the shroud of black velvet darkness, without covers.

This morning Grey and I clutch each other to stay warm. I pull my fuzzy pink robe up. Roll it around my hands and tuck them under my chin. I want to feel my mother nearby. Ask her what I should do, but she never answered that question with anything but a question. "I don't have to live with your decision. You do. So, what are your options, Alexandra?"

And this relentless process of introspection, exploring every road I can imagine, became part of me. I didn't always talk through my options with her, especially if it concerned doing something bad, like shaving my legs for the first time when she told me not to, but she read my mind always, would ruffle my hair and say, "Whatever you decide, you need to be able to look at yourself in the mirror and like who you see. And," she would exhale softly, "conduct yourself like a lady. You won't miss all of life's storms, Allie, but you'll weather them."

The indecision storming through my mind isn't about shame or blame versus being proud of my reflection. It's about settling for less from both Bill and myself. It wasn't a long deliberation.

So, before dawn this morning, my mind travels road after road to decide the best route to take with Bill Brady. We've grown close over these past few months. He's easy to talk to. It's even better because he calls me, his mind racing, full of questions or excitement to tell me things, but it's easy to be tied up with Jo or just want a night to myself, not care he isn't there.

He told me he thinks I'm his intellectual equal. Because of the surprise in his voice, I didn't take this as a compliment, but as confirmation that he initially discounted me. I know. I'm nit-picking now. Trying to find fault.

I'm dabbling in more than a few dark arts these days: resurrecting the past, anticipating the future, warding off that little demon, Cupid, with his quiver of arrows and trusty bow. There are practices, rituals, to maintaining emotional distance. Finding fault is a key one.

Bill is a career single. A flirt. Fun to fuck.

That sounds too crass, but that's what sex without commitment is. It's just sex. Maybe some good conversation. The instant you let it become more than that, if you catch yourself waiting for their call or text, someone can get hurt. It's like standing on the sidelines watching everyone else have fun.

I think the word is vulnerable. Sometimes I am. Hell, vulnerability, and gullibility are like my panties. I don't leave home without them, I just cover them up with different outfits. Sometimes their outline shows more than others.

Like the afternoon in late September, when we went to lunch together, Bill was excited when I told him I'd never eaten at the boutique restaurant perched on a dirt hill behind a row of flat-front brick stores on Route 66.

"Best fish tacos you've ever eaten," he bragged. He's more of a foodie than I am, but he is so right this time. My mouth waters after the first bite. The breaded strips of red snapper snuggled in a flour tortilla with finely diced avocado, peppers, mango chutney, fine cabbage and laced with some kind of sour cream sauce, are the best I've ever tasted.

All of a sudden, he says, "Don't turn around, but Alex Hershey just sat down in the far corner with two other people." Alex is our head golf professional. We've both known him for years. So, here's the dilemma.

With Bill, I not only agreed, but had requested we keep our relationship under wraps. What I didn't know and hadn't discussed with Bill, is what to do if we got caught sneaking around.

"So, what's our 'secret's blown' procedure? I'm pretty sure you're a master of the clandestine." I asked him. I hear the edge in my voice, too. By the look on Brady's face, it surprises both of us.

"I've paid the bill," he replies. "We just walk straight out the door. Don't let your eyes stray around the room."

My right brow pitches. Silent attitude, but I follow his direction. Before we are out of the parking lot he asks, "Did you make eye contact?"

"No." Strange, but a one-word response can be a crisp monotone. Mine was, as my jaw muscles flex like a body builder's.

We're a couple of miles away when Bill breaks a long silence. "I've got a couple of steaks we can grill tonight. Would you like rice or a baked potato to go along?"

"Neither." I stare straight ahead and concentrate on the rise and fall of each breath. It's the method used in meditation to slow the mind down.

Grey is spinning like she's caught in a gerbil wheel. A few more slow-silent breaths and my feelings came into focus. Walking out of that restaurant may not have been a moment of insight but it was damned revealing. The old me would have kept my mouth shut, chewed on the distaste for a while then spit it in the trash like a wad of rubbery bubble gum.

I'm not that girl anymore, I silently tell Grey. The swell inside my chest on the next breath is her puffing with pride.

Once we're parked in my driveway, I turn to look at Bill.

"I felt cheap." There is no accusation or anger in my voice. I can't blame him for holding up his end of our bargain. I didn't know my end would heist my self-respect without a weapon in sight.

"Aww, come on. Why would you feel cheap?"

"I pretended not to see a friend that I'm pretty damned sure saw us."

"It's nobody's business what we do. I don't want to be the subject of gossip that fuels the kingdom."

"Great. So instead of two free-to-be-consenting adults, we sneak around like we have something to hide. He saw us pretend not to see him, for crying out loud. That's an integrity breech. I remember telling you I wanted us to stay under the radar, but I just realized the difference between keeping a secret and lying. I'll keep our secret. Won't tell anyone about us up to this point, but..."

"But what?" he asks, after a brief pause.

"I won't do this covert, casual relationship anymore. Turns out I'm not a closet kind of girl, Bill."

"So, you're giving me an ultimatum? Make our relationship public or else?" It's his turn to have an edge.

"No." This time the single word is a whisper, soft with no edges. "I'm not asking you to make a choice, Bill. I'm telling you that I just did."

I got out of the car. He met me by the back bumper, kissed me, put his arms around me. I laid my head on his shoulder and said, "I had a good time." I pulled free, squared my shoulders and walked down the fleet of steps to my front door.

"A good time?" I hear him echo.

I don't feel bad about closing the door behind me. I'm proud of myself. I'm not telling you I was right, just brave enough to be honest with both of us. My dating coach's bravado, "Date around, don't ask, don't tell until it gets serious enough to be exclusive," is sound. It's dating and we live in an age where people date without a relationship, have sex without commitment or love. There is a learning curve for sure and I need to study up, and buck up. Pay attention to the lessons.

This time I didn't flunk out. I had no barbed wire to wrestle free. No regrets. An unexpected sense of relief reminds me of the relaxing tingle of slipping into a hot tub.

As I watched him pull out of my driveway, I'm reminded of the quote from Groucho Marx I saw on Facebook. Put at the front of this book.

"You must learn from the mistakes of others. You can't possibly live long enough to make them all yourself."

So, I'm learning, even intend to take a few for the team. Mistakes, I mean. Already have. Maybe that's the structure of the new 'Being Single' play-book. Perhaps I should call it "Skids, Trips, and Tumbles to Learn Bye."

Learning when to say 'GoodBye' is vital.

CHAPTER 40

Game Changers

As I work and walk Houston, my mind eventually gravitates to my love life the way I think about a cup of coffee when my feet hit the floor. It's the Bermuda Triangle of idle moments. I wonder if I'll ever be in love again. Or if I want to be. Is this the end of the road to romance?

Unmarried with children?

As I ponder these things, it's as though the universe pulls me into the introspective arena. Forces me back in the game of 'what do you really want?' I want all the good stuff in a man: strong, virile, passionate, considerate, honest, independent, and faithful is huge. Enormous. Gigantic. But at this stage, I have a few new twists to add to the list. I want to be his perpetual date, not his wife. Not interested in a live-in boyfriend, especially one with a roving eye…to say the least.

Then I received an email that made me appreciate the expanse of my options. I hadn't heard from Georgia, the man who sent me a book for my birthday last year. He'd wanted to come my direction, take the train ride to the Grand Canyon. We'd talked on the phone several times, as well as emailing.

I came to realize he is a widower who hasn't stopped grieving. Through our many communications, it was pretty clear he felt guilty about moving on…being unfaithful to his wife who'd died five years ago. He sent me a picture of the portrait he had painted of her, from a photo. Debra, the dating coach I spoke with from time to time, advised me to steer clear of grieving widowers. You can't compete with a ghost that they remember with ethereal perfection.

Jo asked if I was afraid of getting involved with a man capable of an ever-lasting commitment. I'd wondered the same. I have a hunch a new man in her life will live in David's shadow, so she probably identified with Georgia's tether, guilt and love for his lost wife.

I decided I'm not willing to engage in a losing battle. Don't want to compete in a relationship with another woman, dead or alive. I'd discouraged him from buying a plane ticket out here, but we continued to visit from time to time.

One morning, he sent a long email. Something must have happened, and he needed to open up. Talk to someone. I'll bypass the 'Hi, how are you, haven't heard from you in a while' opening and get right to the show stopper.

I got such a lump in my throat when I read this, I had to do a double swallow to get a sip of my morning coffee down.

"I haven't wanted to tell you," the third paragraph of his email began. "But eight years ago, I had prostate cancer and had my prostate removed. I chose life over death by the 'C' word. Then I found out my wife was dying. Well," he continued. "I have struggled with this since being single and damn if women after sixty are as much about sex as men in their twenties. What's that all about? It's so hard to pursue a romantic relationship with my limitation."

There's a game-changer for you, Grey chimed in, while I could still feel hot coffee draining down my throat. *What do you have to whine about compared to that?*

I'm pissed that Brad, the man I loved, betrayed me time and again. That I'm in my sixties and single for the first time in damned near fifty years. That I get lonely sometimes. All right, a lot of the time. And that I wasn't any smarter than the damned rat in the Skinner box who became obsessed with the lever. Wouldn't give up. Stupid.

Georgia's road to never feeling the intimacy of sex, the rush of an orgasm again, isn't a choice. It's a fact. Then I reasoned, maybe it would make it easier for him to be single than it is for me. But that was as callous and stupid as imagining myself standing at the base of a long hill I had to climb and envying the man in a wheel chair because he didn't need to wonder if he had the stamina. He was going to get a ride.

The damnedest things bring insight and swift kicks in the ass, when needed. And I needed this one. Georgia had gotten a few too many. He isn't happily taking cooking classes or dance lessons, resigned to being alone because he can't have sex. He's lonely, reaching out, tells me he's looking for someone to love, someone who will love him back, without sex.

Are we that simple? Is loving and being loved what fuels us? If we end up alone, can we flip a switch to an alternate, hybrid energy source to drive our life force? Would a spiritual answer fill the void? If it did, our late date dating crowd might thrive on being celibate, dancing, chanting, and free of STDs. There is so much more than sex, but it's a big part. The bigger the better? Sorry. I couldn't resist. Needed to lighten this up.

I want to reply to Georgia's email, but need time to weigh what to say. Surely something that will come from my heart and ring true to this man. Instead of puzzling this over and over, I needed to distract my mind. Let it move and breathe. Distance clarifies perspective for me, rather like turning the focus wheel on a pair of binoculars.

Brad and I have an appointment with our attorney to officially file for divorce next Wednesday. The banks and our new business plan are no longer a worry. I should be celebrating. Why does it feel like a death march, dragging our dead love and life behind me face down in the dirt? Maybe I should invite a few of the girlfriends. Make a party out of it. Champagne for the burial instead of shrouds.

I talk to Houston as we walk. He hauls me back to the present, watching his frisky gait. Even with a leash, he loves being outside. When we arrived home, I got him a fresh bowl of cool water, then reached for the phone to call my mom. My hand froze in midair. Where did that come from? The sudden wave of grief washed over me. It is warm before it chills me to the bone. For an instant, I forgot that I'll never hear her voice again.

I don't recall the last time I cried so hard it hurt my chest. Hard cries are fast inhales. Shuddering, chest-heaving exhales. My nose both stuffs up and runs. I reach for a tissue. If I rub my eyes, I'll smear my mascara and look like a raccoon. By the time tears run around my nose and drip from my chin, it isn't really a choice.

Where did this come from? Georgia has a lot more to cry about than I do. I've gotten better. Don't cry often anymore. Learned to swallow the urge. I've wondered if I've grown callous or stronger. Lost a tenderness inside or learned to accept what I cannot change instead of fighting it tooth and nail.

So now, crying binges have decided they need to take me by surprise, like a mugger grabbing me from behind.

How do we fuck up the 'happily-ever-after' fairy tale so badly? Bad choice of a mate? Expectations too high to ever attain, so we are hurt, or hurt someone we love, or once loved? Is temptation, the hunt, the chase, the thrill of being pursued, the call of the Sirens?

Should marriage rites come with a kit that contains earwax and ropes to leash us? We could call it The Ancient Myth Method of Survival. After all, Circe gave Odysseus sage advice to get him past the lure of the Sirens' song. Odysseus listened, had his crew lash him to the mast of his ship. His men packed their ears with wax and they made it past the singing sensations, only to sail into the clutches of the wicked monster, Scylla. She grabbed and ate six men before the crew, filled with grief and self-pity, sailed away as fast as they could.

Maybe we need to accept that life and love are a constant challenge, brace ourselves, and move bravely forward. Some things we can affect, others we sail past, and then there are those things that can swallow us whole.

CHAPTER 41

Dickens Had It All Wrong

There's nothing great about expectations. They're relationship killers. Georgia's confession that sex was a dead issue caused me to reflect on my relationship priorities, boundaries, necessities, and desires. Is my desire to be loved strong enough to give up sex to get it?

I was reminded of one night, a while ago, when I was still dating Bill Brady. He was trying to be sexy. Make me feel sexy.

"I like you in those skinny jeans. Creamy skin," he'd said, as he put his thumb inside my waistband and ran his hand across my stomach.

"I love the way you feel against the palms of my hands." The comment and compliment raised questions, the way weeds popped up in a field of wild flowers. I need lessons on how to accept a compliment, right?

What scares me is that at my age, sexy, by his standards, has a shelf life. That means I have a sensual shelf life. In ten years, I'll be in my mid-seventies. Tight ass and abs or not, my skin will be a testament that gravity works. So, what then?

I've battled self-image and self-esteem issues too hard, for too long. I need to be enough now. All this mixed up with Georgia's confession has stewed inside me. Late in the afternoon I finally respond to Georgia's revealing email about his prostate surgery. My backspace key got a workout as I wrote and rewrote before I hit the 'send' button.

I began, "You've had so much to deal with. Several of my dearest friends and close confidants are men with your issue or past the age of performance. Incredible men with minds and hearts that enrich my life.

"You've brought up interesting questions that I've been puzzling, through introspection. When not in a relationship, I miss the physical, but I wonder if that is more because I love the physical rush of sex, or that I used it to validate I was wanted. The woohoo moment lasts less than a minute, is attainable by other means and is at times the cause of performance pressure for both men and women.

"In fact, romance gasps for air when men of age turn to...don't know how to phrase delicately. Kink, I guess. And I don't mean just soft porn or lacy lingerie."

I had no intention of telling him about the man I've called B. J. who didn't want me, or even to have sex with me, but only wanted to assault my tonsils or degrade me by squirting all over my face. That he'd tangled his hand in my hair to manage his fantasy of a forceful finality. Gagging optional. Still pisses me off when I think about the bastard. I also didn't want to tell Georgia that from experience, I'm pretty sure that without prescriptions the performance field would be less intense for most men past mid-sixties.

Some of the games and accessories do add variety and intrigue, can be fun, but there was a time all it took was a stiff wind and soft touch. Instead I opted for a tamer dialogue in the response I emailed him.

"I have a hunch that a lot of what you encounter with the active libido of single women in their sixties is that sex equals validation they're wanted and desired. I can't say I'm ready to give it up, but can honestly admit that if I have to choose between an insecure sexual relationship I've had enough of or the companionship of love and passion, I'd go for the latter in a heartbeat.

"This is inappropriate, and I'll probably regret telling you this," I added, "but there is considerable attraction to the idea that the man one is in love with isn't chasing other women because he needs the stimulation of strange. Well, that was a peek inside my baggage trunk, right?

"Wow...this has been a saucy response to a fella I haven't even met...LOL"

Georgia's reply came back within an hour. It touched and warmed my heart.

"I valued life versus dying of cancer, so know it was the right decision. I still would love to meet you someday. That was the sweetest response anyone could hope for and made me feel better. I sense we have a connection of at least friends. I hope to venture west within the next year. If you head to the south, or even east coast, I hope you'll give me a call."

I do hope to meet this man one day. But when I wake in the night with a familiar ache, moisture between my thighs, my breath shallow and fast, I wonder if I lied to us both when I wrote that email. Would I sacrifice the thrill of sex forever, for being loved and wanted?

Then I remember something I said to Brad, after he'd had an illness that made us both fearful of him taking a drug that would increase blood flow and risk an aneurism. I realize I made that choice once. I meant it when I told Brad I never wanted him to try Viagra.

"I could live without sex, but don't want to live without you."

CHAPTER 42

The Power of Perspective

I need to back up a moment, to catch you up on my upcoming trip. Last June, at the beginning of the golf season, Carol, Jo, and I were having drinks and snacks after a Friday night Skins Game. Carol was telling us about this great trip she was taking to Cuba as part of the 'People to People' program out of Washington D.C. She poked me in the ribs with her elbow and said, "You should come with me. Do you want me to see if I can get you in?"

Without a second's hesitation I said, "Yes." Fate? Destiny? It was an opportunity to experience new people, places, and things. I'm still all about that. There is no way I could have realized then how much the trip would teach me about foreign cultures, myself, relationships, and embracing my new single status.

The People to People program was intended to boost American's engagement with everyday Cubans despite a five-decade U.S. trade embargo to the communist island. The licenses allowing Americans to enter Cuba exclude trips that are primarily tourist oriented and require mandatory participation in educational exchange activities. The Treasury Department required an itinerary, an assigned representative to each tour, and an explanation how the exchanges would enhance contact with the Cuban people, support civil society, and/or help promote the Cuban people's independence from Cuban authorities.

The Cuban diplomat who lectured on the fourth night of our stay, didn't get the memo.

"We let you go to Tropicana last night, but only one night. You go again, we arrest you."

A return trip to see the dancers at the legendary Tropicana was not on our schedule. His declaration was a territorial display of power. His way of verbalizing that our group of Americans have been allowed into Cuba but are not welcome.

I don't want to go into the politics of it here, except to tell you I feel a deep sadness for the Cuban people, the dull look of defeat in the eyes of those who've stayed. The desperation that drove others to risk their lives and the lives of their children, to cross ninety miles of treacherous ocean in makeshift boats and rafts to reach Florida.

The average income of the people is twenty dollars a month. Education is free. Compulsory to age fourteen. But what they read, see on media, and hear over the airwaves is censored. Internet is not an option. Such suppression is not 'for the people', it is for those in power. It reminded me that rape is a power trip, too.

All of this opened me from the inside, made space in the tight spots in my heart. I felt empathy for the people, distain for their suppressors, and grateful to have been born free.

I always was free to be, even with Brad, but had not exercised the gift. It dawned on me that being in the shadows, bolstering Brad's ambitions, being mom and grandma, taking care of my mother were not bad things, but propping others up became my crutch. As long as I was busy taking care of them, I didn't have to mess with muddled up me. So much for my halo, right? Needed to hang that baby on the codependent coat rack I've decided to get rid of.

The pace of the trip to Cuba was both exhilarating and exhausting, especially since my digestive system revolted on the second day, and again on the fifth day. Not a good thing when wandering the streets with a guide, no bathroom in sight. My digestive event culminated in hives that surrounded my stomach like a band of red-skinned marauders. That day should have ended calmly after two Benadryl, four Pepto-Bismol, and a couple of glasses of red wine.

I couldn't dodge dealing with my single self during the trip to Cuba. Our tour group was an even number of sixty-four; twenty-nine couples and three sets of single travelers. Asako, was from Tokyo, close to my age. Three years a widow, she still wore her gold wedding band. Carol, though divorced twice, was widowed by her third husband around four years ago. I was the only divorced, or soon-to-be-divorced, single woman. Of the three single men; Gary left his less energetic wife at home, Dr. Xie left his research lab and a girlfriend in New York, and there was the very rich, very good looking Turkish man, twelve years younger than I, who left his manners and view of romance somewhere between Istanbul and Toronto.

Asako had flown from Tokyo to join her husband's first cousin, Louise and her husband, Jack, on this trip. So, Asako joined them for meals and on most of the motor coach transports. Louise, I'm going to guess, is in or very near her early eighties. This trip was a physical challenge, but she was fiercely determined to be independent.

One night she and I were the only women in a group of eight that opted to visit the Museo Hemmingway, that would make us late for dinner. Cuba has not implemented handicap accessibility standards, but who knew there would be steep stairs at the entry, a time limit before our transport back to the hotel had to leave, and a guide on a mission to get us in and out on time. I'm not sure what the Spanish word for 'hurry' was, but it brought Speedy Gonzales, a cartoon character from childhood, to mind. He was always in a hurry.

Bless her heart, Louise displayed an indomitable spirit as she took the steps cautiously. I had stayed close behind her, just in case. If we missed seeing one more nostalgic room or hammered silver necklace more or less, I'd be good.

"You're not going to believe what I practiced, so I could come on this trip," Louise told me, with a sly grin, as she glanced back at me.

"I practiced getting on and off the toilet. You can imagine how important that is." Her thin shoulders shook as she chuckled. I wish I knew why the trip was so important to her, but 'why' didn't matter. It just was.

I liked Louise, admired her courage and determination, but didn't realize at the time she would do more than inspire me.

From the beginning of the trip, Carol and I are comfortable being independent. She spent time with the couple we both knew, who had originally suggested she go on the trip they were taking. Carol likes art galleries. I gravitate to historical places and museums. During meals, we mingled with a variety of couples at tables for six or eight. It didn't take long to realize wives around our age group weren't necessarily excited about single women in their mix of couples, for cocktails or at meals. It's okay. I get it, especially when one evening I wanted to tell one of the husbands where to go and how to get there. Think below ground. Flames. Pitch forks.

On the way to our dinner table, Carol and I stopped by to say hello to Pam and Jerry, a couple who appeared to be in their mid to late fifties. A full week into the trip, we've visited while on walking tours, waiting in line for bathrooms, and at cocktails before dinner. I know they have children the age of my oldest grandchildren.

I didn't flinch when Jerry raised his hand and gripped my hip the way a bronc rider gripped a saddle horn, but my jaw muscles clenched. Pam's eyes caught his move, then caught my eyes. I took a step toward Carol, who didn't see any of it, and excused myself to the Ladies Room.

When I walked out of the bathroom, the son-of-a-bitch was standing in the hallway with a creepy, sidelong "I want to fuck you," glance. He started to step toward me, to say something, but I shoved a 'stop and back the hell up' palm gesture. Then in case anyone walked into the hall, I forced a casual, relaxed pose, even a managed a slight smile as I said, "You're disgusting and if you ever touch me again, I'll break your hand. No bluff," I added with a wicked wink.

Brad was a black belt in Tae Kwon Do. Taught me what they call 'one-time attacks'; how to break a hand when breaking a hold. Leverage. All women should be trained. He was a married man humiliating his wife in front of another woman he barely knew. Bastard.

When I got back to dining room, I found Carol at a table for four, chatting away with Dr. Xie and the Turkish man, Ahmed, whose name I avoided mispronouncing whenever possible. It looks easy, like Amen at the end of a prayer, but nope. The Turks made three distinct syllables, in three exhales out of it; Ah...Ha...Med.

He'd sat beside us several nights at dinner. Half a dozen times when we boarded one of the tour busses, he'd pat the seat beside him. "Come. Sit with me."

I'd shrug, glance back at Carol. She'd wink and then elbow me as she passed. The day I'd gotten sick, before I knew I was sick, he and I walked to a little restaurant not far from our Havana hotel and had lunch together.

He was fifty-five, very handsome, broad shouldered with a trim waist. I learned he'd immigrated to Canada when his now sixteen-year-old daughter was eleven.

"For her. I do this for her," he said. He showed me photos of her on his phone. Photos of his eighty-foot yacht he harbored in the Sea of Marmara, near Istanbul as well.

"Do you go back to Turkey very often?"

"Four or five months a year. My daughter is in a boarding school in Toronto. I want her to have global education. She will succeed in any University around the world."

When he traveled, she stayed at school or with her mother. His ex-wife. At this point, I'm not seriously considering sleeping with him. I don't know if my ego could handle a man used to handling women in their thirties. Plus, he told me he had a girlfriend.

"It's new," he explained. "Maybe six weeks. Too new to bring her on this trip. Besides," he said, as he poured more wine in my glass, "Is good, because I like you."

That did make me smile, but I needed to be honest here.

"I'm more than a decade older than you," I said, with a smile.

"And you are very sexy."

What a great come-back line.

"We not getting married. Nothing like that. Just have some fun, Eh?" He ended that little tidbit like a true Canadian.

Okay. At this point, I'm considering it. Seriously, but there was not time for an after-lunch interlude. We nearly missed our tour bus, leaving for the only tour of the farm and horse ranch. It was the only time we would have to opportunity to go outside the city. See another facet of Cuba. I longed for something to dispel my disillusion with the ghettos outside the window to my room.

He and I sat together on the bus, but when we got back to the hotel in Havana I wasn't feeling well. It was warm out, but I was chilled. Achy. And when I scratched an itch on my side, I realized I had a rash around my back and stomach. Ahmed was with me when I lifted the edge of my blouse and showed Dr. Xie the rash. Turns out, I also had a temp of 101 degrees.

I took the Benadryl and Ibuprofen Dr. Xie handed me, turned to tell Ahmed good bye, that I was going to my room to rest instead of to dinner.

"I'll come see you after the meal."

"Not tonight," I said, sounding like a bored-with-sex wife. "The Benadryl is going to make me really sleepy. Hopefully I'll be back to normal in the morning. Perhaps I'll see you at breakfast." I turned to leave, but he took my elbow.

"Do not worry. It will be good. You will see I am good. I come to your room later. I knock three times."

"Not tonight. I'm on meds, in need of a hot shower and cool sheets." I declared with what I thought was finality.

"I knock four times. You answer or you don't."

"I won't."

"I knock four times. We will see." About the time we reached the corridor to our rooms, he planted a kiss on me, full tongue, and all I remember is that the elevator at the end of the hall pinged. I wonder if I looked like a gazelle with the speed of my escape. I felt bad the next morning, about being so abrupt, but damn it, he licked his tongue across mine in a first kiss?

Grey liked his looks, that he was more than ten years younger and very interested. *It's part of his culture to be aggressive,* she chided. *Give the guy a break. He likes you.*

"He doesn't like me," I actually verbalize back, after I spit toothpaste into the sink. "He wants to get laid. Remember when he said, 'We aren't going to get married, just have some fun, eh?' Did you forget that part?" I spit again for emphasis.

You started that one. Grey reminded me I told him I liked being single. Never wanted to marry again. Shit. Grey never gives me even a little break. I'm wrapping my mind around casual sex, as it seems the only way to have sex without waiting for a relationship to blossom. No blossoms here. Casual is okay I guess, but I need to be more than a receptacle. I should have gotten points for patience. Not pushed.

The next morning the Turk clearly ignored me, evidently his ego bruised by my hives and my response to too much of his tongue.

The, *"I was sick, running a temp, and had hives,"* excuse aside, here's the thing about a first kiss, for me at least. It should be warm, passionate, with a soft mouth, in no rush. Tiny tastes with the tongue at first, the responsiveness one to the other will encourage more...or not. Maybe he was trying to impress me with...his tongue?

So, this morning, he intended to ignore me.

No problem. I sat alone at a table for four and enjoyed my yogurt and granola breakfast. I had my iPad for protection, to look at so I didn't have to meet eyes of couples who wonder if I'm sad or glad to be alone. Carol is a late riser. She made it through the buffet and ordered coffee with barely fifteen minutes to spare before our morning tour departure.

She's embraced being single. I envy her more than she knows. I am still a guppy hiding in the reeds. The water's fine, but I get uncomfortable venturing too far alone in this new environment. I thought I was past this. At home, I had my haunts. Places that I was comfortable alone. Rarely was I in such an exclusively coupled group as I was on this trip.

As we boarded yet another motor coach a few days later for another morning tour, I passed the Turk as I made my way to the back. I tap him on the head with my tour pass and smile as I walk by. Ice broken. He stopped pouting and made a point of sitting next to me at lunch, then asked if I'd have dinner with him. I was afraid to wonder what *he* had in mind for dessert.

Carol is her bubbly, mingling self no matter what. The past few days we've had meals with Lindy and Steve, a couple from Missouri. I think they must be late forties, early fifties, both fit and fun to be with. Lindy is lively, witty and very smart. We talk about books and favorite authors. Steve is an accomplished financial broker and seems relaxed in the company of 'the three blondes', as he called us. I've grown to have an immense respect for confident women like Lindy, and married guys, like Steve who don't flirt, and are safe for single women to be around.

After her first divorce, Carol was single for eight years, when her children were young. She worked her way from a nine thousand dollar a year English teacher's salary, to earning six figures in sales for IBM in the late Eighties. She bought their stock. Eventually, traded payroll for stock options with dividends and split-adjustments. IBM stock increased about 860% since 1990. I doubt Carol knew at the time that she was securing her very lucrative future. On the other hand, she probably did.

I remember watching her act helpless or batting her eyes with a coy smile at mixers back home. I used to think she was a little ditzy, but have come to realize she's sly like a fox. How she pulls off being genuine as well I don't know, but she's real and I enjoy her many facets. She won't miss me tonight at dinner, there's a group of eight, now seven reserved. I tell the Turk, "Yes, I'd like to join you for dinner."

I'm either a glutton for punishment, nursing an overactive libido, or still wounded and looking for validation. Probably a combination of all three, but I am trying to convert from monogamy to casual sex. No strings. I've seen enough of the Turk to know I wouldn't want to keep him in long term, but he thinks I'm sexy. He's young enough, confident enough in his "I am good" prowess, that he just might be.

It was to be a full moon, so the tour directors planned a 'moon walk', that was to begin in the hotel lobby at ten thirty that night. It seemed like a great way to lead with a bit of romance, this walk together under a full moon. Unfortunately, no one alerted the weatherman.

I got dressed and ready with an hour to spare before dinner that night. As I opened the window of my room and looked out over the narrow railing into the neglect-worn ghetto below, an overpowering melancholy swelled inside me. I watched a woman scrub clothes in a tub without suds. Her hair spilled from a morning pony tail. She wiped her brow with the back of her hand. She had nowhere to go. No way out. How dare I feel sorry for myself because I'm single. Alone. I'm also free, with a world of opportunity.

Melancholy transformed into resolve. With a clarity I have only experienced a few times in my life, I picked up my phone to text Brad. It was time. I knew I might regret it, but did it anyway. I have not regretted what I texted him for even a moment.

"After my mom died, you told me I'm a strong woman. You're right. I possess my mother's strength. Because I loved you, you thought I was weak." Now here comes the not nice part.

"You are one stupid son-of-a-bitch." I can't believe I said that, but again, no regrets. And I didn't stop there.

"I'm sorry for a lot of things," he texted right back. "I feel bad about us, but right now I am worried about you. Are you ok? You sound seriously depressed."

Where in the hell was this concern all those years? Grey went on a rant. *We might have stood a chance.* I want to punch him in the nose all the way from Cuba.

"So sorry to convey the wrong meaning," I text instead. "I loved you for so long, getting ready to go out tonight is strange, but it's time. There's a very rich, very good looking Turkish man that just might get lucky tonight. Goodbye, Brad."

I shudder just a bit even now, thinking about what I wrote. But what the hell? His girlfriend has been in my bed, closet, tub, and house for a year now. It's time I projected a visual of my own. *And no*, I scold Grey, before she starts in on me. *It wasn't lady-like, but it felt damned good.*

When I walked down to dinner to meet the Turk, I thought I might get lucky tonight. A bit of romance and sex with a strange but handsome man. The walk under a full moon would be a good start. Unfortunately, the dark clouds and rain that rolled in obscured even a ray of moonlight.

Another unfortunate circumstance is that as we all waited, hoping the storm clouds would pass, the bar was not only open, it was manned by bartenders in white shirts, jackets and ties, determined we would take an appreciation for the Cuban Mojito home with us.

They juiced raw stalks of sugar cane right beside the bar, mixed the syrup with fresh mint, a little water, and a healthy pour of white rum. The Turk handed me a fresh Mojito each time my drink got below the half. Ice did melt in a hurry in this humid climate. I wondered if he wanted to get me drunk? If he did, Grey and I knew he'd be sorry.

Okay, I'm shifting from seeking validation and being vulnerable, to making excuses for letting my hair down and getting a little wild. I was mustering courage to be sexual with a man twelve years younger.

There's an intrinsic problem with me having too much to drink. I've always considered it a gift that my system has a gauge for alcohol. When I reach capacity, it doesn't shut me off or spill down the sides. It spews like Coke from a shaken bottle. This is not conducive to romance, but my date didn't seem daunted in the least when I put my hand over my mouth and bolted for the bathroom. After two untimely trips to the ladies' room to be sick, I asked for a glass of water. Finally. Dumb shit.

"So, I don't kiss you. Is okay. No problem."

Is this guy for real?

"Come, I walk you to your room." He'd been a gentleman this evening, so walking me to my room sounded tame enough. A gentlemanly thing to do.

I own this, at this point. I can't blame him for being aggressive. I'd seen the tip of that iceberg already. Coupled with both of us having too much to drink, I'm only responsible for myself here. After my system evacuates, I'm pretty okay. No slurred words. I'm surefooted, if still a little queasy. I'm the first to admit to overindulgence and my own stupidity. No doubt about it. But then I hadn't thrown up that night Jo and I binged in Atlanta. The only thing I can figure out to explain that, is the greasy food we ate for dinner. I'll keep that in mind before I decide to be an idiot again.

The Turk did surprise me. I figured he knew we'd both need a hot shower, cool sheets, and a good night's sleep, that it was too late for carnal activity.

Nope. As soon as I swiped my key, he reached around, dropped the handle and pushed his way through the door ahead of me. He didn't hold it open for me either. I had to shoulder the plank of wood on huge hinges to keep from being flung back into the hallway. That threw 'gentlemanly' right out the door for me.

In a pretty cool move, he hopped and plopped down in the middle of my bed, stretched out, elbows behind his head propped against my pillows.

Bless her heart, at this point, Grey is nearly hoarse from yelling, and is kicking the hell out of my head from the inside out. I held the door open, gave him a 'thumbs out' gesture as I shook my head. He didn't budge, but intended to argue me into submission.

I never reached Grey's octave, but my 'bad mommy' voice that directed my pack of three boys, made my intent clear and concise. "Out. You are leaving, right now." Again, the Turk was pissed. As soon as he passed into the hallway, I slammed the door behind him.

Grey became a bitch. I want to tell Grey to shut the fuck up, but know I deserve every kick in the ass she gives me. My head was battered, but clear. I'd stood my ground with a man that reminded me too much of B. J. and his Pal Dick. True, this wasn't the same. I wasn't in a secluded house in the woods. But what if I got in a compromising position and he wanted something I did not want to do? I think this guy's a jerk, but not a rapist. Neither was B. J. He changed the venue when I insisted and I left insulted but unscathed.

Tonight, with the Turk, I intended to keep the door to my hotel room open. If he didn't leave my room, I would have. At this point, I could still say "No", or "Hell no!" and get away with it.

I remind myself of what I told my teenage granddaughters:

"No" is a complete sentence. It does not need a qualifier such as, "No, because..."

To the guys out there, take your time. We might surprise you if we feel safe enough to let our guards down. You are physically stronger than us. We know this. We will compensate and become cautious if we feel the least bit insecure.

When the Turk got out and I was alone in my room, my single status blinked like a neon sign through a grimy window. I took my forearm, fist to elbow, rubbed a clean spot on the window, and saw my new life with amazing clarity. It glittered with opportunity. I was free. So what if I'm alone? I'd been lonelier when Brad was beside me. Lonely with a side of rejection.

All of this opened me from the inside, made space in the tight spot in my heart. I felt empathy for the people, distain for their suppressors, and absolutely fortunate to have been born free. To be free.

Strain used to spoke from the edges of my eyes and crease the space between my eyes. As I passed the window I ran my fingers through my hair, pulling it away from my face and glanced at my reflection. I smiled when I realized I looked like I'd been ironed. Not wrinkle free for sure, but crisper. When you start taking care of and caring about yourself, it becomes visible. Sort of like your image in rumpled clothes, to a wrinkle free or pressed outfit. Same clothes, but you wear them differently.

A few more strands of barbed wire sprang loose that night.

CHAPTER 43

I'm Glad You're Here

It was a short, morning flight from Cuba to Miami, where we would spend one last night together as a group before we disbursed to worldwide destinations such as Tokyo, Hong Kong, England, New England, and Toronto. At the cocktail party that night, the Turk made one last stab at it, but I didn't want to stand at the same table with him. He got the message.

I gave Asako a hug, and we promised to keep in touch. She invited me to come to Tokyo. Said her apartment was small, but I assured her I didn't take up much room, and would love to visit.

I'm always startled at how tiny Louise is when I'm beside her. Her wrinkles, earned over eighty some years, deepen the grace of her smile. We exchanged a look, a smile, and then she reached to push the hair from my face and behind my ears before she put her hands on my shoulders. I leaned down, to hug her goodbye.

"Have a good life," she whispered in my ear. My breath caught and I froze. I drew back, and cupped her face in my hands. My lips a tight line, fighting confusion for control.

"Those are the last four words my mother ever said to me," I managed, before tears dripped down my cheeks.

"You already knew she loved you." Louise said sternly. "Her last words weren't about how *she* felt, but what she wanted for *you*. Now do it," little bitty Louise commanded, with a quick, hard grip on my hands. "Have a good life."

It happened exactly like that, and will forever be one of the mystical-magical memories of my life. I chose not to analyze it but to feel my mother nearby, if just for a moment.

CHAPTER 44

The Codependent Three-Step

I got home from Cuba, then rolled into Thanksgiving, and Christmas. I enjoyed my family in the valley over the holidays, and when they came in clumps to Flagstaff to sled and ski after Christmas.

January 8th Jo and I headed back to Cabo and our penthouse accommodation at a bargain-basement, maintenance fee only price. We'd be nuts to pass up the opportunity, especially when she has a ton of airline points, to boot.

Chrissy, Bonnie's daughter, came down for four days, this year, too. We have so much fun together, I wonder why I've fought being single. One afternoon, Jo diverted from the group to find someone that could fix a broken gel nail, while Chrissy and I got twenty-dollar massages. Worth every cent, by the way.

We were going to meet at the Monkey Business Bar, a little open-air place behind Señor Frogs. Turned out, Jo couldn't find any place that did gel nails, so by the time Chrissy and I caught up to her we were one mondo margarita behind. Now these aren't regular margaritas by any stretch. They squeeze fresh limes over ice, add tequila and Cointreau, an orange liqueur, instead of the regular Triple Sec. The salt rimmed glasses are big. Double size, and Jo ordered her second when we arrived.

We decided that we'd better eat, so went to a small Mexican food restaurant down the street. I've learned to eat greasy food if I drink. Don't understand the dynamic, only that it can help.

Jo fell in love with the blue-eyed chef. I took pictures as she patted his generous tummy and looked up at him with amorous eyes. We did drink bottled water, along with another margarita.

It was our last stop at Cabo Wabo that did it, I think. The live band we've come to love was in full swing. An ice-bucket of two-for-one Coronas with lime last a long while as we talked to people at nearby tables, danced. Our wide smiles in pictures on our phones are a testament that we had a great time.

It was two days later that we became a little confused. Chrissy had flown home, to Memphis. Jo and I were getting ready to go to the beach, when I got a text.

"Hello, this is Jeff, from Denver. We met at Cabo Wabo a few days ago. I wanted you to know I've been thinking about you." He sent a picture of the ocean he taken from his lawn chair on the beach that he said was the new La Paz. I've been through La Paz. It could use new.

I have no clue who he is, so now we're on a man hunt. I asked Jo if she remembered a man named Jeff from Cabo Wabo? No luck. I texted Chrissy. Nope.

"Beautiful view," I replied. "Are you enjoying your time in Mexico?"

Come on. I had to improvise.

"I'm going home Saturday," he said. "Am going to Las Vegas for a trade show. I could drive through Flagstaff to see you on my way back to Denver."

I was on the brink of confessing that I had no idea who he was when he sent a picture of himself holding two impressive fish. One in each hand with a note that said, "I'll bring lunch."

Jo and I were at the pool when the picture came through.

"He was the guy sitting at the table on the ledge above us," I said excitedly. She gave me a double blank blink.

"I discounted him when we found out he had a woman with him." She'd been T-shirt shopping and didn't join him at their table until shortly before we left.

"It was his seventieth birthday," Jo finally muffled into the towel she was laying on, face down. "I talked to him too."

"We weren't tequila mindless, we just don't consider men with dates worth remembering."

"Well...maybe a little tequila mind gap," Jo said. She turned to her side and propped a fist under her cheek, with a down frown. "He sent shots to our table and things got a little blurry after that."

"Damn it." I shook my head.

"We need to stay on the beach and out of the bars," I lamented, planting my forehead on the heel of my hand.

I joked about this, but it's no joke. We need to monitor our drinking closely. In my old, before-I-left-Brad life...hell before that night in Atlanta, I didn't know where the threshold to brown or blackout territory was. I always got sick before I got drunk. But I've crossed that threshold a couple of times since, and evidently need to pay better attention. The last night Jo and I spent in Atlanta when we drunk-sexted and regretted it the morning after was my first time. That afternoon outside Cabo Wabo was mild. I had a short gap in memory, but enough to spur me to do a little research.

I learned that when the blood alcohol level is jacked too high too quickly, we don't necessarily 'forget' what happened. Our brains short circuit. We can walk, talk, participate in activities, meaning we may not pass out. But our short-term memory fizzles before it imprints events. We don't 'forget'. We never form the memory in the first place.

I did remember Jeff leaning over the railing. Talking to him over the band and commotion at the outside restaurant at Cabo Wabo. I recall taking the business card. But after one and a half shots of cheap tequila to cap off the afternoon, I don't remember posing for the picture he took of Jo and me while we waited outside for a cab. I don't remember giving him my phone number. My fault. Not his.

We texted, exchanged pictures of our vacation adventures and talked on the phone every day for nearly a month. The first thing I needed to know was about the woman he was with in Cabo. Wife, girlfriend, lover?

"Naw...She's the wife of my best friend who was killed in a car crash a few months ago. I had this fishing trip planned to stay with a buddy of mine and she asked if I'd let her tag along. She needed to get away. Anywhere, for a few days. We toss a king-sized pillow between us in a king-size bed. She's depressed as hell. Falls asleep between seven or eight o'clock most nights."

Did I see the red flag waving? Hell no. I want to cop to adjectives like; trusting, unsuspecting, easily deceived, gullible. You'd think after all the lies and deceit in my marriage I'd be craftier, more savvy. But I wasn't and I'll own that one along with the myriad of other foibles plopped in my 'dumb shit' portfolio along this journey.

I'm on tiptoe at the moment hollering, "Hey!" to Groucho as I catalogue mistakes.

My only defense is that I didn't, still don't want to become too wary and suspicious to trust anyone. I actually would have needed a crystal ball to reveal the real problem in what he just told me and I can't find one at any price.

Shortly after I got home to Flagstaff my attorney called. The judge had our divorce decree in hand and would stamp it that day. The eighth of February I was officially, legally no longer Brad's wife. It was an odd moment. I wanted to celebrate that all the years of heartbreak and hurt were over, but even that thought resurrected rotten memories. Moments are over each second that ticks by, but we keep them alive inside us. The final decree didn't scrub them away, but I was elated that the mediations and meetings were over.

In the past two and a half years, he lost his temper at me in every single one. Stormed out of more than a few. With narcissistic or manipulative personalities, it's about winning. Period. They get what they want, or they get pissed. The meetings were opportunities for him to blow up, tell me how worthless I was, how he'd done it all. Everything belonged to him, especially control.

I could celebrate the end of all that for sure, but our marriage failed. You don't kick up your heels and celebrate getting out of class because you flunked.

"You don't celebrate final failures of anything," I told Jo over the phone.

"Like hell you don't. Peace treaties, truces, the end of wars rate party-hardy celebrations!"

259

Jo showed up within an hour with an ice-cold bottle of champagne. We wrestled with the cork on the kitchen porch, pointing out and away from our faces.

"This damned cork reminds me of me. Doesn't want to let go," I grunted just before it blew off and out of my hand and white suds spewed into the air.

"Here's to your new beginning, Allie." The clink of our glasses was musical, as though we'd hit a new note I'd never heard before. Beautiful. Unforgettable.

I imagine Brad and his girlfriend had two toasts to make that night. One to our divorce being final. The second to opening escrow on the new house he bought in Forest Hillside that same day.

They would move in a long-par-five, dog-leg right away from my house, within the next thirty days. I'd get to see the adorable couple arm in arm at the clubhouse with our old friends.

Since Cindy was married to Brad's best buddy, she wanted to let me know before someone else did.

"Brad says it will be great. When the kids and grandkids come to visit they can go back and forth between his place and yours. Almost like a family again."

Super, I could hang out at the pool with his girlfriend, her grandchildren and mine, while he plays golf. It felt like a home invasion. I get that his life revolves around his golf pals. They golf winters in the valley and summers in Flagstaff. But though several of them have memberships to Forest Hillside, they have houses in other parts of Flagstaff. I don't trip over them at the fitness center, or when I'm eating lunch alone. They'll be at all the holiday events the community puts on and my kids won't feel all warm and fuzzy and family again, they'll feel like yo-yos. Oh well, oh dear. I'll get past this, too.

The second week of February, Jeff who I'd met in Cabo came through Flagstaff on his way home from an event in Las Vegas for outdoor adventure clothing and equipment. It's not really 'on his way', in fact it's close to two hundred miles out of his way, so that counted for something, right?

I met him in town square for dinner. I know. Jeff is the second man I met in Cabo and continued to date once back home. Revenge sex can be and was hot as hell that weekend. I know the 'don't sleep with them on the first date adage' and its sage advice, but we'd talked daily for over a month now and he was from out of town. I didn't have to trip over him again if I didn't want to and I didn't do it for him. I don't know if I did it for me, or against Brad. Don't care. It was great.

He lived in Denver, Colorado, eleven hours from Flagstaff, but swore he didn't mind the drive. He came to see me twice in Flagstaff during February and when I was in California in March he took a flight over to spend four days with me that didn't turn out as planned. Not in the end anyway.

Jeff, a retired doctor, is three years older than me, and has enough titanium in his knees to send airport security into a frenzy if he steps through a scanner. He's a big guy, six feet tall, broad shouldered, with the thighs of a weight lifter.

Besides that, he's cozy, warm and I feel petite in contrast. I sort of like to see his silky white-grey hair messy in the mornings. It's a sign that something defies this alpha male besides his waistline.

It is my psychosis. I'm attracted to alpha males. Beta's are good guys that make huge contributions to the world at large, but alphas emit magnetic auras that draw me in like a tractor beam on a star ship. I'm aware of it. I'm working on it.

When I met Jeff in January he was booked on a three-week trip to Alaska the end of April. The entire trip promised rugged scenery, wildlife, waters of the ocean and Inland Passages.

"With my arms wrapped around you on the deck of the boat some night, we might even see the northern lights," he said. The promise of adventure rates right up there in moments I want in memory for my porch rocker some far-away day.

When he invited me to come along, I told him I'd love to. I got a new down jacket, a Gore-Tex shell, two pairs of gloves, wool socks, round trip tickets on American Airlines, and insisted on paying my fare on the excursions.

In the time before the trip, we managed to spend time together every few weeks. Our daily texts often ended with "I miss you, wish you were here," but there's been no relationship talk. This is good. I'm not ready. He's a friend and a lover. We still have room to wiggle, but after I experienced a moment of insight last night, I realized too much wiggle room can be hazardous to my health.

These moments of insight don't come often and aren't the product of deliberation, or analyzing a subject. As if you're in a pitch-black room, a switch flips and a light bulb makes what is right in front of you crystal clear. For me, these insights have proven to be about survival, emotional if not physical. They are turning points in my life. I have to be honest with myself when they hit, and brave up. At the time this one lit up, I wasn't honest with myself or brave.

Jeff and I were dangling in the uncertainty of a friends-with-benefits relationship. FWB is a relationship stage, not destination. Friends with benefits engage in intimate acts, enjoy physical contact, touch, taste, and pleasure. But it isn't all free fun. Both must balance on the same tight rope, over the same rocky ravine. One step back, and you're fuck buddies. One step forward, and the fairy dust of fate blinds one or both of you into wanting more. There is that watchful tension wondering who will go first and in what direction. That's presuming someone else doesn't stroll by or out of the past, and one of you leaps off the tight rope, whipping the other off balance and leaving them clinging for dear life. With both hands.

This is the only type of relationship I've experienced since I left Brad and my home. I'm most likely the culprit, inching back if they move too close. I know they sense this. Jeff and I are still on the tight rope, but there are markers that have disturbed the balance. The night I fell asleep in his arms, was one. A late-night text of his that ended, "You are what I want." Shit. Daniel had texted the same thing, before he became distant as a newscaster.

Jeff and I were having a great time and the damned winds of romance made us teeter. Then there was also the day I questioned myself when I woke one morning during those four days he spent with me on the California coast.

"How are you feeling?" he asked, when I woke up in bed.

"I have a headache, and I'm sore inside." I pressed my hand below my waist, completely confused. "The last thing I remember is standing at the kitchen counter last night. What happened?"

He laughed. "Do you remember breaking the wine glass on the kitchen floor?"

"Sort of. I got dizzy."

"I had a hell of a time getting you up the stairs. When I got out of the shower, you were passed out across the bed. Naked." He jiggled my thigh and smiled.

"Too tempting to pass up. I couldn't resist. You pushed me away at first, said no, but I knew you'd eventually wake up and want it. I think you had an orgasm." He patted my thigh as though proud of himself.

My face was skewed in question when I looked over at him. I was still foggy and it was nearly 9:00 in the morning.

"Afterwards, later, you got weird though." He stared at the ceiling, curled his bottom lip out and shook his head. "You told me you were going to hit me with a ball bat. Bust me up. Tell your sons on me."

"Oh my God. I don't understand." I plaster both hands over my face and wished I could melt into the covers. "I had the happy hour margarita at 4:30 when we got off the harbor cruise. It was in a short glass with more ice than anything. Then a glass of wine with dinner and I ate the entire cobb salad with grilled chicken. When we got back here, you fixed yourself a Dewar's then lit the fire pit and I opened a bottle of wine, but I only drank one glass. That's not enough to be drunk." Surely it wasn't. "Did you do something that made me mad? Hurt me?"

"Of course not. Did you take some other kind of medication?"

"No. I don't have anything stronger than Excedrin."

I felt horrible as I rambled on, accusing this gentle man of hurting me while I tried to reconstruct the night before, but couldn't scrape anything together. He asked if I remembered taking a bath? No to that one, too.

What in the world would he think of me now? A drunken mess that wanted to hurt him? It was the highest speed WTF moment yet. I apologized over and over.

Since I'd experienced the too-much-to-drink amnesia a couple of times, I questioned myself about that night. I am confident I didn't have too much to drink. One weak, happy-hour margarita and two glasses of wine two hours apart over a four-hour period with a full meal is not blackout territory. But because it had happened before, when I woke up late that morning, sore in all the wrong places, I hopped on the dance floor to do the codependent, take-the-blame, three-step.

I need to interject a few lines about the codependent three-step. The dance of shame, suffering, and self-abuse.

For all that Brad displayed characteristics of NPD, I personified those of a high-functioning codependent. Over nearly fifty years, I learned to judge myself for having the human need and desire to be loved. He told me I was insecure, crazy and...the list goes on. That no matter how hard I tried, I was never enough. The codependent doesn't happen, they develop over time as they adapt, learn to ignore personal needs, scramble for validation, suppress emotions, take responsibility for another's actions.

This does not qualify us for sainthood. I didn't want to be a martyr either. I was strong, decisive, independent everywhere, except about being wanted and loved, when I crumbled like a Scottish Shortbread dunked into a cup of coffee.

For codependents, communicating our needs is tough because we fear rejection, criticism, even the rage of our partner. But denying our base needs leads to resentment and the spin comes in, because we feel guilty about resenting them for denying us what they tell us we shouldn't need or feel.

Codependency is programming. It's insidious. We learn it is easier to take the blame and feel the shame than risk being told we're crazy or wrong or full of shit, even when we know we aren't. The lever might never work again, but we won't give up.

I was mortified about what Jeff told me I said to him. What in the world was happening to me?

He stayed over another two non-sexual nights.

So did the vaginal infection I couldn't seem to kick. That was a hearty gust that hit me hard. I was chafed, red, no real discharge, but itched like the devil. I didn't tell the doctor about that crazy last night with Jeff. It was awkward enough to explain, "I'm divorced, and dating, and by the way, I need you to run tests for sexually transmitted diseases."

Dr. Chaplin smiled. "Sex is a healthy activity," she said. "What sort of protection did you use?"

"Neither of us are dating anyone else," I answered. Lame. Stupid.

"Have you ever been treated for any vaginal infections or STDs before?" she asked, still upbeat. Not brandishing a cross of shame or a Dunce hat for me to wear.

I gave her my history of vaginal infections from when I was in my twenties. So many that the doctor put me on estrogen shots. I remember the vials of candy apple red fluid. I took them for three years, but when we moved to Amarillo and I had to find a new doctor, who said he couldn't in good conscience give them to me. I was desperate. Told him I didn't care what it took, I needed to get rid of these infections. They'd plagued me for so many years. I was twenty-eight by that time.

"It must have hampered your sexual relations with your husband. I'm sorry," Dr. Chaplain said.

"Didn't slow us down a bit," I said. It hurt when we started to have sex, burned, stung, then once things got going…I gave her a smile as I shrugged. But I was ready to try just about anything to get rid of them.

I attempted to give Dr. Chaplain the condensed version. She had a schedule to keep, so I did the wedge-my-heels-in-the-stirrups routine, which is a vulnerable position to say the least, as I continued my vaginal infection history. Gratefully, my history had a happy ending. At least I thought so, at the moment.

"The doctor ran tissue, fluid, and blood tests, and finally treated me for bacterial, yeast, and trichomoniasis infections at the same time. Twice. Back to back. I wanted to bake him cookies, send him on a cruise, resisted the urge to hug him, because it worked.

"The worst part of it was having to take two rounds of Flagyl for the trichomoniasis infection. It gave me beyond migraine headaches the entire time I was on it. Over two weeks. I dropped five pounds though," I teased, even though it isn't a natural thing to do when you're in spread eagle and in stirrups.

"Did the doctor treat your husband, too?"

"Yes, he did. It was the first time Brad took the Flagyl, too. It didn't bother him, though. No headache."

265

"That was possibly the key to your getting rid of the infections at that time, Alexandra. Trichomoniasis is a sexually transmitted disease, but very often, doesn't display symptoms. Especially in men. They just keep passing it back to their partner, over and over again," she finished casually, as she snapped off her rubber gloves.

I pulled my feet out of the stirrups, sat up, and squeezed my hands tightly between my knees. Restraint. I needed to hold myself tight, because I wanted to scream, cry, and kill something all at the same explosive instant.

"Does trichomoniasis...can it be spread any other way? A toilet seat?" I wanted to think of other options, but couldn't.

"No. It's a sexually transmitted disease."

"Do you think the doctor in Amarillo knew that? That's why he wrote Brad a prescription, too?"

The way she shrugged and nodded reminded me of Jo.

"But why didn't he tell me?" I dug my thumbs into my jaw muscles, as I kneaded my temples with my fingers.

"That one of you exposed the other to a sexually transmitted disease poses the possibility of consequences. What year did this happen?" she asked, brow wrinkled in curiosity or concern.

"1976."

"In Texas?" she shrugged again, as she reached for the door handle. "We'll call you when the test results are in."

The linked Tiffany bracelet I'd put on the day I left Brad, snagged on the stirrup when I got off the table. Suddenly, I wanted it off. Frantically tried to pry the clasp open. My thumb nail broke back and tore the edge of my nail bed. Hurt like hell. I didn't need Grey to tell me I was going to go insane if I didn't get a grip now. Moments like this, she gives me a break. I focused on tying my sneakers, freezing my face in calm blankness as I checked out and left.

I didn't want to talk to anyone. Even Jo. I turned the radio off. My face ached. Again.

Of course, it does, Grey finally spoke up. *You're bottling a hurricane inside. My God, you'd only been married for nine years. Jason was barely three years old, when you moved to Amarillo.*

"And I'd been battling the infections for years by that time," I said aloud.

I became obsessed with getting the bracelet off. I didn't care why. I wanted it off. I parked in the driveway the same way I did the day I got back from B.J.'s house. From being used. I got a butter knife out of the kitchen drawer. You'd have to see the clasp that connects the heavy links of the bracelet I hadn't opened in over two years. It wouldn't let me free. Wouldn't open so I could rip it off. By the time Jo answered the phone, I was frantic.

"I need you to get this bracelet off me. Now. Please."

"I'll be right there. Just sit down and settle down. We'll get the damned thing off. Guaranteed."

I can only imagine what I looked like when Jo saw me clutching my wrist. I wasn't thinking clearly. My entire jaw quivered. My breath was ragged. Irregular. We were going to make a ceremony of taking it off, followed by a celebration. That plan was right out the window and she didn't ask why.

"I need a screw driver," she said. I heard her rummaging through the tool box in the laundry room cabinet. It didn't take long once she set the butter knife across the bracelet, used it as a base to pry open the clasp. The platinum and gold bracelet clattered to the floor.

"Okay now," Jo said, in a sturdy tone. "What in the hell is going on?"

She's a good listener and a better friend. Knows just when to interject, 'what a bastard,' or 'that son-of-a-bitch'. In some crazy way when she does that, I don't feel I'm battling these demons alone. She may as well have punched me in the gut when I finished explaining and she finally spoke up.

"You told me you couldn't take estrogen when you went through the change, because of your sister."

My oldest sister, Karen, died at age fifty-six of breast cancer that metastasized. The doctor told us that estrogen replacement therapy she'd taken for eight years didn't cause her cancer, but it cost her fifteen years.

"You think the years of estrogen shots I took had something to do with my breast surgery?" I asked, more in a contemplative statement to the wall, than to Jo.

"Do you?"

"I'll never know. Three years after I stopped taking them I had the bad mammogram and a suspicious biopsy. Pre-cancer. They said the surgery removing the breast tissue would reduce my chances of getting breast cancer by 95%, so I did it. I was only thirty-two. Jason was in grade school." My words shivered. I had to stop and take several breaths. They'd only removed tissue between the skin and muscle; replaced it with implants that Dr. Rowley replaced when I had my tummy tuck.

Jo deftly shifted the subject.

"My first husband went on a trip to New York City, came home and gave me syphilis, and the clap. Two for one fuck."

I knew the story, that she'd been married for six months when she was nineteen, but it was worth retelling at the moment.

"I burned the sheets, towels, mattress pad, and booted his ass out the door." Those were new details I hadn't known.

"Had to finally get a judge to sign off to get my divorce. Couldn't find the bastard."

"He knew you well, then," I sniffed and managed a smile.

"He knew I had a six-thousand-acre ranch, knew how to run heavy equipment to dig a pit and make his sorry ass disappear."

"You sound so tough," I smiled. "But I know how the story really ended. That he had the wheels to disappear in because you gave him your Jeep before he left."

"You know too damned much about me."

"Ditto."

I can't help but wonder what my life would have been like if I'd never married Brad. The stains of his infidelity were spreading, darkening the stains inside me. My sons salvage me at this point. My life with Brad wasn't a waste because of them. If artificial insemination had been an option to conceive them, in retrospect, I'd have jumped on it.

CHAPTER 45

The Waiting Game

I'd waited three days for the test results and finally called the doctor's office Friday afternoon, fifteen minutes before they closed for lunch. I couldn't sit through the weekend and not know. I was supposed to drive to Phoenix the next morning to catch a flight to Denver, to spend the weekend with Jeff.

It was my turn to go his direction, besides, I wanted to meet the other couple with whom we were going to Alaska. He wasn't happy when I told him I'd stopped drinking after that awful night I couldn't remember.

"Aww come on. You can't go to Alaska and not have a Duck Fart or three." He had a great laugh that reminded me of my Uncle Jack. "Every bar and restaurant in Alaska claims to make the best one," he continued.

"I don't know. The only other thing I can think of that I reacted strangely to was Ambien. I took a half of one after a long stretch of sleepless nights a few years ago. Brad refused to tell me what I said or did, but made me promise never to take it again. I have no recollection of anything that night."

"That night in California really scared you, didn't it?" Jeff asked.

"Yes. It absolutely did. I'm not that kind of person. Don't tell someone I'm going to beat them with a ball bat or tell my sons. I can't believe you're not afraid to fall asleep next to me."

"Naw. No worries. We're going to have a great time on the trip."

What I needed at the moment was an answer from the doctor and probably a prescription before I boarded my flight to Denver to see him.

The receptionist put me on hold. A medical assistant finally came on the line.

"Yes, the test results came in today." Then she paused. "Um. I'm going to have a doctor call you back."

"Why? Is there something abnormal? Please, just tell me the results."

They trained this one well. She wouldn't budge.

This is when another moment of insight clobbered me. I was racking them up these days. This one made a long afternoon interminable. I finally called the doctor's office again at 4:55 and was assured someone would call me when they were done seeing patients. Shit. Shit. Shit.

It was after six when Dr. Chaplain called. The test showed I had bacterial vaginosis.

"No, it is not an STD. It's an imbalance of good and bad bacteria in the vagina. Touchy place, that. Moist, dark. Perfect incubator for bad bacteria." She apologized for the delay in the results, but explained that the medical assistant is not supposed to relay anything but 'all clear' results. I asked her to email the test results to me. I wanted to forward them to the date I was going to cancel. I wanted Jeff to see the test, to know I didn't have anything worse.

We were leaving for Seattle, then to Alaska on a three-week trip in just twelve days. Considering the situation, I intended to delay my trip to Denver for another time.

My moment of insight had been roiling in like a tsunami all afternoon. What if it was an STD? I'd watched *Out of Africa*, with Robert Redford and Meryl Streep. He didn't have any symptoms of syphilis. Nothing. Nada, but he gave it to her, and she suffered a grueling death. Brad had evidently kept pounding me with an STD for years while he showed no symptoms.

I'd talked with girlfriends about it. We all concurred that we knew we should use condoms, but nobody did. I'd been careless and beyond stupid. Sure, Jeff was a nice man, but thoughts of where he'd been, with whom, and who they'd been with caused a cascade of idiotic proportions. He'd been in Mexico, for crying out loud.

What had I been thinking? So, he said he hadn't been with anyone in a long time. Define a long time, Alex. Is that a week? Three days? Clearly, it didn't matter. A guy didn't necessarily have any symptoms with trichomoniasis and even syphilis, probably more. He might not know he has it. He could be lying his ass off, too. It was time to find out, so I called Jeff.

"I have a request, I began. "I got test results back today, and have to take medication for bacterial vaginosis."

"Ah. That's no big deal."

"This day has been a big deal for me. The doctor assured me it isn't an STD, but we're having unprotected sex without any discussion of boundaries." I paused, searching for a way to phrase what I wanted to say, instead of just blurting it out.

"What sort of boundaries would make you comfortable?" he asked. "We can use protection if you want."

Wait. What? So, he is having sex with other women? It didn't matter, because my moment of insight had catapulted me way beyond that possibility. Hell, he had a life in Denver before I met him in Cabo. He'd been coming to see me, but then going back to his home turf for weeks at a time. Perfect arrangement for a fellow spreading the love.

"I'm new at this new age of dating and want you to know, I am not casting a net to hoist our relationship to the next level, but sexually, I've decided I have to be exclusive, Jeff. No judgement, just honesty and options."

"You got it, and what may the options be?"

"Being sexually exclusive or giving me the option to opt out." There. That wasn't as hard as I thought it would be. Revealing too, introspectively speaking. Sleeping around is in the new day and age dating diary, just not in mine. It was going to screw up the trip to Alaska, but I didn't care.

I wanted to kick myself, because my sigh of relief was audible when he replied.

"We are good babe. No problem there. You make me more than happy in all aspects. You need to know I do fish tournaments with a lesbian...fishing only," he added, making me laugh outright. I was relieved I'd put it out there. Setting boundaries is new for me. I have to talk myself into them, or like this phone call, make it on impulse and then wing it. It's work.

The twelve days before our trip passed quickly. He was excited to show me around Seattle; lunch at the Space Needle, a visit to Pike's Market for incredible pepper jelly to pour over cream cheese, the fish market where they heaved whole fish from beds of ice to the back to be wrapped. We rode the Ferris wheel, took a three-hour Segway tour, had a huge bowl of fresh shellfish and corn on the cob dumped onto our table top to share at the Crab Pot on the wharf.

The fishing trip through the Inland Passage of Alaska, the hot springs, where I washed my hair and soaked in a steaming water that streamed through my tub from a natural spring and spilled into a glacial bay outside my window, was unlike anything I'd ever done. I met wonderful, hard-working people, helped dump and drag in shrimp pots, caught halibut and rock fish. It was an amazing wilderness adventure that I'll always remember. I did try a couple of Duck Farts. Had a glass of wine or two at dinners, but never came close to intoxication.

By request, he assured me he brought his preferred brand of condoms. Turns out it was wishful thinking for the most part. At seventy, his prostate was on growth-older hormones. Before we left home he told me he was scheduled for a serious session with it, something he called TURP, when he got home.

"The doctor said I couldn't have sex for three weeks after, so I didn't want to do it before our trip, but I couldn't piss." So, he waited until Seattle to tell me, like I wouldn't have understood and encouraged him to take care of himself first?

They gave him an epidural first. I got chills as I imagined the doctor passing an instrument through his penis to scrape the enlarged prostate that was strangling urine flow and hampering performance.

Spending time with a man without having sex was a learning experience for me about myself and him as it turned out. I wondered if his selfish side began to show up on a regular basis because there was no 'reward' to be sought, or because we'd finally spent enough time together he let himself be himself.

His only child side surfaced when he took cuts in line, rushed ahead to throw his duffle into the biggest state room on the boat, didn't hesitate to take the largest or last piece of anything on the boat's buffets. His phone was the worst. He texted during meals, wherever he had dry hands and was on stable ground.

We had a few days left together, but it was time to start inching my way away.

"We talked about being sexually exclusive, but..." I began our last afternoon when we were alone on the fishing skiff.

"Truth is, I don't know how many more years my pal here," he smiled and palmed his crotch, "is going to cooperate."

"I understand," I nodded and winked a smile. "This is so different than when we were young, and single."

"Yup." He confirmed. "I hate those damned latex tube socks on my dick. I'll play roulette with the STD wheel in the time I have left."

"I won't gamble on that one again, and I can't reconcile myself with being part of a harem, either."

"My three weeks are up, and this is our last night together on the boat." He started to reach for me when my fishing pole nearly jerked out of my hands.

"You've got a big one," he suddenly hollered, reaching over to lock the line on the reel of my fishing pole.

"He's good-sized and a fighter," he said, snagging it with the net. It was a twenty-five-pound halibut. They're a flatter than fat fish. So strange that they have a stark white belly they skim the bottom with and both eyes on their top, darker side. Everything about this trip seemed to be a learning experience. I loved it.

We got back to the big boat with an impressive string of rockfish and my halibut to contribute to the dinner grill.

"So, how'd it go?" Bobbie, one of the deck hands asked.

"Great," Jeff said, handing him the fish to contribute to the dinner grill. "We solved the world's problems, now we're going to go downstairs and have sex."

"Great plan," Bobby laughed. You need to realize we'd spent two weeks on a boat, with another couple and three crew members. I have relatives with whom I don't feel as close.

I thumped Jeff on the back of the head, before trotting down the curve of steps behind him. His three weeks were up. It was nice, warm, playful... gloved.

I think I'm getting the hang of and an appreciation for a physical relationship with a man on a parallel path. We said goodbye before heading to separate gates at the Seattle airport. That was nice, too. Perfect timing for both of us.

Endings open the door to new beginnings.

Sometimes.

In Jeff's case, I turned around and ran face first into the door I'd just pulled shut behind me. Hindsight is sometimes like looking through a pair of binoculars. You stop squinting and see things you might wish you hadn't.

CHAPTER 46

A Prick Without a Pin

I came home to Flagstaff and got back to my routines of working out and writing. Running into Brad and his girlfriend for the first time was easier than a sprained ankle or bladder infection, but still...

Jo, Ted, and I were at the bar in the clubhouse visiting with friends when they walked in and sat at a table less than fifteen feet away. Brad came over and introduced himself to Ted and Jo. I went to their table and introduced myself to his girlfriend and welcomed her to Forest Hillside. Strangely, it was okay. None of this was her doing. She wasn't the reason I left him. That night made me sense this was all going to be just fine.

Evidently my dual tendencies are still in play; forever the optimist and the ass-brandishing ostrich. I've even added a new dimension. I like to think things will work out. 'Dumb shit' comes to mind. I have that tendency, too, and not just with Brad, and I'm not just being negative. I already know what happened by the time I wrote this.

I now have to do something else with the excrement that comes along, since I torched my shit sweeping broom. I have a Vitamix and can whip it up to a froth that looks like meringue. Still smells like shit. Would ruin my machine. So no.

A few nights later Ted had put together our weekly group dinner. Ten of us took the large-round table in the center of the clubhouse dining room. Linda, an energetic golf fanatic sat on my left. She was near my age and had been divorced for nineteen years. I was already seated when Judy took the chair on my right. We'd played golf together the first summer after I left Brad, sat together at happy hour more than once. She was going through a divorce at the same time. As it turns out, we could compare notes on Bill Brady's palate and performance.

I wondered how it would feel to associate with the other women I knew he'd been with. My imagination got a little visually frisky for a moment, broke the ice, and then it was no big deal until she slurped down her second glass of wine, ordered a third, and became what Jerry Seinfeld described as 'a close talker'.

She gripped my forearm, leaned in to whisper in my ear. I was glad my hair kept her lips from full contact. I'd love that from a lover, but even Jo wouldn't get that close and get away with it, and certainly not from a mouth I knew had been below Bill Brady's equator. Probably with the same enthusiasm she had for downing white wine. Eww.

"Bill Brady and I are just fuck buddies. We're not dating openly. He's coming over tonight after I get home." She cocked her head and batted her eyes. I bit my lip to wipe the smile off my face. She and Bill are a match made in heaven.

Linda on my left rescued me, because she asked a question that set me on a quest. She'd been single nearly twenty years and had a lot more experience and exposure to the singles scene than I did, especially since she lived in Scottsdale in the winter. Flagstaff any time of year is a barren singles scene. In winter, it's the Gobi Desert with snow.

"I wondered if you'd included anything about date rape drugs in the book you're working on?" she asked. A serious furrow bridged her waxed brows.

"I haven't," I confessed. "I suppose I figured they were a college crowd, party-too-hardy hazard. Not something to be worried about in late-date dating."

"You need to rethink that," she said with a nod and forced smile. Her abrupt shift to grab her purse and excuse herself to the bathroom crisply ended the conversation. No details would be forthcoming. She gave me a seed. It was up to me to plant it and see what in the hell came up.

I've probably mentioned this before, but think I have an aptitude for research. Certainly, an enthusiasm. I knew the librarian's life history before the internet came out. What I discovered about date-rape drugs disturbed me. Deeply. This is when I looked back and smacked my nose on the door I'd closed behind Jeff.

I hadn't even considered that I'd been prey to the all-too-prevalent danger of club drugs or date-rape drugs that crazed night with Jeff. But as I put the pieces together, they fit unnervingly well.

He'd told me about his fantasies. I'd told him they were outside my boundaries.

"No worries," he'd told me.

He's since told me he's aware that he doesn't know how long his package will be able to perform. So, what if he decided the time crunch to fulfill his fantasies justified stepping way the hell out of bounds? My analytical mind suddenly elbowed my codependent self out of the way.

Let's be real here. Honest instead of gullible, Grey chided.

Since I'd experienced the too-much-to-drink memory blank a couple of times, I knew what precipitated it. The very worst time I'd been that stupid, I remember the last drink I had at 10:30 p.m. and waking at 3:00 a.m. clear headed and sick to my stomach. Because I'd experienced it before, I'd questioned myself about that night in California with Jeff. Trouble was, I didn't have too much to drink that night. I took the blame too quickly.

I'd heard of date rape drugs, but didn't imagine they invaded my circle. Certainly not from a man I'd been intimate with for months.

The image of a man in his seventies dealing with a drug dealer was too far-fetched, but then I read that Ambien has replaced roofies as the rape drug of choice. It's easy to get. Legal. Deal is, it's a sleeping pill you have to be laying down before swallowing, and it renders you as unable to resist sexual assault as any street drug. And as a bonus, you won't remember a damned thing. That night I'd gotten dizzy, broken the wine glass at 8:30, and woke up groggy and foggy sometime after 9:00 the next morning. My insides hurt from the inside, and my pelvic floor felt the same pressure I had with bearing down pains, without the pain.

Why in the hell had he told me that I'd said no, but he didn't stop, swore I woke up...eventually. Then told me I'd threatened him with physical violence. I'd never done that in my life.

I kicked off my codependent dance shoes with such fury I'll never find them again. I was furious with myself and this time at that son-of-a-bitch, Jeff, too. I called him, ran through the scenario and asked him if he'd given me Ambien that night.

"I don't even know what Ambien is," the doctor that had been retired less than five years lied.

I wondered how many prescriptions he'd written to patients for Ambien as I unfriended him on Facebook. Blocked his number on my phone. I wondered if he'd forgotten I told him my half-an Ambien story, after the incident when I was puzzling through it. I figure I got a cheap education and it may one day serve me well. I wondered what happened to Linda, but will never invade her privacy and ask for details.

If you think it can't or won't happen to you, even with someone you've been dating a while who might be eager to fulfill a sexual fantasy, have a night with you that you won't remember, but he will...please reconsider. Be vigilant.

If your date keeps signaling the bartender or waiter to bring you another, or keeps refilling your glass if you're at his place or yours, think about it. I don't know a man who enjoys a sloppy-drunk, weaving, puking date. Please wonder if perhaps he wants you less inhibited, or even incapacitated, and at his pleasure. You drink too much. He adds a kick. You're all his and you won't remember a thing. You may suspect something later, but because the drugs have such a short life in your bloodstream, you'll have a hell of a time proving it.

Those are best case scenarios.

Please don't become paranoid, but do be aware and educated. Trust is an admirable trait, but misplaced, it can be dangerous. Even deadly.

CHAPTER 47

The Gift Horse Has Great Teeth

O n the ex-front, I was in a more volatile zone than I realized. I was getting used to tripping over them in Forest Hillside. The end of June, Andrew, Jason, Brad, and I scheduled the semi-annual meeting as the board of directors of our newly founded umbrella company; our device of divorce that kept the wheels of our business on the ground and running smoothly. Brad rushed in ten minutes late, shook hands with the boys and when I reached to shake his hand, he leaned in and hugged me.

"After nearly fifty years together, we can't just shake hands," he said. I'm sure I'd heard that line before. Affable Brad. Hmm...maybe since everything was settled between us, things would finally settle down.

Within fifteen minutes he was on his feet, jabbing his index finger at me, eyes shriveled in hatred and flashing fire. His lips turn chalk-white when he does this. Even if I make a comment, express an opinion that by the nature of a four-person board is absolutely up for discussion, not demand, he explodes.

I've heard that his tempers in his workshop when he can't find a tool or at anything or anyone he considers a slight or challenge to what he wants, have intensified. He rages so hard his fists shake all the way to his shoulders. If he punches the door of his brand-new vehicle again he'll risk damaging himself and his insurance rate.

He doesn't know what to do with the explosive energy when it bunches up inside him, but he has a leash on it. When it jolts to the end of that leash he punches or throws things: walls, tools. Pens become projectiles. Golf clubs cling to the branches of trees to escape him, but these are inanimate things. He never hit or even threatened to hit me, our boys, or anyone else that I know of. I don't envy him the torment he must wrestle to mask and restrain this torrent.

I was used to his tempers. I still look down and away, instead of responding, partially because my old programming commands me to retreat in confrontational settings with him. Largely because I believe he is beyond reason when in a rage. I can hold my own with others, but am still handicapped with him.

I wonder that genetics play a part. I've seen that look in his brother's eyes, as well as his mother's, directed at people or things they professed to love. I've been told her mother was the same. I also wonder if instead of genetics it is the perpetuation of abuse tumbling down from one generation to the next. Whatever it is, I am again grateful for my mother. I'm not betraying her because I'm grateful for my dad, too. He did hurt her, but he was always good to me. I believe this is how my boys feel about their dad, and I am grateful for that too, for their sakes.

Fortunately, Andrew and Jason exercised restraint to Brad's tirade in that board meeting. Whether I know what drives or has driven Brad, I do know my sons. Jason was on my right when Brad bolted to his feet and started jabbing his finger at me. When I looked down, I saw Jason's hand beneath the table dig into his thigh. I shifted my eyes left toward Andrew. As his chin dropped down, he looked up through his now shriveled brow. I caught my breath when his jaw muscles bulged. Brad must have seen it too, because he abruptly swept his papers into one arm and plowed out the door with the other.

Intellectually, I don't quake if Brad's mad anymore. I'm fed up with him. He's lost his temper in nearly every counseling appointment, meeting, or mediation we've had since I left him. Those were the first times other people witnessed it...not his temper, but his tantrums directed at me.

I fear over forty years of being ballroom champs doing the dance between the narcissist and codependent kicks in behind our backs. He bullies to get me under control. My reaction to being yelled at, belittled, and demeaned is still on auto-pilot. My breaths shorten, lips tighten, I blink back tears and that infuriates me.

The instant the door slammed shut behind Brad, Andrew slapped his palm on the table.

"That's it. This will not happen again. Ever. I'll send out emails if we need to make decisions as a group, but this is the last fucking meeting we'll ever have." Andrew jabbed his finger at the door, not me. "I was ready to throw this table over."

I shook my head. That kind of confrontation between the boys and Brad would be tragic and so unnecessary. Jason has a slower fuse than Andrew but is a force to be reckoned with when pushed too far. He gripped the edge of the table with four white-knuckled fingers and leaned back against his chair. In a husky voice he said, "Agreed."

I nodded consent. No reason it wouldn't work to communicate on paper instead of in person. They love their father, Ben does too. They also know his temper. They just had not realized the extent or ferocity of it that has been focused on me, until this last year. To some degree, neither had I.

True to his pattern, by the time the boys got back to the office Brad told them how sorry he was. I understand he apologized over and over. I wondered if he dented his mask when it bounced off the table, hit the floor and he stomped on it this time...again.

When he said he wanted to reach out and apologize to me, Andrew told him to leave that one alone. Andrew and Jason saw the mask when their father hugged me and watched all hell break loose in a blink when he ripped it off. They needed distance between Brad and me, more than I did. Insulation.

Initially after that board meeting, I did the codependent buck up and brace up again. But when I drove back to Flagstaff that afternoon, my home didn't feel like a refuge anymore. Brad and I living within three career golf shots of each other was as prudent as circling an angry grizzly. Unarmed. In his habitat.

On the way home, winding through the mountains, I imagined running into Brad at the clubhouse after he'd had a few shots of Johnny Walker Black. Some imagination...because we actually ran into each other the next night. I figured 8:00 p.m. would be late enough he'd have had dinner and gone home by then.

When Jo and I went to find our spot by the fire pit we love, Brad and his girlfriend were on barstools in the only two seats that faced the entrance. Everyone who walked in the room got a face shot of them, even though more than half the place was vacant. Intentional?

Brad smiled and did an elbow on the table parade wave. I didn't smile back, especially when his girlfriend stuck her nose in the air and turned her back on me. Jo and I got our glasses of wine and took our view seats outside and out of sight.

"I feel invaded." I talk better through my teeth than Brad does.

"The love birds are leaving," Jo said, jerking her thumb like a hitchhiker toward the entrance behind us. Brad and his girlfriend had an arm around the other's waist as they walked out the front doors.

"He's following the NPD textbook," I said. "You left me, but look how in love and better off I am without you."

"He has to save face."

"I so want out of here, but it could take years for my house to sell. Look how long yours has been on the market."

"I looked at condos downtown yesterday, when you were in the valley. I need out of here, too. I live in the house David and I built, sleep on his side of our bed, I need to start over as badly as you do. Never belonged to the country club scene here, but I was one hell of a golfer," Jo finished with a lilt. I know this nearly brings her to tears.

"You're right on all counts. I'm sorry you had to give up golf." After David died she played all the tournaments and every chance she got. "The grounds keeper celebrated when I quit hacking the fairways up," I laughed. "I don't fit in here either. Besides being a lousy golfer, I forget to put on earrings. Haven't worn a diamond since I took off my wedding rings and never was into designer clothes."

"So, they don't roll out a red carpet when you walk into Nieman Marcus?" she laughed.

"I don't breathe the air in that store. I have a Target credit card for an additional 5% off. I love those sweaters we got last week."

"Me too. It's the love of the bargain hunt." Jo has the greatest cheeks when she smiles.

"That said, I should stay put until my house sells. Be sensible." Even I know I've receded again.

Suddenly Jo turned to me and turned serious.

"If you stay in the danger zone with the wreck of your ex that just flaunted his way out that door, you do it by choice, not necessity. One of these nights he'll have been drinking, his gal pal might egg him on. He might need to impress her or his friends. Maybe you've been drinking. It could get messy and the two of you still have a family, holidays, graduations, weddings."

I lifted my chin and look into her eyes as seriously. She challenged me back.

"Again," she said sternly, leaning in. Damn it, I hate when she points her index finger the same way Brad does. But she does but in slower motion. She's making a point, not wishing she could punch me in the chest with it.

"If you stay because you feel guilty about spending money you have, and don't leave before your house sells, then you need to be ready to take responsibility if there's a situation you or your sons are compelled to react to. Pony up, cowgirl."

"I can't react to him, Jo. Unleashing decades of suppressed hurt and fury scares me more than his temper does. Besides that, I'd look like a jealous bitch, and I like the view from the high road." I was swept up by sudden inspiration, as I punched my index finger for emphasis...but I was smiling when I said, "And I'll like a view of the ocean even better."

That was the instant I decided not only that I was leaving Flagstaff, but where I wanted to go. My house would be on the market by tomorrow afternoon and I was seeking sea level.

"It's about damned time you grew a pair."

"I still feel guilty because I have options so many others don't have. Lots of people work hard, sacrifice."

"You didn't win the lottery or inherit a dime, Allie. Things happen for a reason. Brad being a bastard is exactly the shove you needed to get the hell out of here."

"Ya think?" I asked, lines of worry melting.

"I think if you keep looking that gift horse in the mouth, he's going to knock you on your ass," Jo retaliated. "This is the last trimester of your life. Damn it, Alex, choose to be free because you have the choice. Be grateful you do."

"I am." Palms together, my templed index fingers tapped the end of my nose, just before I turn to Jo. "And I'm also out of here." Conviction is unmistakable, steely eyes, formed features and for me, my pitched right brow. I'd forgotten what it felt like.

That shift inside me was a full eight points on the Richter scale. Instead of disbelief and resentment that Brad had moved into the neighborhood, Jo was right. It was time I left. Past time.

Jo's proverbial gift horse materialized the next morning when I poured my first-frothing cup of coffee, filled my chest with fresh air, lifted my chin, listed my house, booted up my computer and searched the internet for apartments to rent near San Diego.

By the next morning I'd DocuSigned the listing papers, had made a few appointments to see apartments, packed a bag, and was heading west on I-40. When I glanced in my rear-view mirror I swear I caught a glimpse of that gift horse grinning so big his block teeth showed. I didn't care that he could use a tooth brush and floss, he was bold and beautiful...inside. Where it matters.

CHAPTER 48

Playdates and Playmates

I'm not holding myself together with barbed wire anymore. I enjoy the field of wildflowers that sprouted up here and there over these past few years. The butterflies are beautiful when they emerge from their protective cocoons, flutter from flower to tree, but are too delicate and dainty for me. I want to fly with the untethered falcons. Six months ago, I'd have wanted to fly with the eagles, but after seeing them litter the landfills in Juneau, Alaska like buzzards, the falcon is my favorite.

I'm leaving the house in Flagstaff furnished the way we bought it and I packed in two stages. First setting out only the things I wanted to take with me, packing and labeling the boxes and hauling them to the garage. After I checked with the boys about anything they wanted, I boxed and bagged everything else in my closets, cupboards and drawers for donation.

This is an enlightening process on so many levels. I learned to let go of things I once valued and suddenly they became what they were all along. Things. Stuff. With each box and bag taken into the donation truck, another tangle of barbed wire sprang free and rusted to dust.

My new apartment is tiny and perfect. I don't open a closet or cupboard I need to clean out or weed through, or feel guilty because I haven't hung that picture or used those dishes or worn those clothes in eons.

The fickle hand of fate is having such a blast that I'm both tempted to grab it by the wrist to get a grip and yet to let her go. She's on a roll.

The first new person I met once I settled in San Diego once taught relationship/dating classes. I'm not making this up, and Jo keeps reminding me that things happen for a reason. I spent four hours with this woman and learned more about dating than I have by stumbling around for the past two years.

"Chuck the 'sex by the third date or he'll dump you' rule," she said. "Write down your relationship goals. Date a lot of men in the first stage I call being a play date. First, always identify three things about him you find manly, intriguing. If you can't find three, find the nearest exit." She went on from there and I was mesmerized. I'll relate some of what she said as best I can.

You want to make friends at the play date stage. Kayak, hike, go to the theatre, movies, dinner – whatever you both like. If he pressures you for sex, dump him. This stage isn't about 'relationship dynamics', it's to find out if you can be great friends. Don't tease, but tell him you're a fun date and if it moves to the next stage, you're worth the wait. Be real here. If he pressures you or is no fun, move on.

Your play date becomes a play mate when you become intimate. That's stage two. At this point cull the others from the herd and be exclusive. You'll know very soon if you two are meant to move on to the third stage, life partner or soul mate, or not. If not, break it to him gently and hit the road or hitch up to the friends-only corral post.

Don't string men along. Don't give him a blow job if you hate them. Again. Be real. Some country comedy guy once said; 'Women marry men thinking they'll change. Men marry women thinking they won't.' Truth is, we all change, just be your true self wherever that leads you.

I don't know where life is going to lead me, but I'm no longer stuck in a rut. I'm not sad or sorry I left Brad and am on my own. That gift horse and I have become pals. No bridle or saddle. Don't need one. He's gentle. I've developed a rhythm to his gait. Feed him apples and carrots with an open palm so he doesn't inadvertently bite one of my fingers with those blocked teeth of his. I love his grin.

I still don't want to handle the bracelet, and my wedding rings are stashed in some dark safe deposit box miles away. No. I don't want to transform them into something else like a necklace and earrings.

Maybe someday, *I'll* be transformed enough to give those diamonds a different look. A new sparkle. Until then...I don't miss them at all.

Whatever circumstances render you single and alone, get a grip and get ready to ride it out, to be thrown for a loop on that damned roller coaster along the way. Hang in there long enough and you'll find it's strange to say or do something you would never have said or done before. Your laugh will take you by surprise. So will needing to plop down and have a good cry. That will come out of nowhere too, but less and less often as time goes by. I don't mind the creases in my cheeks from smiling. No more fat fillers. They're my lines. Contours of the character I've grown to be.

I've been close enough to see the ocean in the distance, if I get on my tip toes, for a week now. Little by little the fog clears, my path has smoothed out, and I'm mending – standing taller, stronger and redefining my direction. I've come to realize each day, each step, each decision I make determines my path. I need to own it. Want to. Even when the rocks and gravel that still get in my shoes cause me to stumble every once in a while, I pause, shake my shoes out, and know the rocks and gravel are a hell of a lot better than walking on eggshells.

There is so much more I could tell you, moments too stupid, careless, and damned dangerous that though I own them, have learned from them, I did not have it in me to share. I've even spared Jo some of the gritty details.

She won't love the congestion and traffic where I've settled, but I want to show her around Alpine, about thirty minutes east. It's horse country and quiet. We have a knuckle-bump agreement to stay friends forever. I don't know what I'd have done without her. That rancher's daughter helped me cut and untangle the barbed wire that once held me together.

Ted's put a deposit down on a retirement condo in Carlsbad, thirty minutes north. My sons and grandchildren are excited to come and visit. They'll love the ocean, there's so much to see and do...and it's some of the best weather in the world. I'm not manufacturing enthusiasm to have a happy last chapter, it's real and I'm beyond grateful.

And now?

I'm going to take a shower, blow-dry my hair, and get ready.

I have a date tonight and a new determination to be and enjoy a play date.

I miss sex, dream about it, but won't become a playmate, until it feels right. No judgement here. Everyone gets to figure out their own boundaries. I sure as hell tested mine. I yearn to be held and to handle and hold a man that cares about me. It might not end up being life-long love and commitment for either of us, but he'll remember my name and me long afterward. And I him.

I won't promise I'll never have another fling, if it feels right either. That's the key. Not what I do, but why I do it. I no longer see sex as validation. I'm valid just as I am.

So, the man I'm off to meet for dinner isn't going to get lucky tonight... but maybe, if he or another man in my future is willing to wait, we'll both get lucky.

I have a chance to find someone to love who will love me too, and I won't settle for lopsided or less ever again. I sent that ostrich packing...dragging a knapsack of barbed wire and broken dreams. Don't worry, I packed my old pal a lunch and a bottle of water. We're going in different directions.

I have things to do. Places to go. Adventures to chuck into my 'moments to remember' folder with the new smile I found along the way.

EPILOGUE

I hope that this book has made you laugh a bit, cry a bit, and recognize you are not alone. If in my story you see some of yourself, recognize some of what drives or has driven you or your partner or spouse in the past, I have been successful.

If I accomplish nothing more than giving you permission to assess your situation and make a conscious decision about it, give you insight and hope knowing you're not alone, the hours at the keyboard will have been worth it.

If someone who didn't get it, didn't understand you or what you've been through reads this, lessens their judgement, reaches out to embrace you, it will be a triumph.

As I look back on the last two years through the laughter, tears, self-doubt, and rebirth, I will be forever grateful that I found it in me to begin again.

ACKNOWLEDGMENTS:

My sons and grandchildren are the loves of my life. Their support and encouragement has been monumental, especially since I asked them to swear never to read this. I'll continue to thank you in person. Words can't begin to express my love and gratitude.

Even though I scuffed my knees over and time again as this book and my life spilled onto these pages, Jo grabbed me by the scuff of the neck and kept me from face planting, at least staying down long enough to drown. We formed a fulcrum as we leaned against one another, ignited our laughter, love of life, our real and at times raunchy sides, pressure release vents we needed to revive to thrive again. I don't know what I'd have done without her. Thank you.

I wonder that my older sister doesn't have soot on her cheeks for allowing me to vent, believed me, even before she knew the truth, and as always, leaned in with solid support. It mattered more than you know. Thank you isn't enough.

My sincere admiration and thanks to Ted, his great laugh, lists of questions that made me examine my motives and direction so many times. I still laugh when I remember the way Jo and I made him blush red, then watched him rally and return the volley. He's fun, fascinating, and real. Thank you for listening and caring. You're incredible.

Antoinette Kuritz, Senior Partner of Strategies Public Relations has worked with and mentored me since I pitched five bare-bones chapters about late-date dating experiences. Her confidence, encouragement, and guidance helped lay the foundation for the scope and complexity I didn't want or dare to share in the beginning, but it helped me heal. She's a cookie baker, favorite meal maker, all about her kids and grandkids, mom and grandmother, with a huge heart, but on a book project the woman also carries this prod she doesn't hesitate to use if she believes I can do it better. She must have had a first-aid kit stashed in her desk because when I ripped off scabs, bled on pages, argued against it, bitched, moaned and cried, she bandaged me up and then picked up that wicked prod again. Thank you lady, for all that you are and mean to me, and to the completion of this work.

ABOUT THE AUTHOR AND MORE...

ALEX DELON can attest that beginning again after an over forty-year marriage is both a challenge and adventure. At first, much like rappelling down the face of the Eiger, or breaking a land-speed record in a Ferrari with bald tires; but the regeneration garnered as she found the courage to begin again is as exhilarating as winning the Boston Marathon, a torch of triumph in hand. Her sons and grandchildren cheer her on. That she landed in the beautiful San Diego area makes it even better.

Finishing her first book gave way to the creation of a website that is taking on a life of its own, as it enriches hers. Research for fresh blog and article content on relationships, dating, intimacy, safety, and just-for-fun tips surprises, shocks, outrages, and entertains her every day. She doesn't run short of conversation topics or questions anymore, and once you join the lively conversation, neither will you. The site also has book club questions and links to a wide variety of resources to explore. She hopes you'll join in, use the additional features on the interactive site and perhaps activate the translate tab so we can share and learn about ourselves and others around the world or here at home where we might bridge a language barrier in our own neighborhood. Welcome to alexdelon.com.